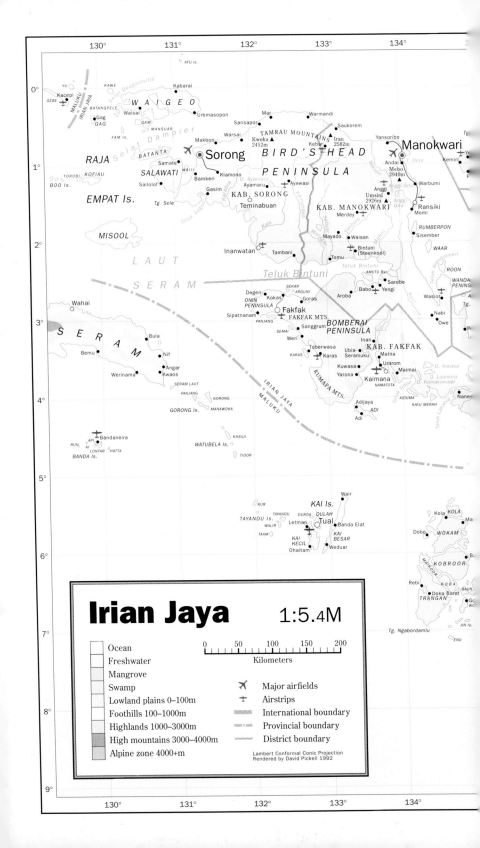

Irian Jaya

1:5.4M

Ocean	
Freshwater	
Mangrove	
Swamp	
Lowland plains 0–100m	
Foothills 100–1000m	
Highlands 1000–3000m	
High mountains 3000–4000m	
Alpine zone 4000+m	

0   50   100   150   200
Kilometers

✈ Major airfields
✚ Airstrips
▬ International boundary
▬ Provincial boundary
▬ District boundary

Lambert Conformal Conic Projection
Rendered by David Pickell 1992

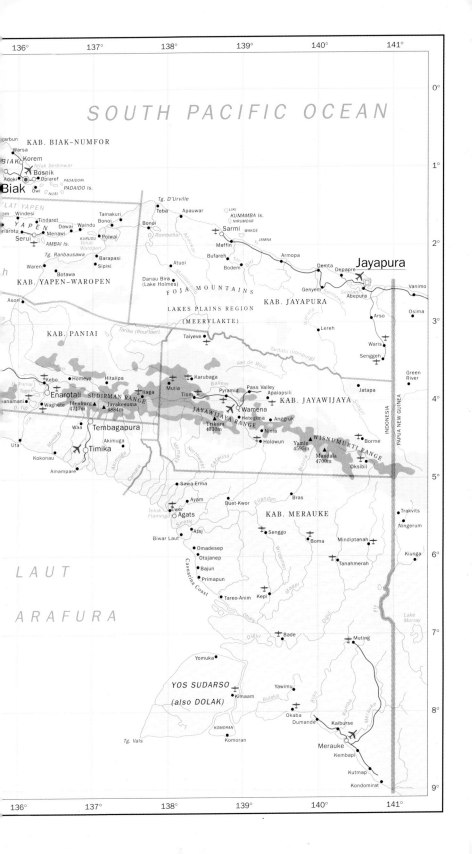

NEW GUINEA

Journey into the Stone Age

Text and photographs by
KAL MULLER

Edited by David Pickell

PASSPORT BOOKS
a division of *NTC Publishing Group*
Lincolnwood, Illinois USA

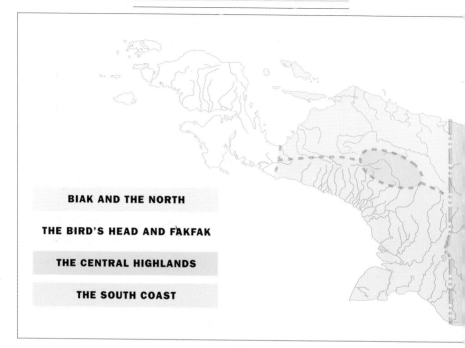

BIAK AND THE NORTH

THE BIRD'S HEAD AND FAKFAK

THE CENTRAL HIGHLANDS

THE SOUTH COAST

This edition first published by Passport Books, a division of NTC Publishing Group, 4255 West Touhy Avenue, Lincolnwood (Chicago), Illinois 60646-1975 U.S.A. Originally published by Periplus Editions (HK) Ltd.

Publisher: Eric Oey
Designer: David Pickell
Production: David Pickell
Cartography: David Pickell

Printed in the Republic of Singapore
ISBN: 0-8442-9901-4

Author Kal Muller has explored, photographed and written about Indonesia for over 15 years. His work has appeared in dozens of books, as well as in the pages of *National Geographic, Geo,* and many other magazines. Muller now spends half the year in Indonesia, and the other half at his home in Mexico.

Cover: Men painting themselves for a demonstration of war canoes in Biwar Laut.
Page 1: Dani huts in the Baliem Valley.
Pages 4–5: A brown river near Amamapare.
Pages 6–7: Traditional dancers on Biak Island.
Frontispiece: The mummified remains of war *kain* Werapak Elosarek in Akima Village.

Passport's Regional Guides

BALI
The Emerald Isle

NEW GUINEA
Journey into the Stone Age

SPICE ISLANDS
Exotic Eastern Indonesia

JAVA
Garden of the East

BORNEO
Journey into the Tropical Rainforest

SULAWESI
Island Crossroads of Indonesia

SUMATRA
Island of Adventure

EAST OF BALI
From Lombok to Timor

UNDERWATER INDONESIA
A Guide to the World's Best Diving

WEST MALAYSIA
and Singapore

EAST MALAYSIA
and Brunei

The Passport Regional Guides of Indonesia and Malaysia offer an in-depth, region by region look at this diverse and fascinating corner of the globe. Each volume contains over 150 stunning color photographs, as well as authoritative essays on history and culture. Comprehensive, up-to-date travel information round out these books, making them the most practical travel guides available on the region.

Contents

PAGE 29

PAGE 50

PAGE 103

PART III: *The Bird's Head*

PART IV: *The Highlands*

PAGE 127

PAGE 175

AUTHOR'S DEDICATION

To IMBC
*for inspiration
above and beyond*

Many people have given generously of their time to help with this book. Among them are: Phil Reid, the best of travel companions; Paul Lundberg, who offered crucial introductions and corrected errors; Beni Wenda, a friend and the best of guides; Wayne Knight, a superb helicopter pilot; many Catholic fathers and brothers; friends Leroy and Philomena Hollenbeck; and John Cutts, a most dynamic and intelligent son of Irian.

THE AUTHOR

Kal Muller has explored, photographed and written about Indonesia for more than 17 years. His work has appeared in dozens of books, as well as in the pages of National Geographic, Geo and many other magazines. Muller typically spends at least half the year in Indonesia, and the rest at his home in Mexico.

CONTRIBUTORS

John Cutts arrived in Irian Jaya in 1954. His parents were pioneering missionaries in the highlands, and he grew up with the Moni, Dani and Nduga in the Homeyo and Hitadipa areas. His wife Joy and two daughters, Jaime and Jenna, have also lived with the Moni for many years. Cutts now works as a community liason for Freeport Indonesia.

George Chaloupka works with the Museum of the Northern Territory in Darwin, Australia. He is an acknowledged expert on Australian Aboriginal and Melanesian rock art.

Kal Muller shows volume one of this book to dancers in Dukum.

DAVID PICKELL

PART I

Introducing Irian Jaya

As the 19th century wound down, only one of the world's great lands still remained cloaked in mystery: New Guinea. Here was a place where pulp writers could indulge their fits of fancy, populating this great unknown island with strange beasts and even stranger people, and no one could yet prove otherwise.

The Baliem Valley, where agriculture had been going on for 9,000 years, and which supported a population density of almost 1,000 people per square kilometer, first felt the gaze of an outsider in 1938.

Today hardy travelers can still get a special thrill pulling out a good, U.S.-produced flight map of Irian Jaya and seeing the words "Relief Data Incomplete" printed across great swaths of territory.

Irian's 1.6 million people form a patchwork of ethnicities, speaking, by most estimates, as many as 250 distinct languages. The island's great size and rugged terrain have isolated them from one another for thousands of years, and each has developed a distinct culture and lifestyle.

The Dani of the central highlands, perhaps the best-known of the Irianese, live in communities of tidy little thatch-and-wood huts, surrounded by neatly kept gardens of sweet potato vines. The scene has reminded more than one writer of the farm country of the American Midwest, and as such it is a remarkably incongruous sight on an island otherwise unmarked by the hand of man.

Although the stone axe was unceremoniously abandoned as soon as steel became available a few decades ago, the Dani remain resolute in sartorial matters: penis gourds for men, and fiber skirts for women. Even a concerted effort by the fledgling Indonesian government failed to convince Dani men that pants were superior to their *horim*.

If the Dani are Irian's most famous group, the Asmat of the South Coast are the Island's most notorious. Historically, Asmat culture was centered around a cycle of head-hunting.

Fresh enemy heads were necessary to bring about the periodic spiritual rejuvenation of the village.

As long ago as 1770, Captain Cook's landing party was sent packing from their territory with volleys of arrows and frightening bursts of lime, but the Asmat's most famous victim may have been Michael Rockefeller, who disappeared after his boat capsized off Irian's southern shore in 1961. He could just as well have met a more prosaic death by drowning, however, or been devoured by a saltwater crocodile.

Today, the mention of cannibalism—or ritual warfare in the highlands—yields embarrassed smiles and shrugs, and it has of course been banned by the government. But there are still pockets of this great island where the missions and government haven't yet reached, and no one can say what cultural practices exist there.

Modernization, and tourist infrastructure, have come to Irian Jaya, if in a much more limited way than in western Indonesia. Wamena, in the heart of the Baliem Valley, is an hour-long, daily flight from Jayapura, Irian's bustling and modern capital on the North Coast. Other points, including the swamps of the South Coast, require quite a bit more patience and organization.

The rewards of a visit to Irian are manifold: snorkeling in the clear, coral-filled waters off Biak; smoking a clove cigaret and cracking pandanus nuts in a warm hut in the highlands; or laying back in a canoe, a livid sunset lighting up the sky, the only sounds the rhythmic strokes of the paddles and the sweet, mournful singing of the Asmat.

Overleaf: *One of Irian Jaya's most distinctive birds, the* mambruk *or Victoria crowned pigeon,* Goura victoria. *Photograph by Alain Compost.*
Opposite: *A Dani man, sitting on the straw floor of a* honai *in the central highlands, plays a traditional mouth harp of split bamboo.*

GEOGRAPHY

A Vast and Rugged Island

The island of New Guinea is enormous, spanning 2,400 kilometers end to end, and 740 kilometers at the shoulder. Covering 792,540 square kilometers, it is the world's second-largest island, behind Greenland, and just ahead of Borneo.

The island is neatly bisected at longitude 141°E, with the western half being the Indonesian province of Irian Jaya, and the eastern half being part of Papua New Guinea, an independent country. Irian's 421,981 square kilometers constitute a whopping 22 percent of Indonesia's total land area.

The shape of New Guinea has been likened to that of the cassowary bird, and the westernmost peninsula, nearly cut off from the "body" by Bintuni Bay, is called the Bird's Head—"Kepala Burung" in Indonesian, and "Vogelkop" in Dutch.

A 2,000-kilometer-long cordillera of craggy mountains running the length of the island is New Guinea's most distinctive topological feature. The crests of the main divide top 3,000 meters in many places, and a handful of rocky peaks soar above 4,500 meters. Small permanent snowfields and relict glaciers still grace the highest elevations.

Towering cordillera

Irian's mountains are geologically quite recent, consisting largely of sedimentary limestones, sandstones and shale that has been uplifted and faulted on a massive scale by plate movements. The central cordillera traces the exact line where the Sahul Shelf and the Pacific Ocean Plate meet.

Volcanic rock is not common in the mountains, but in one of the few places an igneous intrusion has appeared—in the Sudirman Range—the outcrop has proved to be incredibly rich in copper, gold and silver. (See "Tembagapura" page 51.)

The central mountain chain comprises three contiguous ranges: the Wisnumurti Range, running westward from the Papua New Guinea border; the Jayawijaya Range, defining the southern reach of the Balien Valley; and the Sudirman Range, extending west to the Paniai Lakes.

[Note: The Dutch names for these ranges beginning from the border, were: Star Mountains, Oranje Mountains and Nassau Mountains, sometimes all simply called the

Snow Mountains. At least one contemporary source has incorporated the Wisnumurti Range into the Jayawijaya Range.]

The Wisnumurtis are topped by Gunung Mandala (formerly Mt. Juliana) at 4,700 meters and Puncak Yamin at 4,595 meters. Gunung Trikora (formerly Mt. Wilhelmina) crowns the Jayawijaya Range just southwest of the Baliem Valley, reaching 4,743 meters.

Irian's highest peak is the pride of the Sudirman Range: Puncak Jayakesuma (formerly Carsensz Top), or simply Puncak Jaya.

Reaching 4,884 meters (although it is often marked, incorrectly, 5,029 meters on maps), this is the highest point between the Himalayas and the Andes. Several other peaks in the area top 4,000 meters, including Ngga Pulu (4,860 meters).

Coastal swamps

The south-facing slopes of the mountain chain fall off sharply, yielding to dense forest and then coastal swamps. In the west—near the island's "neck"—these slopes are steep ridges of sedimentary rock, scarred by landslides and cut by short, powerful rivers which spill from great gorges just a few kilometers from the coast.

East of Puncak Jaya, the southern coastal forest broadens, and the swamplands around the Casuarina Coast are vast, reaching 300 kilometers inland. Several rivers here are navigable almost to the mountains, and the land is so flat that tides affect river height far inland.

At the far southeastern corner of Irian Jaya, near Merauke, there is a large, anomalous stretch of dry, grassy savannah. This environment, which seems to belong more to Australia or Africa than New Guinea, supports great numbers of deer and wallabies.

The Lake Plains region

The northern slopes of the mountains descend gradually, yielding to foothills and then the vast Mamberamo basin. This is the Lake Plains region, or Meervlakte. It is flat and swampy, full of nipa palms and lowland forest, and little explored.

The Mamberamo and its two main tributaries—the Taritatu (formerly Idenburg) flowing from the east, and the Tariku (formerly Rouffaer) from the west—are slow, silty meandering rivers. Thousands of oxbow lakes, and other shallow, sometimes seasonal lakes dot the region.

The Bird's Head

Bintuni Bay cuts deep into Irian, and its inner reaches form one of the most extensive mangrove swamps in the world. North of Bintuni is the Bird's Head, which is made up of lowland forest to the south, and more mountainous regions to the north, marked by the Tamrau Mountains, and the Arfak Mountains near Manokwari.

Parts of the Bird's Head exhibit karst formations, the tropical climate having weathered the limestones to fantastically shaped spires and gorges.

The island fringe

Yos Sudarso Island (also called Kimaam) is very large—170 by 100 kilometers—but low, swampy and separated from the mainland only by a narrow channel. Off the Bird's Head are the Raja Empat islands: Waigeo, the largest; Batanta and Salawati, near Sorong; and Misool, which takes its name from a medicinal bark prized by the Javanese. Cenderawasih—"Bird of paradise"—Bay (formerly Geelvink), is the site of numerous small islands, and to its north are the large islands of Biak, Supiori, Numfor and Yapen.

Opposite: *Despite the tropical latitude, permanent snowfields cap the Sudirman Range near Puncak Jaya.* **Above, left:** *The silty mouth of the Timika River, emptying into the Arafura Sea.* **Above, right:** *Irian's lowland swamps in places reach 300 kilometers inland.*

The Geological History of New Guinea

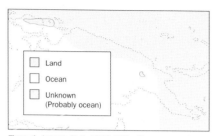

Figure 1. Jurassic Period (170–140 million years ago)

Figure 4. Oligocene Epoch (37–24 million years ago)

Figure 2. Cretaceous Period (140–63 million years ago)

Figure 5. Middle Miocene Epoch (15 million years ago)

Figure 3. Eocene Epoch (53–37 million years ago)

Figure 6. Pliocene Epoch (5–2 million years ago)

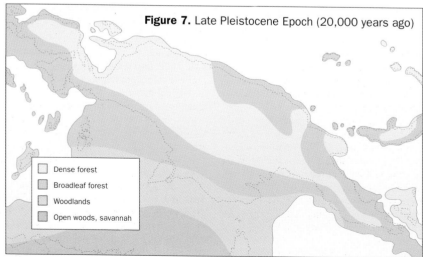

Figure 7. Late Pleistocene Epoch (20,000 years ago)

After Timothy Flannery, *The Mammals of New Guinea* (1990)

FLORA AND FAUNA

A Strange Assortment of Creatures

Irian Jaya is rich in unique plants and animals, some of them beautiful and others downright weird. The largest indigenous land animal is not a mammal but a bird, the flightless, ostrich-like cassowary. Many of the island's native mammals are marsupials, and one, the hedgehog-like echidna, lays eggs.

In addition to this collection of oddities, Irian is also home to some of nature's most glorious creatures—the birds of paradise and the great birdwing butterflies.

Diverse plant life

Irian has the richest concentration of plant life in all of Indonesia, and perhaps in all the world. Scientists estimate there are 16,000 species of plants growing in New Guinea, including hundreds of species that are of medicinal importance. At least 124 genera of New Guinea's flowering plants are found nowhere else, and botanists suggest that further research may find 90 percent of all the flowering plant species here to be endemic.

So far, 2,770 species of orchids have been recorded here, most growing in the rich lowland forests, but the small, bright flowers of some can be found even in the subalpine meadows of the highlands.

Some species are quite unusual. Pitcher plants (*Nepenthes* spp.) have evolved a very interesting adaptation to nitrogen-poor soils. Their leaves form cups of enzyme-rich water, which attract and drown insects, providing an important source of fertilizer.

In the high scrublands in the central cordillera, one can find the giant anthouse plant (*Myrmecodia brassii.*) These epiphytes grow outward from trees, looking like a large, very spiny pineapple. The bulbous base of *Myrmecodia* is honeycombed with passageways just teeming with ants. Even small frogs and lizards have been found to live inside this strange plant.

Mangroves and nipa palms ensnarl the brackish estuaries of the coast, particularly in Bintuni Bay, the South Coast, and the edge of Cenderawasih Bay. Further inland—in the Lakes Plain region, and in the south—swamp forests replace the mangroves.

Swamps to alpine meadows

Irian's swamps harbor the most extensive stands of sago palms (*Metroxylon* spp.) in the world. Starch extracted from the pith of this tree serves as the staple for all lowland Irianese. Though western visitors often decry it as bland and gummy, sago has the distinct advantage of being the least labor-intensive of all of the world's staple crops to collect.

Further inland, the swamps give way to lowland forest and forested foothills. Here grow a variety of tropical evergreens, with

ALAIN COMPOST

palms, ferns, rattan and many species of orchids covering the understory.

At 1,000 to 3,000 meters the forest changes. In areas with constant cloud cover, one sometimes encounters the eerie moss forest, in which all the trees are encrusted with lichens and mosses in huge streamers. The pandanus grows here as well, producing huge fruits full of rich nuts.

The farmers of the central highlands have exploited the fertile soil surrounding some of the river valleys, most famously the Baliem. In most of the lowlands, with few exceptions,

Above: *The unusual hornbill, called* burung tahun *(year bird) in Indonesian.*

the soil is leached and barren.

Past 3,000 meters, the forest thins out and gives way to strange, prehistoric-looking tree fern (*Cyathea*) savannahs. Here also are sub-alpine scrublands of rhododendrons and stunted conifers. Beyond the tree line (3,900 meters) one finds subalpine and alpine heaths and swamps, then just rock, snow and ice.

Unique biogeographical region

Sir Alfred Russel Wallace opened the world's eyes to Irian's magnificent biological diversity. Between 1854 and 1862, Wallace sent a total of 125,660 specimens back to England, including a staggering 83,200 Coleoptera (beetles). A talented and scrupulously honest writer, Wallace estimates that he traveled

14,000 miles within the archipelago on some 60 to 70 separate journeys.

Wallace was the first to recognize the marked change in faunal types as one moves east of Bali from the Asian to the Australian biological regions. The large area of biological overlap in between, including Sulawesi, the Moluccas, and Nusa Tenggara, is now called "Wallacea" in his honor.

New Guinea is well on the Australian side of Wallacea. Since the Arafura Sea is quite shallow, the rising and falling of the sea brought on by the Ice Ages have caused the two land masses to have periodically connected. Because of this—and because of the existence of marsupials and monotremes in both

places—New Guinea is typically considered part of the Australian faunal province.

But recently biogeographers have suggested that the Australian influence may be exaggerated. For example, the land bridge connecting the two was always a dry savannah belt (see map page 20), which would have been a very effective barrier to rainforest species. Further, the majority of the amphibian species and many of the small mammals (e.g. rodents and bats) in New Guinea are Asian in origin.

Colorful avifauna

So far, biologists have identified 643 species of birds in Irian Jaya (712 in all of New Guinea), and there are some real gems in this group. The Victoria crowned pigeon (*Goura* spp.), the world's largest pigeon, is a brilliant lavender with a delicate crown of feathers and bright red eyes. Parrots, cockatoos, and lories brighten up the forests with red, yellow and purple.

During his eight years in the archipelago Wallace spent six months in what is now Irian, three months on the shores of Dore Bay and three months on Waigeo Island. Approaching the coast for the first time, Wallace tingled with anticipation, knowing that "those dark forests produced the most extraordinary and the most beautiful of the feathered inhabitants of the earth"—the birds of paradise (See "Birds of Paradise" opposite.)

Irian is home to some strange birds as well. The megapods or brush turkeys, which bury their eggs in sand or piles of vegetation are found here. Bowerbirds, industrious creatures that decorate their large nests with bright objects such as flowers and berries, sometimes collecting small piles of objects of a single color, are present here in 9 species.

One of the most famous of Irian's birds is the cassowary (*Casuaris* spp.), a large, flightless bird with a nasty reputation. These ugly customers have powerful feet ending in large claws, powerful weapons that have disemboweled more than one human victim. These birds are sought by hunters everywhere they are found, and the hair-like feathers are a common decoration on hats and other items.

Strange mammals

Marsupials dominate the list of mammals indigenous to Irian. Unlike placental mam-

Above: *The magnificent riflebird,* Ptiloris magnificus. *Some 36 species of birds of paradise are found in Irian Jaya.*

Birds of Paradise

Long before the world knew anything of the habits and habitats of the beautiful birds of paradise, their feathers enhanced the appearance of the rich and powerful. Paradise bird plumes graced the headdresses of fierce janissaries at the 14th century Turkish court, and were de rigueur at the Nepalese court, and the courts of other colorful potentates. In the 1880s, the Paris fashion world discovered the plumes, and thousands of birds were slaughtered to adorn capes, hats and other accessories. The trade was banned in 1924, but the ban has been as full of holes as the smuggler's ocean is wide.

Malay traders called them *manuk dewata*—the gods' birds. The Portuguese called them *passaros de sol,* "birds of the sun." A learned Dutchman, writing in Latin, coined the name, *avis paradiseus,* "bird of paradise."

A great body of myth has developed around these birds, and well into the 18th century Europeans still believed that the birds came from Paradise. They had no feet, and thus remained always in the air, living on the dew of heaven and the blossoms of spice trees. The female, it was believed, even laid her eggs and incubated them on the back of the male.

In 1598 the Dutch navigator Jan van Linschoten, wrote: "[N]o one has seen these birds alive, for they live in the air, always turning towards the sun and never lighting on the earth till they die, for they have no feet or wings." Even in 1760, Carolus Linnaeus, the famous Swedish taxonomist, christened the largest species *Paradisaea apoda:* "footless paradise bird."

All these myths were simply the result of the Aru Islanders method of preserving the skins: the wings and feet were cut off, the body skinned up to the beak and the skull removed. The birds have been hunted for centuries with bow and arrow, and more recently, with mist nets.

Paradisaeidae comprises 42 species, 36 of which inhabit New Guinea and its neighboring islands. The family is quite varied, and includes birds of paradise, riflebirds, sicklebills and manucodes. All have beautiful coloration and odd feathers—iridescent breastplates, shaggy napes, fans, and strange "wires." The most characteristic are the *Paradisaea* spp., crow-like birds, the males of which in the breeding season sprout beautiful nuptial plumes from their sides.

The greater bird of paradise (*Paradisaea apoda*) and the lesser bird of paradise (*P. minor*) are relatively common inhabitants of Irian's lowland rainforests, but seeing them can be difficult. Paradisaea are omnivorous, eating a variety of insects and being especially partial to nut-

meg and mahogany fruits. Groups of males display together, often in the main food tree in the area, which makes for a spectacular sight (it also makes them very vulnerable to hunters.)

According to observations in the Asmat region (on the coast near Otsjanep) the greater bird of paradise was in full breeding plumage and displayed from August to early September, for a few hours in the morning, beginning at 6:15 a.m., and again at 2:30–5:45 p.m.

Above: *An Asmat hunter with two greater birds of paradise,* Paradisaea apoda.

mals, young marsupials complete their gestation in an external pouch. Wallabies and tree kangaroos, found in the lower mountain regions, are the largest of Irian's native, land-dwelling mammals.

Other marsupials include bandicoots, possums and cuscus or phalangers, these latter woolly, tree-dwelling creatures with prehensile tail. Unfortunately for the cuscus, its fur is much appreciated for personal adornment, as is its meat. Some cuscus are said to be so docile that capturing one requires nothing more than finding it and picking it up.

Huge bats, called flying foxes because of their long snouts, roam the forests on 1.5-meter wings seeking fruit, and an astonishing variety of tiny insectivorous species roam the night skies.

Perhaps the most unusual mammals in Irian are the spiny anteaters or echidnas which, along with the Australian duck-billed platypus, are the world's only monotremes, unique egg-laying mammals. The short-beaked echidna (*Tachyglossus aculeatus*) is also found in Australia, but the long-beaked echidna (*Zaglossus bruijni*) is endemic to New Guinea. When threatened, the echidna uses its powerful front claws to dig into the ground, presenting a would-be predator with a back-full of stout spines.

Reptiles and amphibians

Two species of saltwater crocodiles frequent the coastal swamps and estuaries of Irian, and both are giants. An estuarine crocodile (*Crocodylus porosus*) that had been terrorizing the Asmat village of Piramat was finally killed in 1970. This rogue beast was 7 meters long and was known to have taken 55 human victims. Crocodile skins have been an important export from the early 20th century, and they have been almost wiped out in some areas. Hunting wild crocodiles is now at least technically illegal, and some 25 farms in the province raise captive animals for their skins.

A great variety of snakes and lizards are found here. Varanids or monitor lizards are common scavengers and predators on small animals. The largest of these, the beautiful emerald tree monitor (*Varanis prasinus*) may reach three meters in length, although it is shy and not dangerous.

The same cannot be said for the death adder (*Acanthopsis antarcticus*) or the taipan (*Oxyuranus scutellatus*). These two are extremely venomous, but fortunately are rarely encountered. The most beautiful snake found here—perhaps anywhere—is the green tree python (*Chondropython viridis*), a harmless creature with strikingly green coloration and jewel-like markings.

The only amphibians native to the island are frogs (the large marine toad has been introduced), but there are more frogs in New Guinea than anywhere else, with well over 200 species, some hardy ones found up to 3,850 meters.

Beautiful and rare fishes

The swampy south coast of Irian is too silty to allow the growth of coral, but around Triton Bay near Kaimana, off the Raja Empat Islands, and around the islands of Cenderawasih Bay are some of the finest and least disturbed coral reefs in the world.

Since it is so close to the epicenter of species diversity for the vast Indo-Pacific region, New Guinea coral reefs probably harbor some 3,000 species of fish. Important food fish—tuna, jacks, mackerel—support a large fishing industry off Biak Island.

Irian's freshwater lakes and streams contain 158 species of rainbowfishes. These small, and often colorful fishes are found only in New Guinea and Australia and are favorites with aquarists.

The Archer fish (*Toxotes* spp.) is a small, unremarkably colored inhabitant of some of Irian's lakes, slow rivers and swamps. This animal's talent is the ability to spit a gob of water—with astounding accuracy—to bring down insects. The insects are gobbled up as soon as they strike the surface of the water.

Some of Irian's freshwater species are giants. The sawfish (*Pristiopsis* spp.) prowls the large river systems and some of Irian's lakes, including Lake Sentani. These distinc-

Above: *The striped possum,* Dactylopsila trivirgata, *is a common small marsupial in Irian.*
Opposite: *The frilled lizard,* Chlamysosaurus kingii, *looks fierce, but unless you are an insect, the animal is quite harmless.*

ive animals can reach 5.2 meters, and weigh almost half a metric ton. The people living around Sentani believe their ancestral spirits live in these sawfish and refuse to eat them. Lake Yamur, at the base of the Bird's Head, is said to be one of the very few places in the world that one encounters freshwater sharks.

Birdwing butterflies

The colorful princes of Irian's insect fauna are the birdwing butterflies (*Ornithoptera* spp.), which can be found in all parts of New Guinea but reach their greatest numbers and diversity in the Arfak Mountains just inland from Manokwari. These butterflies are covered with shimmering colors. Recently, a captive farming project has begun to raise these creatures for the lucrative export market in dried and mounted butterflies.

New Guinea probably has almost 100,000 insect species, and many of these are still undescribed. In the forests one can find great stick insects and katydids—some of them startlingly accurate mimics—as well as tens of thousands of species of beetles.

The capricorn beetle, a tank of a creature, lays its eggs on the sago palm, and its large larvae are prized as food by the Asmat of the South Coast. The sago grubs are an essential feature of every ceremonial banquet.

Spiders, too, are found here in great numbers—some 800 species. These include the formidable giant bird-eating spider (*Seleno-cosmia crassides*), whose size and aggressiveness allows it to reverse the usual order of prey and preyed upon.

A precious environment

New Guinea has the world's second-largest rainforest (after the Amazon) and Irian has the largest tracts of undisturbed lowland rainforest in all of Southeast Asia. These lowland alluvial forests contain valuable timber reserves, making them a major target of the logging industry.

In the mid-1980s, through the efforts of the World Wildlife Fund, an ambitious program of conservation areas was adopted for Irian. Today, almost 20 percent of the province's land area is a conservation area of one kind or another, making Irian Jaya—at least on paper—one of the best-protected pieces of real estate in the world.

Although the problems of exploitation are still great, Irian's inherent ruggedness and isolation will do a lot to insure the protection of its forests. Also, unlike, for example, Borneo, Irian Jaya is not very rich in the most valuable species of tropical hardwoods.

It is the marine areas around Irian that are most in danger. Great fields of the giant tridacna clams (which can grow to 1.5 meters across and live two centuries) have been stripped, the meat canned and frozen for the Asian market, and fish-bombing has destroyed nearshore reefs in many areas.

PREHISTORY

Papuans and Austronesians in New Guinea

Prior to the arrival of the Portuguese in the early 16th century, there appear but scant references to New Guinea and its inhabitants.

Frizzy-haired men and women appear on some of the friezes at Borobudur, the great 8th century Buddhist stupa in central Java, but these could just as well represent peoples from islands closer to Java.

The Negarakertagama, a 14th century panegyric poem dedicated to the East Javanese king of Majapahit, mentions two Irianese territories, Onin and Seran on the southwestern side of the Bird's Head peninsula, but direct control from Java must have been practically non-existent.

It is certain however that *prahu*-borne trade between some of the Moluccan islands—and perhaps even Java—and the western extremity of what is now Irian existed long before this. Items such as bird of paradise skins and massoi bark, unquestionably of Irianese origin, were well-known trade items. And the Sultan of Tidore—a tiny, but influential clove-producing island off Halmahera—long claimed areas in and around western Irian.

The Papuans

The indigenous Irianese, black-skinned, hirsute and frizzy-haired, are physically very distinct from Indonesians in the rest of the archipelago. Just when these so-called "Papuans"—and the Australian aboriginals—first arrived in the area is still mostly a matter of conjecture.

Most scientists now believe that *Homo sapiens* developed more recently than had been thought, and linguistic and genetic evidence points to a single African origin. Our species arose in Africa, perhaps no more than 200,000 years ago, and it was 100,000 years later before any of these early humans left the African continent.

There is no longer thought to be any link between so-called "Java Man" or *Homo erectus,* an extinct humanoid that lived a half-million years ago in Java (and elsewhere in the world), and any of today's people.

What has been established is that 100,000 years ago humans began to fan out from Africa, and some 30,000–40,000 years ago they settled New Guinea, Australia and points in between. These original Southeast Asians related to today's Australian aboriginals, Papuans and Melanesians, are the direct ancestors of the Irianese.

The Papuan migrations

How did the Papuans reach New Guinea? The first clues date from the Pleistocene era when periods of glaciation reduced sea levels 100 to 150 meters below their present levels. The history of man and animals in insular Southeast Asia is intimately linked with the resulting submergence and emergence of two great continental shelves at opposite ends of the archipelago: the Sahul in the east and the Sunda in the west.

At no time was there a land bridge stretching all the way across what is now Indonesia and vast stretches of open water had somehow to be crossed. Man was successful in making this crossing, but other placental mammals—except for bats, which flew, and rats, which tagged along—were not.

Right: *Asmat stone axes. Photograph courtesy of the American Museum of Natural History.*

The earliest tentative figure for human presence in New Guinea, based by inference on Australian paleoanthropological evidence, is 60,000 years ago. But there is in fact little hard evidence arguing for a date prior to 30,000 to 40,000 years ago. This is nevertheless very early — fossils of modern man are found throughout the Old World only from about this time.

Even for the more recent dates, however, linguistic comparisons are unable to relate the distribution of contemporary languages to the earliest migrations, and we have no way of knowing if there were one or many. And the archaeological evidence is meager. A dig has recovered 39,000-year-old stone tools from the Huon Peninsula, but little else from this earliest period.

A later Papuan migration may have coincided with the last glacial peak, which occurred some 16,000 to 18,000 years ago. After that, as the earth's atmosphere warmed, the seas rose as much as 6 meters above their present level.

The Papuans of 18,000 years ago lived in a New Guinea radically different from the one we find today. Ice sheets covered 2,000 square kilometers of the island and the snow line stood a mere 1,100 meters above sea level. (Today, there is only 6.9 square kilometers of glacier left.) The tree line stood at 1,600 meters below the present one and temperatures averaged 7° Centigrade cooler.

For many millennia after reaching the island, the Papuans expanded within New Guinea and to neighboring islands. Their aboriginal Australian cousins adapted themselves to a radically different ecology. The two gene pools have been isolated from one another for at least 10,000 years, and probably longer.

A linguistic Babel

Linguistic studies show, moreover, that the various Papuan groups have evolved in relative isolation from one another for many thousands of years, partly because of the island's rugged geography but also because each group was typically in a perpetual state of warfare with its neighbors. As a result, New Guinea, with only .01 percent of the earth's population, now contains 15 percent of its known languages.

Estimates of the number of distinct languages spoken by the 2.7 million people of New Guinea vary from a whopping 800 down to about 80, depending on one's definition of what constitutes a distinct language. Some languages in Irian Jaya today are spoken by just a handful of people, and the 1.6 million Irianese probably speak 250 languages.

In trying to bring order to this linguistic chaos, experts have been forced to divide Irian's many tongues into at least four distinct phyla or families. (Languages in a phylum share less than 5 percent of their basic vocabulary with the languages in another — and by

Language Groups

- Trans–New Guinea Phylum
- Geelvink Bay Phylum
- East Vogelkop Phylum
- West Papuan Phylum
- Austronesian (Non-Papuan) Languages

way of comparison, most of the languages of Europe fall into a single family, the Indo-European phylum.) These are the East Bird's Head phylum, the Cenderawasih Bay phylum, the West Irian phylum (which includes north Halmahera) and the Trans-New Guinea phylum. The last is the most widespread on the island, comprising 84 percent of Papuan speakers and 67 percent of the languages.

As the climate of New Guinea warmed, more ecological zones became suitable for human habitation. Farming may have begun more than 20,000 years ago, but for most Irianese, hunting and gathering remained the basic source of food for many thousands of years later. A lack of systematic archaeological work leaves us with hypotheses and conjectures for the next stages of human development, but it is likely that agriculture, based on taro as the staple, was already in progress 6,000 years ago, and there is evidence of agriculture in the highlands from 9,000 years ago.

The seafaring Austronesians

The peoples who are known today as Malays, Indonesians, Filipinos and Polynesians share a common ancestry that can be traced back to a handful of hardy seafarers who left the coasts of southern China some 6,000–7,000 years ago. Collectively they are known as Austronesians (older texts call this group "Malayo-Polynesians").

The accepted wisdom had been that the original Austronesians moved down through mainland Southeast Asia and hence to the islands. But contemporary linguistic evidence suggests that this group underwent a gradual expansion, as a result of advancements in agriculture and sailing techniques, with Taiwan as the jumping-off point. From there they voyaged through the Philippines to Indonesia and out across the vast reaches of the Pacific and Indian Oceans.

The Austronesians brought with them a social organization distinguished by what are called bilateral, or non-unilineal, descent—wherein both biological parents are recognized for purposes of affiliation. This contrasts with the unilineal societies of New Guinea and Melanesia which are mostly patrilineal, wherein descent, as in European societies, is recognized through the father. (Or sometimes the mother, but rarely both.)

Austronesian speakers appeared in the islands of Indonesia by about 3,000 B.C. and over the next two millennia, through superior technology and sheer weight of numbers, they gradually displaced the aboriginal popu-

lations who then lived here. This seemingly inexorable displacement process never took place in New Guinea. The Papuans were never displaced from New Guinea, it seems, because of the terrain and the existence of stable, well-established groups of agriculturally sophisticated Papuans.

The two groups intermingle

Although the Austronesians never penetrated to the interior of Irian, they settled and intermixed with Papuans along the coast and on the nearby islands, mingling their genes but imposing their languages. At about this same time—2,000 B.C.—a major expansion of the Trans-New Guinea phylum of Papuan language speakers also occurred, west from New Guinea to the islands of Timor, Alor and Pantar, where they replaced earlier West Papuan language speakers.

These islands had already been settled by Papuan speakers long before the Austronesian arrival, and there were probably two phases of Papuan settlement here: a first taking place many thousands of years earlier and a second contemporaneous with the Austronesian arrival.

The second Papuan expansion was perhaps due to an agricultural "revolution" that included the domestication of pigs and tubers in New Guinea by at least 4,000 B.C. The Trans-New Guinea languages, strongly influenced by Austronesian loan words, also expanded into the island's central highlands by about 1500 B.C., wiping out traces of earlier diversity there.

A sweet potato revolution

The introduction of the sweet potato (*Ipomoea batatas*), ranks among the most crucial factors in New Guinea's evolution. The sweet potato is a New World plant, and it was once thought to have been introduced a few centuries ago by early Portuguese and Spanish navigators. Recently, however, some plant geneticists have said that the plant must have arrived at a much earlier date, perhaps A.D. 500. How it could have gotten there at this time remains a mystery.

Whenever it started, the *Ipomoea* revolution brought high yields at healthy elevations. Unlike taro, the sweet potato grows well up to 1,600 meters above sea level, allowing its cul-

Opposite: *Women tend their sweet potatoes in the Baliem Valley. The nutritious sweet potato offers a high yield and grows well at high elevations. Its introduction was a revolution.*

ivators to settle out of the range of the malarial *Anopheles* mosquito and exploit the fertile oils of the Central Highlands.

The sweet potato allowed for much more intensive agriculture, which together with healthier conditions, resulted in relatively higher population densities in the highlands. Crucial also was the development of a technically brilliant system of parallel or gridiron irrigation ditches, which allowed for fallow times equal to that of the cropping cycle. Older slash-and-burn techniques used elsewhere on the island require 10–20 years of fallow time between crops, resulting in much lower population densities.

In the southeast corner of Irian, the Marind-Anim experienced their own agricultural revolution. Beds of earth, surrounded by drainage ditches, were here raised in the swamps and planted with yam and taro alternating with bananas, and areca and sugar palms. These efficient gardens provided food for similarly dense population settlements.

Prehistoric trade

Trade in the eastern islands of the archipelago began long before the common era. Fragrant Timorese sandalwood and Moluccan cloves are mentioned in early Han Chinese texts, and the latter have also been found in Egyptian mummies. In early times this trade was undoubtedly accomplished through many intermediaries, with east Indonesian products ending up in China and Rome only very indirectly via the powerful maritime kingdoms of western and central Indonesia. It is unlikely that ocean-going sailing ships from China, India and the Middle East, which relied upon the seasonal monsoon winds, made regular voyages to eastern Indonesian waters much before about A.D. 1000.

Large, elegant bronze kettledrums provide the earliest concrete evidence of contact between mainland Asia and the New Guinea area. A fragment of one of these drums, cast by the lost wax process, has been found in western Irian. These drums—or more properly, metallophones, since they are more gongs than drums—were produced between about 400 B.C. and A.D. 100 in the area of Dongson, in what is now North Vietnam.

Although metals were widely worked in Southeast Asia by 1500 B.C., no earlier metal artifacts have been discovered in Irian, and it is thought that these drums, which have been discovered elsewhere in the archipelago, were trade items brought from other areas of Southeast Asia.

Wet-rice agriculture, another import from the Asian mainland, was introduced in the archipelago between about 1000 B.C. and 500 B.C., albeit on a small scale. Because of the soils and climate of the island, and the local preference for tuber crops such as taro and yams, rice culture never developed on any large scale in Irian.

IRIANESE

The Province's Diverse Ethnicities

Even today, members of groups unknown to the outside world occasionally step out of the forests of Irian Jaya. The most populous groups of the highlands and the coasts have become rather worldly, and their languages and customs have been recorded by western and Indonesian anthropologists. But a vast area between the coasts and the mountains remains concealed by a canopy of thick vegetation, and little is known even of the topography of these areas.

As recently as 1987, two previously unknown groups surfaced. Representatives of the first, apparently shocked by what they saw, disappeared again immediately. Those of the other took the first tentative steps into the outside world, accepting modern medicine and steel axes. These latter tribesmen, sartorially distinguished by long, quill-like ornaments jutting straight up from holes in their nostrils, spoke an unknown language.

The Irianese speak a bewildering 250 different languages. Many, perhaps most, are barely known outside their own ranks, and only a handful have been thoroughly studied by ethnographers. The best known are the Ekari of the Paniai Lakes region, one of the first places where the Dutch colonial administration seriously established an outpost, the Dani of the Baliem Valley, and the Asmat of the South Coast. The economies and customs of several other groups have been systematically recorded, and at least the basics of the languages of many others are known.

Any attempt to properly describe such a diverse group of people and cultures in such a limited space is bound to fail, so we will try to mention just the better-known groups, and to fit them into a classification according to geography and agricultural practices.

People of the coastal swamps

Although malarial, uncomfortably hot, and often thick and impenetrable, Irian's lowland swamps are blessed with an abundance of sago palms, and nutritious game such as birds and seafood: fish, turtles, crabs, prawns and shellfish. The trunk of the sago palm provides and easily harvested staple, and the game the necessary protein.

Sago is collected, not farmed, and in areas where stands of the palm are widely dispersed, people lead a semi-nomadic life, living in "portable" villages. Large stands of sago and the rich waters at the mouths of major rivers can support populous, more or less stable villages of up to 1,000 inhabitants.

Sago collecting is the most efficient way to obtain starch. Although the tough palm must be chopped down, the bark removed, and the pith tediously pounded and rinsed (the glutinous starch must be washed from the woody

pith), sago gathering requires fewer than half the man-hours required to grow, for example, paddy rice.

The long, wide swamps of the South Coast support the Mimikans of the coastal area south of Puncak Jaya, the Asmat of the broad coastal plain centered around Agats, the Jaqai inland of Kimaam Island around Kepi, and the Marind-Anim around Merauke in the far southeast. Along the North Coast, the Waropen groups of the coastal swamp around the edge of Cenderawasih Bay and the mouth of the great Mamberamo River live a similar lifestyle.

Of all these coastal people, the Asmat are the best known. Their fierce head-hunting

ulture, powerful art, and the unfortunate dis-
ppearance of Michael Rockefeller in the
egion in 1961 have succeeded in making
hem infamous. (See "The Asmat" page 162.)
Many of these coastal peoples were at
east semi-nomadic, and their cultures
evolved around a ritual cycle of headhunting.
Nomadism and headhunting are, of course,
igh on the list of established governments'
most loathed practices, and both have been
anned and discouraged in Irian.
. The Mimikans, the Asmat and the Marind-
nim have all suffered from the loss of spiritu-
l life that came about with the ban on head-
unting. None of these groups is particularly
uited culturally to organized education, busi-
ess or any of the other limited opportunities
hat have come to them with modernization.

The Austronesians

ome of Irian's coastal areas have been set-
led by Austronesians, and here garden and
ree crops replace sago as staple foods.
Particularly on the North Coast and the
eighboring islands, many ethnic groups
peak Austronesian languages that are very
different from the Papuan languages found
hroughout the rest of the island.

The Austronesians have historically been
nvolved in trade with the sultanate of Tidore,
he Chinese, the Bugis and other groups
rom islands to the west. Bird of paradise
kins and slaves were the principal exports,
long with whatever nutmeg could be taken
rom the Fakfak area.

Austronesian influences can be seen in the
raja" leadership system practiced among
hese groups, perhaps adopted from the sul-
anates of Ternate, Tidore and Jailolo. With
heir political power cemented by control of
rade, some rajas ruled wide areas embracing
everal ethnic groups, from seats of power in
he Raja Empat Islands, in the Sorong area,
round Fakfak or in the Kaimana region.

A somewhat different system was found in
he Austronesian areas around Biak, Yapen,
Vandaman Bay and east of Manokwari. Here
ome villagers practiced a system of heredi-
ary rule, and others were ruled by self-made,
harismatic leaders or great war heroes.

The inland groups

nland from the coastal areas, in the foothills
nd valleys of Irian, scattered groups live in
mall communities that subsist from small
arms, pig raising and hunting and gathering.
hey usually grow taro and yams, with sweet
otatoes being of secondary importance.

Since they were intermediaries between the
highlands groups and the coastal people,
some groups in this zone were important
intermediaries in the trade in pigs and cowrie
shells, both, until fairly recently, serving as
"money" in the highlands.

In the interior of the Bird's Head, the
Maibrat (or Ayamaru) and surrounding
groups carried on a complex ritual trade
involving *kain timur*—antique cloths from
eastern Indonesia—which were obtained
from the coastal Austronesian traders in
exchange for pigs and food from the interior.

Every two years the Maibrat "Big Men"
(shorthand for a kind of charismatic leader)
organized a huge feast involving payments to
relatives and economic transactions between

groups. The Maibrat believed that death and
illness were the work of ancestral spirits.
Good relations among the living, achieved
through gift-giving, were essential lest the
ancestral spirits be angered.

The people living in Irian's lowland forests
between the coastal swamps and the highlands are the least known. Nowhere is there a
very high population density, and many of
these people are nomadic.

Opposite: *A Biak islander wearing a mantle of
cassowary feathers. The people of Biak are of
Austronesian descent.* **Above:** *A Dani woman,
dressed in marriage finery. The Dani, like most
of Irian's highlanders, are Papuans.*

The Kombai, Korowai and scattered other groups living between the Asmat area in the south, and the southern ranges of the Central Highlands in the north, have proved to be among the most resistant people on the island to the entreaties of missionaries and others who would have them join the so-called modern world. One group has for years systematically rejected, with spears and arrows on occasion, missionaries, government workers, and even gifts of steel axes, nylon fish nets, and steel fishhooks.

Cannibalism is frequently reported and surely still practiced here. These unregenerate forest dwellers—inhabiting the area in the upper reaches of the Digul River watershed and scattered other locations in the foothill

forests south of the central cordillera—live in tall tree houses, perhaps to escape the mosquitos, and the men wear leaf penis wrappers.

Highland Irianese

People have been living in Irian's highlands for 25,000 years, and farming the relatively rich soils here for perhaps 9,000 years. The altitude of the rugged mountain chain produces a more temperate climate than the south, and perhaps more important, is outside the worst of the range of the malarial *Anopheles* mosquito.

Highlanders practice pig husbandry and sweet potato farming. Sweet potato cultivation, featuring crop rotation, short fallow peri-

ods, raised mounds and irrigation canals attains a peak of sophistication in the Baliem Valley. Irian's first highlanders relied on taro and yams, adapting to the subsequent introduction of sugar cane, bananas, and much later, the sweet potato.

One sartorial trait distinguishes all of Irian's highlanders: they all wear "phallocrypts" (penis coverings). Or at least all *did* until this striking wardrobe caught the attention of some puritanical missionaries. However, there is less pressure on the highlanders to wear clothes today than there has been in the past, as both the Christians and the government have toned down their campaigns.

The well-known Dani are but one of many highland groups living in Irian's highlands (See "The Dani," page 122.) West of the Dani are the Amung, Damal and Uhundini groups numbering about 14,000 and sharing a language family. West of the Damal are the Moni, numbering about 25,000. (See "Growing up Moni," page 130). Further west in the vicinity of the Paniai Lakes, the westernmost extent of the central mountains, are the Ekari, numbering about 100,000.

East and south of the Dani, living in some very rugged terrain, are the 30,000 Yali speaking several dialects. Three related groups live east of the Yali: the Kimyal, some 20,000 of whom live around Korupun, the 9,000 Hmanggona who live around Nalca, and the 3,000 Mek or Eipomek who live around the village of Eipomek.

The Western Dani

The Western Dani, sometimes called Lani live in the highlands from east of Ilaga to the edge of the Grand Baliem Valley. The introduction of the Irish potato, which can withstand frost and cold, has allowed the Western Dani to plant up to 3,000 meters.

The Western Dani have been responsive to the efforts of missionaries and the government, and have historically been far less warlike than their neighbors in the Baliem, as they farm far less fertile soil and consequently have less excess population and time to expend on warfare. The Baliem Dani's proclivity for warfare is considered to be a product of the spare time resulting from good soil and sophisticated agricultural techniques (For more on the Baliem Valley Dani, see "The Dani," page 122.)

The Yali

The Yali live in the area west of the Baliem Valley, from Pass Valley in the north to Nini n the south. There are at least three dialects of the Yali language, with speakers centered around Pass Valley, Angguruk and Ninia. The language is related to Dani, and their name comes from the Dani word "yali-mo," which means: "the lands to the east."

[Note: Many common Irianese ethnic designations come from other groups, for the simple reason that many languages do not have a term for "we" or "us" that is not non-exclusive of members of other groups, or that refers to a group larger than the immediate political community or confederation. For example, the Dani have a word for "people," but this is in contrast to "ghost" or "spirit," and is not exclusive of any other people. The word "yali" has a cognate in the Yali language that also means "east," and the Yali will use it to refer to people living east of their territory. It is perhaps important to note also that this "east" is not a compass point per se; it really refers to a specific end of the common trade route, which, in this case, is east. Many of the terms coined by western anthropologists for ethnic identifications have gained currency among the highland Irianese, through the bi- or tri-lingual guides around Wamena. For example, "koteka," an Ekari word for a penis gourd, is universally understood in the Baliem Valley, even though a Dani word (horim) exists. Some people call this bahasa baru, the "new language."]

The Yali are immediately distinguished by their dress, which consists of a kind of tunic constructed of numerous rattan hoops, with a long penis gourd sticking out from underneath. They maintain separate men's and ritual houses, which unlike Dani huts are sometimes painted with motifs reminiscent of Asmat art. The Yali are farmers, growing sweet potatoes and other highlands crops in walled gardens.

The terrain of Yali-mo is formidable, which delayed the arrival of both missionaries and the government. Though contacted in the late 1950s by the Brongersma Expedition, the first permanent outside presence was a Protestant mission established in the Yali-mo valley in 1961.

When the first airstrip was built at the mission, one or two cowrie shells was still an acceptable daily wage and most of the Yali had only heard rumors of steel axes. The missionaries traded axes to acquire land and pigs, introducing the metal tool's widespread use. The Protestants began a school and offered medical aid including a cure for frambesia or yaws, a virulent rash caused by the spirochete *Treponema pertenue*. This disfiguring disease was eradicated in 1964.

Also in 1964, anthropologist Klaus Friedrich Koch arrived in Yali-mo, where he learned the language and conducted anthropological research that led to the book *War and Peace in Jalemo*. Like the Dani, the Yali are farmer-warriors, but they live in a much more hostile environment. The Yali responded eagerly to the mission-sponsored introduction of new plants such as peanuts, cabbage and maize, as well as to animal husbandry—placing great demands on the first imported stud hog.

By the time Koch left the field in 1966, there were already six landing strips in Yali-mo, opening this area to the outside world.

But the next year, the mission maintained by the Dutch Protestant Gerrit Kruijt and his Biak preacher encountered a serious public relations problem. The preacher and his assistant were having sexual relations with the local women and, as Robert Mitton writes in *The Lost World of Irian Jaya,* "the locals decided that they had had enough of the Good Word, burned down the missionary's house and ate his Biak preacher and twelve of his assistants. Fortunately for them, the [Dutch] missionaries were on leave."

Opposite: *An Asmat man from Biwar Laut, on the south coast of Irian.* **Above:** *A Moni man from the highlands near the Kemandoga Valley.*

The Kimyal

The 20,000 Kimyal were one of the last major groups to take their place on the ethnographic map. Writing in the mid 1970s, Mitton called their territory as "True cannibal country." In 1968, two Protestant missionaries, Australian Stan Dale and American Phil Masters, were killed and eaten while hiking from Korupun to Ninia (see "Missionaries," page 46). In the same area several years later, anxiously awaiting their helicopter amidst hostile natives, Mitton writes: "we could have been eaten and defecated by the time it got to us." When they were finally rescued, the Kimyal shot farewell arrows at the helicopter.

Linguistically and culturally related to the Kimyal are the Eipomek, or simply Mek, living around Eipomek, east of Nalca. (Older texts refer to this group with the silly, and unflattering moniker "Goliath pygmies.")

The Eipomek are short-statured mountain people, and dress, much like the Yali, in rattan hoops. Many of the men wear nosepieces of bone and feather headdresses. Unlike many highlanders, the Eipomek play long, thin drums, decorated in motifs much like Asmat drums.

The Ekari: born capitalists

Furthest to the west of Irian's highlands, in the fertile Paniai Lakes and Kamu Valley region, live the 100,000 Ekari. The Ekari (in some texts, called Kapauku) have been among the most successful of Irian's ethnic groups in making the transition to modern ways of life. One anthropologist, Leopold Pospisil, has called them "primitive capitalists" for their acquisitiveness and culture based around property ownership.

[Note: as of this writing, the Paniai Lakes region is off limits to tourists.]

Of all highland groups, the Ekari have proved the most responsive to government programs such as improved animal husbandry and agricultural techniques. The first contact with the West came in 1938. One subdivision of the group came under strong Roman Catholic influence after 1948 while others hosted Protestant missionaries.

Many groups in Melanesia are led by non-hereditary chiefs called "Big Men" who achieve their status through personal initiative. In Irian, such Big Men rise to their position through skills in war, oratory and trade, in varying combinations. The Ekari chiefs are an extreme example of wealth-accumulating Big Men, depending on successful pig breeding, which in turn requires a large, polygamous household. This enables the leader to extend credit by lending pigs and to show his generosity to his followers.

The Ekari have no concept of a gift—everything is leased, rented or loaned with elaborate calculations of credit and interest. Just about everything can be settled with suitable payments, including crimes such as rape, adultery and murder. A fee was even charged for raising a child.

After Dr. Pospisil gave the tribe a lecture on agriculture, he was given several chickens—the Ekari remembered what he had told them earlier about being paid to lecture to students in the United States.

The Ekari, who keep all accounts in their heads, work with a highly developed decimal system, which repeats at 60. Numbers are crucial. When Pospisil showed them a photo of a pretty smiling girl, the Ekari counted teeth. In a photo of a skyscraper, it was the number of windows. Boys considered it a special favor to be allowed to count the white man's "money," a collection of various shells and beads. The anthropologist was kept well advised, ahead of time, when his cash flow was getting behind. Not surprisingly, the Ekari became experts at mathematics when schools opened in their homeland.

Most unusual for a traditional culture, the Ekari have no communal property. Everything is owned, including each section of an irrigation ditch, a part of a road or footpath, even a wood-and-liana suspension bridge.

Conspicuous consumption is taboo: the most valuable shell necklaces are loaned or rented for ceremonies. Persistent stinginess can lead to capital punishment—execution by a kinsman's arrow.

The Paniai Lakes region is fertile when properly cultivated. In addition to the three existing lakes, Paniai, Tage and Tigi, there is another that began to dry out some 15 centuries ago, leaving behind the swampy Kamu Valley. Lake products are harvested exclusively by women, who collect crayfish, dragonfly larvae, tadpoles, waterbugs, frogs, lizards, birds' eggs, vegetables and fruits.

Traditional Ekari religion

The Ekari creator was omnipotent, omniscient, omnipresent and…nonexistent. Only after missionaries arrived did the Ekari name their creator, Ugatame. They believed that since all good and evil came from this being,

Opposite: *A Moni woman and her child.*

man had no free will—a most Calvinist phi-
osophy. But religion occupied little of the
people's attention. Of the 121 tenets of Ekari
belief compiled by Pospisil, only 14 dealt with
the supernatural.

Christian missionary efforts ran into prob-
ems. The Ekari refused to come to church
after one of the missionaries stopped giving
out free tobacco upon attendance. "No tobac-
o, no heleluju," said the men. And because
the highlands get awfully cold at night, the
Christian hell didn't seem like such a bad
place—warm, and nobody had to gather
wood. (See "Missionaries," page 46.)

First contacts with the west

In 1936, the Ekari saw an airplane fly overhead for the first time. The pilot, a certain
Lieutenant Wissel, was credited with discovering the area and the lakes were named after
him. (In 1962, the name was changed to
Paniai.) Even many years after the event, the
Ekari clearly remembered exactly what they
were doing when the plane came.

In 1938, a Dutch government post was
established at Enarotali and missionaries
soon followed. World War II interrupted the
process of modernization. The Japanese soldiers forced the tribesmen to participate in
labor gangs and to feed them, leading to
resistance and deaths on both sides.

After the war, the Dutch returned and the
pace of change picked up. Thanks to the good
advice of Roman Catholic priests, the Ekari
radically improved the utilization of their
lands by building large-scale irrigation ditches to prevent flooding.

The construction in 1958 of an airstrip at
the western edge of the Kamu Valley, which
brought in cash wages, ended the Ekari
youths' dependence on loans from their rich
elders, leading to a loss of influence and prestige for the older generation.

The Ekari became long-distance traders.
They even began to rent missionary airplanes
to take pigs and other trade items to outlying
areas. Dr. Pospisil, who wanted a ride on one
of these flights, was told he could—for a fee.
He was directed to sit in back with the pigs.
When he objected because he wanted to take
photos, he was allowed to sit next to the
pilot—for an added charge.

The ending of warfare and the speedy
acceptance of western medicine led to a great
population increase, and many Ekari have left
to seek a livelihood outside their homeland,
especially after a road connected the Kamu
Valley with the district capital of Nabire. By
1975, over 2,000 Ekari had settled there.

In Nabire, the traditional Ekari pragma-
tism and economic philosophy has served
them well. Ekari couples are famous for their
thrift, hard work, and purposeful accumula-
tion of capital. No other highland tribe has
entered Indonesia's modern economy with
nearly as much vigor.

EUROPEANS

Rumors of Gold and Exotic Trade

Within a few months of the conquest of Malacca in 1511 by the Portuguese, an expedition was dispatched to locate the fabled spice islands. Some sources state that Antonio D'Abreu, the captain of this pioneer expedition, sighted Irian's coast in 1512, but this is doubtful. But soon thereafter, references to New Guinea begin to appear in the western literature.

In 1521, 27 months out of Spain, Antonio Pigafetta, the chronicler of Magellan's epic world circumnavigation, received a first whiff of information about Irian while loading cloves in Ternate: "...the king of these heathens, called Raja Papua, is exceedingly rich in gold and lives in the interior of the island." This, however, was a decidedly false lead.

In 1526, the first Portuguese governor of the Moluccas, Jorge de Meneses, landed on Warsai (which he called "Versija") on the northwest coast of the Bird's Head, not far from Sorong. Meneses was on his way to take up a new post at Ternate, when he was driven eastward by adverse winds. He baptized the island Ilhas dos Papuas from the Malay *orang papuwah,* meaning "frizzy haired man."

Search for the 'Isla de Oro'

After this initial forced landing, the more dynamic Spaniards made contact with Irian as a result of their colonization of the Philippines. In Mexico, on the other side of the Pacific, Hernan Cortez, that prince of the conquistadores, also heard reports of this island of gold. Already in Mexico, and soon in Peru, the Spaniards had plundered a vast store of gold from the Aztecs and Incas. But this had been accumulated over generations, and after their initial euphoria, the Spaniards had to settle for the more mundane mining of silver. But if the Americas held no El Dorado, why not seek one on the other side of the Pacific?

In 1528 Cortez equipped and sent one of his lieutenants, Alvaro de Saavedra, to relieve a Spanish outpost under siege at Tidore by the Portuguese—and, not so incidentally, to discover and conquer the island of gold. While trying to return to Mexico from the Moluccas, Saavedra reached Biak, which he promptly dubbed "Isla de Oro." Spending one month among "naked black people," Saavedra made plans for further discovery and settlement even though not a trace of gold was

ound. He tried twice to return to Mexico along the equator but was turned back both times by contrary winds. Later, the Spaniards discovered that the only way to reach the Americas from Asia was to sail north to the latitude of Japan before catching the winds that would carry them east.

In 1537, the ever-optimistic Cortez directed Hernando de Grijalva to discover the island of gold. The expedition ended in disaster—not only did they find no gold, but the crew mutinied and murdered their captain. The disintegrating ship was abandoned in Cenderawasih Bay, and the seven survivors were captured and enslaved by the natives, becoming Irian's first white "settlers." Years later they were ransomed by the Portuguese governor of Ternate.

In 1545, Ynigo Ortiz de Retes, another Mexican-based Spanish captain, gave New Guinea its name, while at the same time claiming it for the King of Spain. He chose the name "Nueva Guinea" either because of the people's resemblance to Africans, or because of the island was on the other side of the globe from Africa. New Guinea first appeared on Mercator's world map in 1569.

Retes' explorations dispelled the illusion of easy gold for the taking, so Spain soon lost interest in the island. (There in fact is plenty of gold in New Guinea, but the first gold rush, in Laloki, near Port Moresby, did not take place until 1878.)

In 1606, the last Spanish exploration of New Guinea took place. Luis Vaez de Torres, a Portuguese in the service of Spain (as had been Magellan), sailed the length of New Guinea's south coast and, in two places, landed and claimed possession for Spain. The annexation was ephemeral, but the strait Torres discovered still bears his name. He was first to prove that Australia was separate from New Guinea. Spain maintained the fiction of its claim to New Guinea, based on Torres' voyage, until the treaty of Utrecht in 1714 formally "relinquished" the island to Holland and England.

In an era of conflicting claims, might made right. In her push for a monopoly on the spice trade in the Moluccas, Holland muscled aside the Spaniards, the Portuguese and, for good measure, her own English allies. Nor did the Dutch neglect explorations to the east.

In 1606, the same year that Torres made his discovery, Dutch navigator Willem Jansz sailed along New Guinea's west and south coasts. Also looking for gold, he touched land at various points, including the mouth of what

Opposite and below: *Luigi D'Albertis ascending the Fly River in the* Neva, *in 1876. D'Albertis harrassed the people of the Fly by shooting off fireworks and stealing artifacts. He made few friends even among his own crew, one of whom he beat to death in a fit of anger, but he did make it 930 kilometers upriver.*

has since been called the Digul River.

In 1616, two more Dutchmen, Jacob le Maire and Willem Schouten, surveyed New Guinea's north coast, including the islands of Cenderawasih Bay. Then, in 1623, Jan Carstensz sighted snow-capped peaks while sailing along Irian's southern coast. His reports were ridiculed in Europe, as no one believed that there could be snow so near the equator (4° S). None of the doubters bothered to check with the Spaniards about the Andes, and 200 years would pass before whites saw the snows of Kilimanjaro.

Birds of paradise and slaves

Although Irian harbored no gold, there were nonetheless valuable trade items emanating from the island, as the Dutch belatedly discovered. Javanese, Bugis, Bandanese and Seramese traders were conducting highly profitable forays to the west coast of Irian. In exchange for Javanese brass gongs, Chinese porcelain, cloth and metal implements, the traders received *massoi* bark (a medicinal prized by the Javanese, taken orally or as an oil smeared on the body to cure various illnesses, including venereal disease), an inferior quality of nutmeg (whose export irked the Dutch monopolists), *trepang* (dried sea cucumbers, a Chinese delicacy), tortoiseshell, pearls, bird of paradise skins and very valuable slaves.

From their bases in the nutmeg islands of Banda and clove-producing Ambon, the Dutch sent out their own trading ships but soon ran afoul of the "treachery" of the Irianese. Not without justification, the Dutch blamed the hostile attitude of the Irianese on the forcible capture of slaves by other traders.

Muslims from Seram Laut practiced the most effective means of control of Irian's trade. A contemporary Dutch account states that the Seram Muslims married Irianese wives ("in which they are not very choice," it gratuitously adds) and then instructed the children of these unions in the Muslim faith. Through these relatives, the Seram Laut men controlled Irian's trade.

In 1660 the Dutch East India Company recognized the Sultan of Tidore's sovereignty over "the Papuan Islands in general" while signing an "internal alliance" with the sultan. The treaty stipulated that all Europeans, except the Dutch, were forbidden in the area. The Dutch also reinforced the brutal Tidorese tribute-collecting flotillas to increase the sultan's authority and wealth.

While the Dutch were quite successful in maintaining a spice monopoly in the Moluccas, Irian was too far away for effective control. The great French explorer Compte de Bougainville initiated a round of expeditions to New Guinea in 1768, and the prince of navigators, James Cook, having made a series of historic discoveries in the Pacific rediscovered the Torres Strait in 1770 (then had a run-in with the Asmat of the south coast). Other early sailor-geographers to visit New Guinea included William Dampier Dumont d'Urville and two particularly bothersome (to the Dutch) Britons.

In 1775, Thomas Forrest of the British East India Company landed at Dore Bay, near present-day Manokwari. He was looking for a source of spices outside the Dutch sphere. Forrest was told that no Dutch "burghers" traded there—only Chinese, who easily obtained passes from the Sultan of Tidore and flew Dutch colors. They were trusted not to deal in spices. Forrest learned that these traders brought steel tools, weapons and porcelain to exchange for *massoi,* ambergris *trepang,* tortoiseshell, bird of paradise skins and slaves.

Another Briton, John McCluer, stopped on the southwest coast of Irian in 1791. His name then stuck to the gulf which he correctly mapped as almost cutting off the Bird's Head from the body (now called Berau Bay). McCluer found some nutmeg in Irian, but of the inferior elongated variety, not the prized round type.

European outposts established

Irian's first European settlement was an unmitigated disaster. In 1793, Captain John Hayes, an officer in the Bombay Marine (the British East India Company's navy) led an expedition to Irian to establish an outpost. Based on an account of Forrest's brief stopover, Hayes chose Dore Bay for his settlement, dubbed New Albion. He named his little harbor Restoration Bay.

Hayes claimed the land for Britain, but his expedition was totally unofficial and was backed with private money. He found nutmeg trees, dyewood and teak, and dreamed of the area being the center of a British-run spice trade. His little community of 11 European settlers and an equal number of Indians planted *massoi* and nutmeg trees and hoped for the best.

They built Fort Coronation to defend themselves against local hostilities and an expected Dutch attack. The Dutch did not need to bother—after 20 months, native arrows, a lack of supplies and disease forced the evacuation of the colony. All the men who had not been killed or taken as slaves by the natives were by this time very sick. The quality of spices gathered was very disappointing, and the British East India Company expressly banned any further private attempts to settle New Guinea.

[Note: Things might have been different if the settlement hadn't taken place just as the Napoleonic War put the Dutch East Indies temporarily in British hands.]

The next European colony did not fare much better. Stung into action by false rumors of a British trading post somewhere in southwest Irian, Pieter Merkus, sent the Dutch governor of the Moluccas, sent an official expedition in 1826 to claim New Guinea's south coast up to the 141st parallel. Expedition leader Lieutenant D.H. Kolff published a most interesting account of the effort.

In 1828, based on Kolff's report, a government post and colony named Merkussoord (after Merkus) was established on Triton Bay, a beautiful—but malarial—bay near present day Kaimana. Fort du Bus, built of stone, was named for the Belgian Viscount du Bus de Ghisignies, Governor-General of the Dutch East Indies.

The fort's garrison consisted of a lieutenant, a military doctor, 11 unhappy Europeans and 20 despondent Javanese soldiers and their families. A scowling group of 10 Javanese convict laborers were stuck with all the dirty work. Some Malay Muslims voluntarily joined the colony and Seramese trading boats called regularly. After 10 years, malaria finally forced the abandonment of the colony.

In 1848, again prompted by British activities the Dutch reinforced the Sultan of Tidore's nominal control of Irian's north coast. An 1850 report of the sultan's yearly tribute-gathering *hongi* expeditions describes them as unabashed exercises in pillage, rape and abduction.

Official accounts of this period indicate that Irian's most important exports to Ternate were *trepang,* tortoiseshell and *massoi,* with lesser quantities of cedar, ebony, sandalwood, rubber, pearls and copra leaving the island. An indeterminate number of slaves and bird of paradise skins round out the list.

The plumes were traded to Persia, Surat and the Indies, where the rich wore them in their turbans and used them to decorate their horses. Europeans who ridiculed the Asian penchant for these feathers were soon obliged to buy their wives French-designed hats

made from them.

The Dutch claimed sovereignty over New Guinea early on, but were a long time in following up with direct administrative control. Finally, developments on the other side of the border prodded them into action.

In 1884, a British protectorate was proclaimed at Port Moresby in eastern New Guinea and, in the same year, the German Imperial flag was raised on the Island's northeastern coast. Fifteen years later, the Dutch finally established two permanent posts in the west, at Fakfak and Manokwari. The boundary with the British was settled in 1895, and with the Germans in 1910. It followed the 141° E line with the exception of a slight westward blip at the Fly River.

In 1902 a post was founded at Merauke as an embarrassed response to complaints that the theoretically Dutch-controlled subjects regularly crossed the 141° E meridian to bring back British-administered trophy heads. The habits of the people of southeast Irian, in this case the fierce Marind-Anim, were responsible for the Dutch names given to two rivers in the area: Moordenaar (Murderer) and Doodslager (Slaughterer).

Above: *Catholic missionary Father H. Tillemans poses in the Irian highlands with a Tapiro man. Irian's first explorers were traders and naturalists; later these were replaced by missionaries and anthropologists.*

EXPLORATION

Naturalists, Mountaineers Map the Island

Long after the Dutch took formal control of Netherlands New Guinea, their administration still amounted to little more than a name on a map. One contemporary observer described Netherlands New Guinea as: "the stepchild of the Indies, neglected backwater against foreign intrusions, a place for tours of punishment duty by delinquent civil servants and of exile for nationalist leaders."

While the Indies administration ignored Irian, a small but hardy group of explorers—Dutch, English, and American—charted the island's wildlife, geography and peoples.

English biologist and collector Alfred Russel Wallace was the first in a line of distinguished biologists to visit the island. In his eight years in the archipelago, he collected more than 100,000 specimens, and postulated the existence of a biogeographical boundary dividing Asian and Australian species—now called the Wallace Line—where glaciation never lowered the seas sufficiently to allow for an overland spread of wildlife species. (See "Flora and Fauna," page 21.)

Wallace spent three months on the shores of Dore Bay and three months on Waigeo. In addition to a description of his biological work, his famous work, *The Malay Archipelago,* includes accounts of the lives and habits of the people in the areas he visited as well as an account of an early Dutch expedition along Irian's north coast.

In 1872, Italians Luigi Maria d'Albertis and Odoardo Beccari became the first scientists to explore the interior of western New Guinea, spending many months in the Arfak mountains inland from Dore Bay, collecting birds and insects, for which they traded Venetian beads.

[Note: The first scientist to explore the interior of New Guinea was the young Russian Nicolai Mikluho Maclay, who in 1871–2 spent 15 months around Astrolabe Bay in what is now Papua New Guinea. Maclay later spent four months at Triton Bay in western New Guinea.]

In 1876, the colorful, and indomitable, D'Albertis led an expedition in the *Neva,* a small riverboat, eventually traveling 930 kilometers up the Fly River, which begins on the southern coast of eastern New Guinea and loops north to barely touch the edge of present-day Irian Jaya. His crew near mutinied,

he beat a Chinese assistant to death, and he continually terrorized the people whose land he passed through by launching fireworks over their river. He was a singular individual, and perhaps thankfully so.

The Dutch explore Irian's interior

At the beginning of the 20th century, after a late start, Holland unleashed a veritable flood of exploration: 140 expeditions to the interior between 1900 and 1930. The most important of these were military-sponsored missions that began in 1907. At times the parties included over 800 men and had budgets totaling millions of guilders. Blanks on the map were quickly filled in and the newly discovered peaks took the names of Dutch royalty.

In 1905, the Dutch steamer *Valk* chugged 560 kilometers up the Digul River's winding course from the south coast, a distance of only 227 kilometers as the crow flies. A new snow-crested peak was sighted and dubbed Wilhelmina Top (now Trikora) in honor of the Dutch queen. Other expeditions steamed up the Mappi River to a lake of the same name, then onto the Eilanden (Islands) River—now Pulau Pulau—and its tributaries, the Vriendschaps (Friendship) and Wildeman.

While the upriver jaunts were relatively comfortable, overland treks to the central highlands tested the mettle of the toughest explorers, and the logistics of keeping such teams supplied were mind-boggling. The high glacier fields and snow-capped peaks were the most challenging sites to explore, not so much because of the mountaineering skills required (the Himalayas, Andes and even the Alps require greater technical proficiency), but because of the effort required simply to arrive at the base of the mountains. As was the case earlier, it was the British who spurred the Dutch into action. Competition with the British Ornithologists' Union led to a race to the untrodden equatorial snows of the Lorentz Range in south-central Irian.

A race to the peaks

Both the British and Dutch teams found that the best porters were muscular Dayaks from the island of Borneo. Quite a few were sent to Irian, most of them having been jailed by the colonial government for head-hunting. The Dayaks were accustomed to the cool climate of the highlands. But if Dayak porters were equally available to all comers, fair play stopped there. Taking advantage of their bureaucracy, the Dutch held up the British teams with stacks of paperwork.

Opposite and below: *The Sea Gull was the first airplane to fly in New Guinea, leaving Port Moresby in 1922. It was flown by Andrew Lang, and rigger Alex Hill and photographer Frank Hurley (below) came along on the expedition. Photographs courtesy the American Museum of Natural History.*

The Dutch left the competition filling out forms and set out from Irian's south coast in 1909. Led by Dr. H. A. Lorentz—who proclaimed "I shall be first on the snow"—they eventually reached the snowline of Wilhelmina Top (now Trikora). Each of the 82 Dayak porters was rewarded by a tattoo showing a snow-capped mountain and a dragon, to symbolize the hardships. The British finally obtained their permits and gave chase, reaching an elevation of 4,532 meters before turning back. Neither team made the summit.

In 1913, a group led by Dutch Captain Franssen Herderschee finally scaled Wilhelmina Top's 4,743 meters. The Dayak porters celebrated with a snowball fight.

Carstensz Top (now Puncak Jaya), Irian's highest peak, remained for some time the most obvious challenge. In 1913, Wollaston had reached the snows of the Sudirman Range, but no one had yet climbed the higher peaks. Prodded by rumors of yet another British expedition in 1937, national Dutch pride was aroused and an expedition was quickly launched.

By the time an attempt was finally made on the Carstensz, logistics had improved considerably. The first airplane had flown out of Port Moresby in 1922, and in 1926, a Dutch-American team became the first expedition to rely on air transport, the seaplane *Ern*. In 1936, the Dutch pilot Lieutenant F. J. Wissel discovered, from his plane, the Paniai Lakes

which for a while bore his name.

The Dutch were now ready for Carstensz Toppen, named after the first white man to sight it and report snows in the tropics in 1623. The *toppen* is a series of peaks, some ten of which are higher than 4,700 meters high. The explorers misidentified a peak called Ngga Pulu (4,860m.) as the highest of the lot, and this was their goal.

After Wissel's aerial reconnaissance in an amphibian Sikorski, the expedition, led by Dr. A. H. Colijn, plotted a course from the south coast. Once the party was underway, Wissel made two supply drops by parachute then paddled upriver himself to catch up with the group. On December 5th, 1623, after a four-hour climb from the base camp, they reached the peak. The mountaineers celebrated by devouring a tin of marzipan.

Unfortunately, Ngga Pulu was not Carstensz' highest peak, and Puncak Jaya, at 4,884 meters, was not scaled until 1962 by the Austrian Heinrich Harrer.

The Meervlakte

While the explorations of the highlands proceeded apace, other teams made their way inland from Irian's north coast. The only logical route was up the Mamberamo River, navigable for over 150 kilometers.

In 1909, Captain Franssen Herderschee (who later climbed Wilhelmina) ascended the short stretch of rapids through the Van Rees

Mountains and reached a large crescent-shaped basin that he dubbed the Meervlakte, or "Lake Plains."

The basin is formed by the Taritatu River (formerly Idenburg), which flows from the Jayawijaya Range (Oranje) in the east, and the Tariku River (Rouffaer), coming from the Sudirman Range (Nassau) in the west. The two rivers unite to form the Mamberamo.

Although several expeditions subsequently also reached the Mamberamo, the upper reaches of the Taritatu remained uncharted until the 1950s.

By the 1920s, monstrously large teams of up to 800 men (mostly porters) headed inland, supplied by flying boats. They did not always meet with a warm welcome from their hosts, and aviators tell of arrows bouncing off their fuselage.

The Baliem Valley discovered

The discovery of the Baliem Valley in 1938 by American explorer Richard Archbold was the grand prize of New Guinea's exploration. Peering from a giant seaplane dubbed the *Guba*, Archbold was the first white man to lay eyes on the jewel of the highlands, a fabulous 60 by 15 kilometer valley.

The 50,000 Dani living in the valley had at this time had no previous contact with the outside world. A couple of Dutch expeditions had passed close, but missed this rare pocket of flat, arable land—the highlands' largest and most fertile. Surveying the scene from his plane, Archbold described the valley's neat geometric gardens and irrigation ditches as being "like the farming country of central Europe." He later ferried in 30 tons of supplies and a team of 195 men, mostly Irianese porters backed up by 72 hardy Dayaks.

Dutch captain Teerink, one of Archbold's team, was the first to reach the valley with a few porters. When a fuel drop floated off on the river, the captain sacrificed his only bottle of gin to the generator to maintain communications with the base camp. (See "Archbold Expedition," page 118.)

The post-war Dutch era saw two major explorations: The Wisnumurti (Star) Range was reached from the Sibyl Valley at the headwaters of the Digul River; and a joint French–Dutch effort, led by Pierre Dominique Gaissau, crossed the widest part of Irian overland. The record of this harrowing trek from the southern Asmat coast to Hollandia became a spectacular film, *The Sky Above and The Mud Below,* and Paris Match photographer Tony Saulnier produced a first-class book of still photographs.

Opposite: *Explorers of the Paniai Lakes region, posing with Ekari men. The explorers, left to right: F.J. Wissel, Jean-Jacques Dozy, and Dr. De Hartog.* **Above:** *The ice fields at Ngga Pulu, once thought to be the highest of Carstenz Toppen's many craggy tops.*

WORLD WAR II

MacArthur's New Guinea Campaign

For many, the Second World War put New Guinea on the map. Though the Japanese at first swept quickly through the Dutch East Indies and on to east New Guinea, their seemingly inexorable advance was finally stopped 50 kilometers from Port Moresby—from which Australia was but a short hop away.

Vicious jungle fighting by tough Australian troops slowly pushed the Japanese back. As the war progressed and American might came into play, churning out airplanes, ships, weapons and fighting men, the Allies slowly acquired the means to sweep back the Japanese invaders. After the reconquest of east New Guinea, the pace quickened.

By the spring of 1944, when the Allies were prepared to mount an assault on the area, the northern coast of Irian was defended by some 55,000 Japanese troops, backed by considerable air power and substantial naval forces based in the secure waters of the Moluccas, to the west. Thanks to intercepted Japanese communications and broken codes, General Douglas MacArthur learned about the defensive weakness of Hollandia (now Jayapura): although 11,000 Japanese troops were stationed there, only about one-fifth were combat soldiers.

Risking an attack on his exposed flank, MacArthur then bypassed Japanese troop concentrations at Wewak and Hansa Bay and launched a daring assault on Hollandia itself. Control of the skies made a landing possible. The U.S. Air Force, with 1,200 planes, wiped out the Japanese air fleet at Sentani, destroying over 300 craft. Only 25 serviceable planes were left by the American pilots.

The Hollandia campaign

For the Hollandia landing, at the time the largest operation in the Pacific, MacArthur employed 217 ships and 80,000 men, led by 50,000 combat troops. The initial objective was to seize a coastal strip some 40 kilometers wide, between the landing points at Hollandia and Tanah Merah Bay. The lack of Japanese resistance was a godsend, as a chaotic debarkation took place amidst heavy rain and over difficult terrain. When the beachheads were secured on April 22, 1944, MacArthur and his staff celebrated by quaffing ice cream sodas.

The next day, as a landing craft ferried the commander-in-chief to the beach at Tanah Merah, a lone Japanese plane appeared and gave everyone a thorough scare. But the pilot, unaware of the landing craft's passenger, flew on to seek a more sizeable target.

The Hollandia campaign, considered by war historians as a model strategic maneuver, cost the Allies only 159 lives. More than 4,000 Japanese were killed and 650 prisoners were taken. About 7,000 Japanese tried to escape to Sarmi, a stronghold over 200 kilometers down the coast, but disease, starvation and wounds claimed all but 1,000 men.

Meanwhile, Allied engineers reinforced and enlarged the roads and airstrips at Sentani, as the Japanese-built runways were neither sturdy nor long enough for the U.S. B-29 Superfortress bombers. A total of 240 kilometers of roads and airstrips were laid. Sides of mountains were carved away, bridges and culverts were built across rivers and creeks, gravel and stone was poured into sago swamps to support highways "as tall as Mississippi levees."

Building a command post

Almost overnight, Hollandia mushroomed into a city of 250,000, with 140,000 Australian and American troops and support personnel. The area became one of the war's great military bases, with most of the southwest Pacific command operating from here during the summer of 1944. MacArthur chose the best spot for his sprawling headquarters complex—a 250-meter hill overlooking Lake Sentani. Rugs and furniture from the general's Brisbane, Australia office filled prefab army buildings. One of MacArthur's staff described the view:

"[The] deep green hills of central New Guinea formed a backdrop of peaks, ravines and jungle growth that was almost unreal. Little cone-shaped islands, with native houses on stilts clinging to their shores, dotted the lake."

Opposite: *Allied bombing and shelling prior to the Hollandia invasion destroyed all Japanese shipping to and from the area, including this unfortunate craft, now rusting in Yotefa Bay.*

War correspondents, not always in awe of the quick-tempered MacArthur, filed a story about the general's million-dollar mansion with lavish furnishings and a custom-built drive. MacArthur was furious. After the Philippines had been secured, his wife decided to stop at Hollandia on her way to Manila to be reunited with her husband. She wired him, "I want to see that mansion you built—the one where I'm supposed to have been living in luxury!"

Those present did not dare record even a censored version of MacArthur's reply. Another wartime story, probably apocryphal, recounts that it was while gazing out on island-dotted Lake Sentani that General MacArthur conceived his famous island-hopping strategy.

The huge airfield complex at Lake Sentani was to eventually house 1,000 planes. An almost equal number of ships ferried in countless tons of supplies and equipment. Humboldt Bay, with hundreds of ships linked by catwalks and lit up at night, was described by war correspondents as "a city at sea."

The north coast falls

Because soil conditions at Sentani precluded the speedy completion of a bomber base, the Allies set their sights on the Japanese airfield on Wakde Island. After two days of bitter fighting, with 760 Japanese deaths as against 40 on the Allies side, the strip fell. More tough fighting was needed to secure the shores of Maffin Bay on the mainland near Wakde, essential as a forward staging area. The final toll here was 4,000 Japanese killed and 75 taken prisoner, with 415 U.S. casualties. The Tornado Task Force secured all important positions, but at the end of the war there were still some Japanese soldiers holed up in nearby Sarmi.

Despite increasing Allied control of the air and sea lanes, the Japanese tried to send 20,000 troops to Irian from China. The reinforcements never made it. Allied submarines sank four transport ships, drowning 10,000, and the rest of the convoy fled.

The next Allied objective, Biak Island off the north coast of Irian, stopped the U.S.-led blitzkrieg cold. The 10,000 Japanese troops on Biak were well-organized and well-prepared. (See "Biak," page 64.)

The last Allied offensive in Irian occurred on the northern shore of the Bird's Head. Amphibious landings at Sansapor and Mar here went unopposed. These beachheads were only 150 kilometers west of Manokwari, the headquarters of the Japanese 2d Army. Quick work by engineers soon yielded operational airfields from which the next objective, Morotai Island off northern Halmahera, could easily be reached.

In just four short months, from April to July of 1944, the whole north coast of Irian had fallen to the Allies.

MISSIONARIES

Bringing the Word to a 'Heathen' Land

Missionaries have been active in Irian for well over a century. When in 1858 Alfred Russel Wallace arrived in Dore Bay (near present-day Manokwari), he met Johann Geissler and C.W. Ottow, two missionaries sent by The Christian Workman, a Dutch Protestant mission. Although these two (and a third who followed) learned the local language and eventually established four stations in the vicinity, during the next 25 years more of their party died in New Guinea than natives were baptized. One account refers to these deaths as "rather prosaic martyrdoms of malaria."

Protestants and Catholics

During the 1890s and the first part of this century, as Dutch administrative control spread through West New Guinea, many more missionaries arrived. The colonial administration, in the Boundary of 1912, created a duplicate of Holland herself, decreeing that Protestants should work the north and Catholics the south.

The results of this division are still visible today, with more Catholic converts found in the south and more Protestants in the north. Since 1955, however, the various faiths have been free to proselytize anywhere, and consequently have made inroads into each other's "territories." Recently, American fundamentalists have made great progress in the highlands.

Protestant Christianity is the religion of over 200,000 Irianese highlanders as well as most inhabitants of the coastal areas, except for the cities, where many of the recent arrivals are Muslims from other parts of Indonesia. The Mission Fellowship, an umbrella organization which coordinates the activities of nine separate Protestant groups in Irian, comprised 182 individuals at last count. Most Protestant missionaries are married, and the majority are Americans. Many Protestant churches are also now run by Indonesian pastors.

The Catholic missions, staffed by 90 priests, 26 brothers and 95 sisters, are divided into four dioceses. The diocese of Merauke claims more than 100,000 Catholics, Agats 20,000 plus, Sorong 20,000 and the Jayapura diocese some 70,000 converts, with about half of them living in the Paniai Lakes region. The Catholics claim that 220,000 Irianese—about one-fifth of Irian's total population—practice their faith.

Converting the highland tribes

In 1938, a year after the Paniai Lakes of western Irian were discovered, the Dutch opened their first post at Enarotali. This same year, the first Roman Catholic missionary arrived at the westernmost extremity of the highlands. Shortly thereafter, the first American Protestant missionaries arrived, following an 18-day, 100 kilometer hike through torrential rains from the coast.

As the result of a "gentlemen's agreement," the western highlands were divided into two spheres of influence—the Catholics took the area around Lakes Tigi and Tage (as well as in the Moni enclave of Kugapa in the east) and the Protestants the Ekari territory on the shore of Lake Paniai.

One of the immediate results was hyperinflation in the native currency of cowry shells, as the missionaries brought with them huge supplies of shells to finance their operations with native labor. Gone were the days when one cowrie shell would buy a 5-gallon

in of sweet potatoes and 50 of them fetched a wife or a fat pig. It soon took 2 steel axes and 40 blue porcelain beads to convince a porter to carry a pack on the 13-day trek from Enarotali to Ilaga.

Life was not easy for these early missionaries in Irian. Hob-nailed boots were essential for hiking across moss-covered logs, slippery trunk bridges and frequent mud. A pair of these tough boots could be worn out in a week. Exhausting treks were necessary to scout out locations for new missions. Months of hard work by natives paid with steel axes were required to carve airstrips out of the steep slopes. Small planes first dropped in supplies and then, when the strips were complete, transported missionary wives and children and a plethora of goodies with which to tempt the Irianese.

Cargo cults

Irian's highlanders, for their part, often confused these strange foreigners with powerful ancestral spirits who were believed to help their descendants if proper rituals were performed. Thus when the whites arrived with their enviable material possessions, the natives assumed that rituals performed by missionaries, such as eating at tables, writing letters and worshipping in church, were responsible for the arrival of such goods. One can imagine how it appeared when spoken appeals to a metal box led to a seemingly endless supply of steel axe heads, metal knives and food being dropped from the sky.

This led to the development of "cargo cults"—mystical millenarian movements (the highlanders also believed in a "second coming"—a golden age of immortality and bliss). In Papua New Guinea (where there has been more research), these cults led to the construction of model airplanes and mini-airstrips in hope the spirits would send them planeloads of goods ("kago" in pidgin English).

The cargo cult mentality, which was widespread throughout Melanesia, gave a boost to the missionaries' message in western New Guinea. Many people at first thought of the whites as demi-gods, both for their incredible material possessions and for their "magic" in curing disease. This belief was heightened because the whites murmured mysterious incantations over their patients as they cured them (with a quick shot of penicillin) from the disfiguring skin called yaws that plagued the highlands.

Cargo cultism no doubt contributed to the American fundamentalists' success in the

highlands, but great energy and sacrifice also contributed to the evangelical drive. Particularly effective were the native preachers, first from a Bible school on Sulawesi and then from among the highlanders themselves.

Success among the Damal

Following the Allied victory in World War II, the Christian and Missionary Alliance (CAMA) established its headquarters in Enarotali on the Paniai shore. Following up on their pre-World War II work, Protestants trekked east from the Paniai to their former post in the Kemandora Valley. From here, a station was built in Homeyo, among the Moni tribemen controlling the highlands' best brine pools.

By 1954, the missionaries reached the Ilaga Valley, about halfway along the 275-kilometer path between Paniai and the Baliem Valley. The Ilaga region is the hub of a wheel of valleys where fertile soils provide abundant harvests of corn, beans and peas, in addition to the staple sweet potato. The abundance of raspberries here led to the practice of using raspberry juice, along with chunks of sweet potato, for communion. The first converts were 1,200 Damal tribesmen living here as a minority in a Dani area.

While victories were being won for Christ in the Ilaga, back at CAMA headquarters serious difficulties had arisen. A widespread pig epidemic was blamed on the spirits' displeasure with the foreigners. The Ekari at Enarotali revolted, killing their Christian tribesmen as well as an Indonesian preacher and his family. They also destroyed the mission airplane, which was crucial for ferrying

Opposite: *A missionary nurse administers antibiotics to a family in East New Guinea. Photograph courtesy of the American Museum of Natural History.* **Above:** *The mission station at Pyramid, run by American Protestant missionaries, is the largest in the highlands.*

supplies to the highland stations. The trouble-makers were finally subdued—not by Dutch rifles and mortars, but by well-aimed Christian arrows.

On to the Baliem Valley

In 1955, under pressure from the influential Roman Catholic political party, the Dutch parliament finally passed a bill allowing unrestricted activities on the part of all mission societies in Irian. After some brief explorations and the establishment of a station at Hetegima at the southern end of the Baliem Valley, Protestants began expanding into the previously off-limits Baliem at a rapid pace.

The mission at Pyramid, at the northwestern end of the valley was the first to be established. A major trade route already led here from the Western Dani centers of Bokondini, Karubaga and Mulia. Because of its strategic location, more missionaries were sent to Pyramid than anywhere else, and the mission retains its importance today.

The western valley station at Tiom, and one at Seinma in the Baliem Gorge area south of Hetegima, were both opened in 1956, one year before the Dutch government established its first outpost in the valley, at Wamena. In 1958, a year after Wamena was established, Catholics entered the valley.

When Dutch control came to the Valley, the various Protestant sects—CAMA, the Australian Baptist Missionary Society, the Regions Beyond Missions Union, and the United Field Missions—joined forces for financial and logistical reasons as well as to counteract the Roman Catholic presence. The Catholics' more flexible policy toward native beliefs was a sore point with more fundamentalist Protestants. Said one polemicist, "the Catholics' attempts at accommodation have at times produced hybrid creeds scarcely recognizable as the continuation of historic, Biblical Christianity."

With the competition for souls heating up, gone were the "gentlemen's agreements" of old. But old-fashioned Protestant missionaries who, for example, insisted on clothing being worn in church, were also fading. Younger, more open-minded Americans who had taken university courses in anthropology and linguistics after their years of Bible college were now joining the ranks. This new breed of missionaries enjoined only against those practices that were in direct conflict with the Bible—killing the second twin born, spirit worship and the execution of women accused of witchcraft.

Fearing a Catholic monopoly on education, the Protestants also agreed to participate in secular educational programs sponsored by the Dutch government. And, albeit reluctantly, the Americans also participated in setting up a government-subsidized public hospital at Pyramid.

'Pockets of heathenism'

In the early 1960s, the pace of missionary activities slowed. The country was undergoing a difficult transition from Dutch to Indonesian rule, and the frenetic pace of evangelical advances had left numbers of unbelievers as well as "pockets of heathenism" in the minds of the recent converts. It was time to consolidate gains.

Preachers found that even well-behaved flocks were sometimes operating with pretty strange notions of Christianity. The Irianese held such beliefs as that sitting in church would result in immunity from sickness, and that forgetting to shut one's eyes during prayers would lead to blindness. Missionaries responded to these setbacks and superstition by swearing to persevere against this "black magic," which one called "Satan's counteraction to God's perfect will for man."

The Protestants, resolving their internal difficulties, at this time planned a two pronged strategy to conquer the remaining Western Dani—moving eastward from the Ilaga Valley and northwest from Pyramid. Setting aside jealousies and theological differences, the Australian Baptist Missionary Society joined forces with Regions Beyond Missions Union to help the United Field Missions build an airstrip at Bokondini. Areas thus opened up were divided into exclusive spheres of influence.

From Bokondini, missionaries trekked to Mulia to spread the gospel to the "crazy people"—Danis suffering from huge goiters and giving birth to cretins. Disease in this tragic place, the "most concentrated goiter pocket in the world," was soon cleared up with iodine injections and prayers. By 1963, a conference in Bokondini attracted 51 Dani church leaders. In the same year, Bokondini became the site of a teacher-training school.

While the Gospel swept into Western Dani areas, the Baliem Valley offered surprisingly stubborn resistance. Powerful war chiefs here resisted the new creeds, correctly viewing them as as a direct threat to their author-

Opposite: *American missionary John Wilson poses with a Dani man at Pyramid.*

ty. A man who has more than 20 confirmed kills to his credit isn't going to give up his hard-won prestige to a religion that proposes that "the meek shall inherit the earth." Many leaders also objected to the secrets of salvation being revealed to women—religious lore had always been a male preserve.

There were other reasons for a slowing of proselytization here, too. With the civil government providing medical care and newly arrived merchants offering essential material goods, Bible preachers lost some of their punch. In fact, the greatest concentration of Dani who today refuse Christianity live in and around the administrative center of Wamena.

Life among the cannibals

The life of a missionary in Irian was not easy. (This is not to celebrate their suffering; missionary efforts in Irian have inflicted great hardships on the Irianese.) One story involves Stanley Dale, an abrasive former Australian commando, and Phil Masters, an American, who were dispatched to convert a group of Yali villagers in the area east of Ninia, between the Heluk and Seng Rivers.

For a while, the Yali believed that the two newcomers were reincarnations of two of their deceased leaders, turned white after passing through the land of the dead. But they soon realized the missionaries were ordinary humans, and following several misguided attempts at "reform"—including mass fetish-burning—killed them. In 1968, the bodies of the two men were found riddled with arrow shafts "as thick as reeds in a swamp."

Another tale involves Dutch Reverend Gert van Enk, 31, a tall, tropics-cured veteran of five year's service, who has been working among the Korowai tribe, around the upper Becking River, in what he calls the "hell of the south." The Dutch Reformed Church has been trying to proselytize the 3,000 Korowai for ten years and so far has not celebrated a single baptism. Van Enk is not allowed into most of the tribal territory, and if caught there would be pin-cushioned with arrows. But he has no thoughts of giving up. His countrymen, he says, took centuries to become Christians.

Missionaries and progress

Although the methods and mission of Third World evangelical Christianity are today routinely questioned, missionaries in Irian Jaya have often played a positive role in easing traditional Irianese into the 20th century. They have brought medicine, and have often served as an important buffer between the government and the people.

The sensitivity of the church to local customs is today greatly improved. Even fundamentalist Protestants now allow worshipers into their churches wearing penis gourds, and local Irianese are groomed to take over positions of leadership within the church.

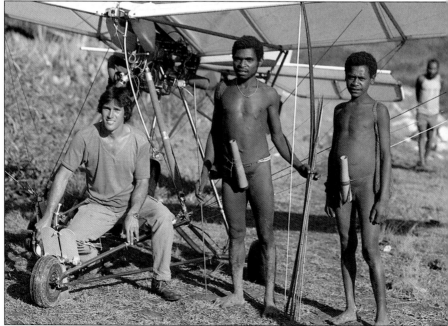

TEMBAGAPURA

A Giant Copper Mine in the Sky

In the shadow of glacier-capped Puncak Jaya, Irian's highest peak, steel jaws travel along the world's longest single-span tramways, carrying up to 17-ton loads of ore across some of the most inaccessible terrain on earth. A huge mineral concentrator processes the ore into liquid slurry, which is then pumped through the world's longest slurry pipelines to a port on the mangrove flats 118 kilometers away on the coast.

With operations higher than 4,000 meters, daily rainfall, and situated in some of the strangest and most forbidding terrain in the world, this mine stands as one of the greatest engineering achievements of our time.

It is also—quite literally—a gold mine for its owners, Freeport Indonesia, majority owned by Freeport–McMoRan in Louisiana. In addition to billions of pounds of copper reserves, making it one of the five largest copper mines in the world, a recently discovered deposit now gives the mine the single largest gold reserves of any mine in the world: 27 million ounces.

[Note: Visitors are not welcome at any of the Freeport installations. Only the head office in Jakarta grants permits to tour the areas, and these are granted for professional reasons only.]

A mountain of ore

The story begins with a jet-black outcropping of ore discovered in 1936 by Dutch geologist Jean Jacques Dozy. Literally a mountain of copper, Ertsberg ("ore mountain" in Dutch) stood 179 meters above a grassy meadow, 3,500 meters up in the highest part of Irian's rugged cordillera. High-grade ore lurked in the rock below to a depth of 360 meters. Ertsberg—or Gunung Bijih (also "Ore Mountain")—as it later came to be called—was so exposed because the softer rock surrounding it had been carved away by glaciers. This was the largest above-ground copper deposit in the world.

The Freeport mines have already provid-

Opposite: *John Cutts, the son of missionaries, grew up with the Moni near Enarotali. The mission's ultralight airplane allowed him to land at even the tiniest of bush strips.*
Below: *The 91 kilometer road to Tembagapura was painstakingly cut by flown-in bulldozers.*

ed the world with 3 billion pounds of copper. The Gunung Bijih deposit, which harbored 33 million metric tons of ore, has been exhausted, and all that remains is a pit. But three additional deposits have been discovered just a stone's throw from Gunung Bijih: Gunung Bijih Timur (including two separate deposits), Dom (Dutch for "cathedral," a hill of marble), and the greatest prize of all, Grasberg (Dutch for "grass mountain").

And the future is very bright for Freeport. As of 1991, proven reserves at the mine total 447 million metric tons of ore, estimated to yield 14 billion pounds of copper, 19 million ounces of gold, and 35 million ounces of silver. At current rates of extraction, this means an annual revenue of $800 million, more than $1 million per day in profit.

Mining costs are relatively high at Freeport, now averaging 46¢ per pound of saleable copper, and falling copper prices have at times made the mine temporarily unprofitable. But now that copper stands near $1 per pound, the mine earns Freeport more than $1 million a day.

'Copper City'

Mine workers live in Tembagapura—"Copper City"—a company town of 8,700 people nestled in a 1850-meter-high valley near the ore deposits. The setting is stunning, with the western flank of Mount Zaagham providing a spectacular backdrop.

A melting pot of ethnic groups labor in the mines. A Javanese welds and reshapes the huge steel teeth of a monstrous ore crusher. A Buginese from Sulawesi checks the rollers under a long conveyor belt that brings blasted chunks of ore to the crusher. A highland Irianese rewires a complicated fuse-box. And a team of two men from Biak efficiently maneuvers a pneumatic drill at the far end of a side tunnel to prepare a section for blasting.

Freeport employs about 6,900 people, of whom 92 percent are Indonesians. Of these 13 percent—about 900—are native Irianese. The company has been criticized for the relatively low number of Irianese working there, although training programs are beginning to show improved results.

For the workers, Tembagapura is pleasant, but remote. As an Irish expat said: "All you have to think about is your work—everything else is laid out for you." And very well laid out, with modern homes following the gentle slope of the creek-split valley. After a heavy rain, and 7,600 millimeters fall each year, 50 waterfalls spring from the tropical vegetation or bare rock on the vertical face of Mount Zaagham.

Facilities at Tembagapura include schools, tennis courts, a soccer field, a complete indoors sports complex, the latest videotapes, a subsidized store, clubs and bars—including the so-called "animal bar," frequented by workers. Hard liquor is taboo, but copious

uantities of beer are served.

Supplies to Tembagapura must be trucked over a steep, narrow gravel road from imika, 75 kilometers away in the lowlands. ust keeping the men fed is a major feat of ngineering. For example, Tembagapura equires 110 metric tons of rice a month, 88 etric tons of meat, and 33 metric tons of sh. The men eat a hearty breakfast, and equire 91,000 eggs *every day.* (Freeport's eet of trucks uses up 200 tires a week.)

Within the relatively narrow valley, real state is at a premium. This means that many f the married workers cannot bring their milies to Tembagapura, which makes for a t of lonely men. It was once suggested that me ladies of pleasure be "imported" and eriodically checked for disease—a practice many Indonesian company towns. But the lea was shot down.

Tembagapura has changed drastically nce the early days, when a German visitor xclaimed, "Mein Gott, Stalag 17." But it is ill an isolated, tight-knit community. As a vanese jokingly said, "Irian is the Siberia of idonesia." He was referring to being so far om home, cut off from familiar surround-gs. But in Tembagapura, he could also have een referring to the cold weather. The mps of Siberia never had the creature com-rts of this town, however.

Most of the Indonesians at Tembagapura e content with their lot. They work hard—9 ours a day, 6 days a week—but they get paid uite well, and they get 5 weeks off each year, ith the company paying the airfare home.

pposite: *Tram cars at the Freeport mine carry 1–17 metric tons of ore at a time along the orld's longest single-span tramway to the efining plant below.* **Above:** *Gunung Bijih, a ountain of nearly pure copper ore, has been xhausted, leaving an open pit. But half a llion tons of ore remain.* **Right:** *A skilled anese miner wields a jackhammer.*

Ertsberg rediscovered

In the early 1950s, Forbes Wilson, chief exploration geologist for Freeport Sulphur of Louisiana, was conducting some library research on possible mining areas. He chanced across a report by Jean Jacques Dozy, published in 1939 by the University of Leiden, but subsequently forgotten in the upheavals of World War II. Although the report states that it would be hard to imagine a more difficult place to find an ore deposit, Wilson was thrilled.

"My reaction was immediate," Wilson said. "I was so excited I could feel the hairs rising on the back of my neck."

Wilson was determined to view the marvel himself and to take enough samples to determine if mining operations would be justified. In 1936 it had taken Dozy 57 days to reach Ertsberg after a parachute drop.

Taking advantage of post–World War II U.S. military organization and financing from Freeport, Wilson sent in an advance party and hopped on a chartered plane from Biak. He landed on the south coast of what was then Dutch New Guinea. The landing strip was a former Japanese airfield used for bombing raids on Darwin, Australia.

Wilson's party canoed as far upstream as possible, then hiked in with mountain Irianese who, paid in axes and machetes, served as porters. The porters, the mining

engineer writes, ate "anything that walks, creeps or crawls," including humans, which they called "long pigs" and found much juicier than pork.

It took Wilson 17 days to reach Ertsberg, scaling a sheer cliff face 600 meters high where the tramway now smoothly ferries passengers and ore. The trek was worth it—as he chipped through the stone's oxidized layer he saw the gleaming golden color of chalcopyrite, a sulfide of iron and copper. Spending several days at the Ertsberg collecting samples, Wilson also saw malachite stains on a distant cliff, part of what is now called Gunung Bijih Timur ("Ore Mountain East").

Wilson's initial estimates, relayed excitedly by radio, proved quite accurate: 13 million tons of high grade ore lay above ground and 14 million tons more below. But, as he describes, this was "perhaps the most remote, primitive and inhospitable area in the world." The copper was there all right; the problem was getting it out.

Wilson even had problems getting out himself. Not only was he apprehensive of his cannibal porters, but he wore out his seventh and last pair of boots before reaching the canoes. But he made it, bringing back several hundred pounds of samples, which confirmed his opinion of their high copper content.

Freeport needed more samples before investing the millions of dollars required to build the mine, however. One problem—insurmountable at the time—was transporting the huge diamond drills needed to take deep samples. Even disassembled, the parts were too heavy for choppers in the early 1960s, which could then lift only one passenger and 113 kilos to a height of no more than 3,600 meters.

Technology and politics

Clouds of political instability combined with technical problems to block the project, as President Sukarno began a military campaign to wrest Irian from the Dutch. The project was put on the back burner in the hopes that eventually the situation would change.

After Suharto took over the reins of government, a 1967 Foreign Investment Law once again encouraged investment in Indonesia. Freeport hired Ali Budiarjo as a consultant and things began to look up. Budiarjo was a Dutch-educated Indonesian, a patriot who opposed colonialism, but most importantly, a Javanese well connected to the Jakarta scene.

Wilson and a legal advisor were among the first foreign businessmen to be welcomed back to the country. When they arrived at the Hotel Indonesia, there were only 15 guests attended by 1,800 employees. Freeport's contract with the government was the first to be signed under the new investment law.

In 1967, the last phase of testing was carried out. Helicopter technology had by then

advanced such that there were craft available that could lift half a ton to the required altitude—enough to ferry in the diamond drills needed for core samples. The deep cores confirmed Wilson's estimates.

Financing was the next problem. Wilson had to convince Freeport's board of directors, understandably nervous after Fidel Castro's nationalization of their operation in Cuba, that Indonesia was a safe place to invest. A consortium of Japanese and German lenders finally backed Freeport and the project began.

Bechtel was chosen as the prime contractor, but even these famous can-do engineers were nearly overwhelmed by technical problems at Tembagapura. Bechtel stated categorically that the mine was the most formidable construction feat they had ever undertaken.

Building the mine

Men and supplies were ferried in from Australia in a PBY seaplane (Howard Hughes had earlier converted it to fish salmon in Alaska but later lost interest) and a seaport was hacked out of the mangrove swamps with chainsaws at Amamapare, at the mouth of the Timika River. Men sank up to their waists in mud sawing through a 15-acre morass of mangrove roots, praying all the time that the racket would keep the crocodiles at bay.

Temporary landing pads for the helicopters were carved out by lowering chainsaw-wielding men on lines from the hovering craft. The men, dangling in the air, cut the tops off the trees to get through the thick canopy and, once on the ground, chopped up enough trunks to make a landing platform. Helicopters ferried men and supplies everywhere. Six choppers were on the job by August 1971, shifting 1,604 tons of supplies inland in that month alone.

The 92-kilometer road from the Tipuka River to the mill site was the toughest challenge. Eighty kilometers from the port, the least abrupt incline rose at a 70 degree angle. The mountain was not only steep, but razor-backed—a two-foot wide ridge, with sheer drops on either side. At first, tiny D4 bulldozers, slightly bigger than a lawn-mower, were flown in to carefully shave off the top of the ridge and make room for the slightly larger D6s, which in turn cleared space for the D7s,

Opposite: *Tembagapura, or "Copper City," nestles in a 1850-meter-high valley.*
Above: *Separated from loved ones in isolated Tembagapura, mine workers entertain themselves with spirited soccer games.*

followed by the D8s. By the time the monstrous, 25-ton D12s were done, 12 million tons of earth had been moved, altering the angle of the slope from 70 to 27 degrees—the maximum that could be negotiated by fully-loaded trucks. Not even the steepest streets of San Francisco have such a grade.

A hundred Korean coal miners were flown in to dig a 1,105 meter tunnel through Mt. Hannekam for the first section of the road, at 2,600 meters. From there, the road dropped to 1,850 meters at the site of Tembagapura, then shot up through another tunnel to the future mill site, located at 2,900 meters, 10 kilometers from Copper City.

To move ore from the mine to the mill, an 800-meter tramway was constructed through the rain and fast-moving clouds of the highlands (there are now two). Each of the cars, humming along on dual cables, carries 11–17 tons of partially crushed mineral to the bottom, dumps its load, and then returns to the top in a never-ending procession.

Construction of the unsupported, single-span tramway began when a helicopter towed a 3,000-meter-long nylon rope from the valley to the mine site. Once this was strung, it was used to pull up progressively stronger rope and finally, the heavy cables. But once in place, heavy oscillation derailed the ore cars, flipping them against the rock wall and down into the valley.

An expert mathematician was brought in from Switzerland to solve the problem. He calculated the resonances of all the parts, and made some small but crucial adjustments to the system. "A tramway is like a violin," the mathematician said. "It has to be tuned."

Pipeline to the sea

At the mill, the ore is crushed to a fine powder, and the valuable mineral is separated from the base rock. A concentrated slurry is produced, then pumped into 112-kilometer pipelines that follow the contours of the land to the port of Amamapare on the coast. There the slurry is dried, and loaded on ore ships.

The pipeline gave engineers headaches at first. It repeatedly ruptured until a pump speed of just over 3 miles per hour, with a fairly wet slurry (64 to 67 percent water), was settled on as ideal.

There are no roads out of Amamapare. All travel is by boat, across the ocean or up the river. Some 18 kilometers upriver, the road begins, and here barges unload their cargo. Timika, where a modern airport receives Garuda jets, is 22 kilometers from where the barges unload. The road then runs flat and straight for 40 kilometers to the base of the mountains, past the ricefields of Javanese transmigrants. From the base of the mountain to the 2,600 meter ridge is a quick, switch-back climb. Once at the top, the road follows the ridge before heading through a tunnel to Tembagapura—92 kilometers of incredible engineering.

On Christmas Day 1971, the first convoy of trucks arrived at Tembagapura. A year later, the first shipment of copper concentrate was already on its way to Japan. In the meantime, about $200 million had been spent.

In March 1973, President Suharto gave Tembagapura its name and officially opened the operation. At the same time he ordained that the name of the province would henceforth be Irian Jaya ("Victorious Irian") instead of Irian Barat ("West Irian"), a decision which obliged the Freeport officials to send the dedication plaque back to the United States for re-engraving.

Although the initial investment in building the mine was recovered in just three years, low world copper prices kept profits to a minimum until 1979. From the start of operations in 1973 until the end of 1980, some 521,000 tons of copper concentrate were shipped out, containing 6 million ounces of silver and 463,000 ounces of gold, and resulting in $772 million in gross sales.

Community relations problems

The Irianese living near the mine site were at first simply astonished by all the activity, then began to resent the huge disparity of wealth that existed between themselves and the Freeport workers. At times, groups have claimed ownership of the mine, saying that their land and minerals have been unfairly expropriated.

At one time, the Irianese—who considered the mountain sacred—put up *saleps*, hex sticks in the shape of crude half-meter-high wooden crosses, all around Copper Mountain. Resentment still surfaces today.

In the first years of the mine's operation, a cargo cult grew up in the area. One man proclaimed that he would be able to open the warehouse inside the mountain where the whites and western Indonesians obtain their wonderful possessions, with only a special rodent's tooth. The tooth didn't work, but this longing for material goods continued to brew.

Separatist rebels—members of the Organisasi Papua Merdeka, or OPM, which had been fighting against Indonesian rule since the 1960s—recruited some Irianese near Tembagapura, including a few of the company workers. The conflict came to a head in the summer of 1977, and the slurry pipeline was cut in several places, power lines were ruptured, an explosives magazine was burned and several trucks returned with arrows in their radiators.

Most of the problems the company faces today have to do with displacement, and a growing dependency on the mine. In its setting, the wealth of the Freeport operations is incredible, and even the garbage produced by Tembagapura is very attractive to the people of the surrounding mountains.

Shanty towns sprang up just outside the town border, housing at one time some 1,000 people. The squatters lived off Tembagapura's garbage, stole whenever possible and were a constant sore point with Freeport as well as the government, which tried to convince them to return home or settle in the transmigration site at Timika, 70 kilometers away in the hot lowlands. (Recently, a sudden flood wiped out the shantytowns, and the people were relocated.)

Freeport has regularly sponsored local development projects, but in the past has had little success. Often, the problem has been that the company rushes in with manpower and largess—for example, building a village with company carpenters and wood—and the villages are left with a project that is unsuitable, and for which they have no sense of ownership. New programs are attempting to work more closely with each community, allowing the people to build a political consensus for the type of development they would like to see. This process results in fewer of the kind of flashy projects that look good in a corporate report, but the results are more lasting and valuable.

Opposite: *The monument to Irian's independence in Jakarta.*

IRIAN TODAY

Dutch New Guinea to Irian 'Victorious'

As the Japanese saw their fortunes slipping toward the end of the second world war, they openly encouraged anti-colonialist movements and, in a last-ditch effort to maintain eroding Indonesian support, promised independence after the war. Nationalist conferences were held and the political infrastructure for an independence movement was in place by the time Japan surrendered on August 15, 1945.

On August 17, nationalist leaders Sukarno and Mohammed Hatta declared *merdeka,* "independence."

The Dutch were unwilling to relinquish the territory, howevery, and it took four years of fighting on Java and the threat of a cut-off of Marshall Plan funds to Holland to make the declaration stick. The Dutch formally ceded sovereignty on December 27, 1949, and on August 17, 1950—five years after the original proclamation—the Republic of Indonesia was born. The Dutch East Indies were now independent—all of the Indies, that is, except western New Guinea.

Colonial holdover

The 1946 Linggadjati Agreement, signed by Dutch and Indonesian representatives, states that the Dutch were to relinquish the "whole territory of Netherlands India." But as fighting flared anew before the agreement could be implemented, the Dutch considered it null and void. For their part, Indonesian nationalists always believed that Irian was an integral part of their country.

In the final document ceding control of Indonesia, the status of Irian was purposely left vague. The Indonesians were anxious to get on with building their country, certain that the Irian question would eventually be resolved in their favor. They took to heart Dutch negotiator Dr. Van Mook's assurances that "it is absolutely not the government's intention to shut West New Guinea out of Indonesia."

Holland soon found an excuse to withhold her half of New Guinea, however, when Indonesia turned its agreed-upon federal structure into a unitary republic with power concentrated in the capital and the president. The Dutch regarded this as a breach of the Round Table Agreements that had led to Indonesia's independence. But it was the

internal politics of Holland, more than any other factor, that led to the retention of Netherlands New Guinea.

Right-wing parties at home insisted that the Dutch flag remain planted in at least one portion of the former colony, and the presence of oil around Sorong was most certainly a factor as well. By portraying Irian as an anti-communist bastion in the Pacific, the Dutch also sought and received U.S. backing.

Dutch conservatives wrung support from the Labor Party to obtain the two-thirds parliamentary majority needed to exclude Irian from the Transfer of Sovereignty. Australia, also headed at this time by a coalition of conservatives, supported Holland. In 1952, the Dutch parliament even amended the constitution to incorporate West New Guinea (as well as Surinam and the Antilles) into the Kingdom of the Netherlands.

While the young Indonesian nation struggled to consolidate its scattered islands and peoples, the Dutch tried to make up for their years of neglect of Irian. In the 1930s, 200 Europeans lived in Irian. In 1949, following Indonesian independence, this figure leaped to 8,500—including thousands of Eurasians who fled here, worried about retribution in the young and still volatile Republic. A Dutch exodus from the rest of the archipelago also swelled Irian's expatriate population. Newcomers settled in areas around Manokwari, Sorong and, particularly, Hollandia.

Before the war, Dutch posts along the coast were widely scattered and controlled little beyond their immediate vicinity, and the only inland post was one at the Wissel (Paniai) Lakes, established in 1938. This situation quickly changed after 1949. During the 1950s the Dutch set up a number of new centers in the highlands, and began to take oil out of the Sorong area, nutmeg and mace from Fakfak, crocodile skins and copra from Merauke, and copra from the Raja Empat Islands and the Bird's Head. A new sawmill at Manokwari began to exploit Irian's huge forest reserves. The lion's share of exports headed to Holland and Singapore.

But the cash inflow from exports was dwarfed by Holland's massive subsidies to Irian. While as late as 1957 less than a quarter of Irian's population fell under any sort of administrative control, by 1961 the total had risen to two thirds, with 52 percent of government positions (mainly at the lower levels, of course) filled by Papuans and Melanesians.

President Sukarno and the Indonesian nation viewed these Dutch activities with dis-

may but at first could do little but make vociferous demands that Holland leave. To make matters worse, Dutch elections held in May of 1959 put into power the most conservative and uncompromising coalition since the war.

Early 1960s: the 'Irian problem'

It has often been written that Sukarno focused on the "Irian problem" to rally his nation behind him and draw attention away from pressing domestic problems. Economic conditions in newly independent Indonesia were troubling, and it was only on the strength of Sukarno's personal charisma and oratory that he was able to maintain the delicate balancing act that kept the Army, the Muslims and the Communists in check. But regardless of his motives, Indonesians were very much behind him on the Irian issue.

Sukarno at first tried to work within the United Nations to resolve the Irian question by diplomatic means. His appeal failed, in part because Indonesia was receiving Soviet military aid and the growing strength of the Indonesian communist party scared off potential western allies. When the United Nations rejected Sukarno's demands, he pulled out of the body and nationalized all remaining Dutch-owned businesses.

Failed diplomacy left only one option—the military. Organized by General Suharto, who was given widespread powers as major-general early in 1962, Indonesia began a campaign to infiltrate 1,500 troops into Irian in order to spur the villagers to rebellion. The campaign was a resounding failure, but it showed Indonesia's determination.

While sporadic fighting continued, Indonesia kept up the diplomatic pressure. The key to her eventual success was the United States. Fearing that a protracted military action against the Dutch would draw Indonesia even further into the Soviet fold, the Americans finally decided to support Indonesia in its claim to Irian.

The 'Act of Free Choice'

Soon, Holland saw her only alternatives as an escalating war without U.S. or European support, or relinquishment of West New Guinea. Following mediation talks in the United States, the so-called New York Agreement of 1962 provided for a U.N. transition team to administer West New Guinea in preparation

Opposite: *Regular air service is an important part of Irian's modernization program. This Merpati Twin-Otter is at the Wamena airport.*

or an eventual plebiscite, the "Act of Free Choice." In 1963 the U.N. handed the territory over to the Indonesians, and it became rian Barat (West Irian).

In 1969, instead of a referendum, the Indonesian government chose some 1,000 representatives who eventually voted unanimously to join the republic, and in August of 1969, Irian Barat formally joined Indonesia. In 1973, President Suharto officially renamed the province: Irian Jaya, or "Victorious Irian." The methods chosen by the Indonesian government have been often criticized, but considering the state of affairs in Irian at the time, it would have been difficult to administer a true plebescite.

The Indonesianization of West New Guinea did not progress smoothly. In 1967, aircraft were used against Arfak tribesmen near Manokwari and rebellions broke out on Biak and around Enarotali, near the Paniai Lakes. And a number of early Indonesian government policies were misguided—such as Operasi Koteka, designed to get the highlanders to quit wearing their penis sheaths.

Dissatisfaction led to local unrest, and in areas an independence movement arose: the Organisasi Papua Merdeka ("Free Papua Movement"). The OPM was formed as the result of blunt actions by the government and unrealistic expectations of self-rule, fanned by the Dutch. When the Dutch saw the tenability of their position in Irian fading, they quickly set up elected councils and other trappings of self-rule—with the full knowledge that Indonesian rule was inevitable, and perhaps even desirable. Today, military commanders are still reluctant to open certain areas of Irian to tourism because of rumors of OPM activity.

One of the most controversial of Indonesia's Irian policies has been its transmigrasi program, begun in the 1960s, wherein the government has been relocating people from overpopulated Java to Sumatra, Kalimantan (Borneo), Sulawesi (Celebes) and Irian.

Initially, transmigration encountered some problems, such as relocating Javanese rice farmers on land that was used as a hunting and gathering ground for the local population. Moreover, the land was often not even fertile enough to grow rice. The government now takes traditional land rights into account when settling transmigrants, and the sites are chosen with greater care. It has also dramatically scaled down the program.

Although problems still exist, today Jakarta's Irian policy seems to be following a more enlightened and successful course in bringing the Irianese into modern Indonesia. Roads are being built, an extremely difficult job considering Irian's rough terrain, schools have been built, and an increasing number of native Irianese are participating in government bureaus.

PART II

Biak and the North

Jayapura, on the north coast of Irian, and the large islands north of Cenderawasih Bay are the easiest parts of Irian Jaya to visit, with a well-developed communications and transportation networks, and plenty of hotels and restaurants to choose from.

Biak is the first Indonesian stop for travelers flying Garuda Indonesia from the United States, and most just remember it as a groggy refueling break on the way to Bali or Java. But Biak, and neighboring Supiori, Numfor and Yapen Islands, are charming places to visit in their own right.

Biak is the best-known of the former Schouten Islands, and the most populated. The town has some lively markets, and an interesting harbor. Inland, one can visit the eerie caves where Japanese soldiers hid during World War II, and a small museum full of relics. Further out from the town, one encounters beautiful waterfalls and reefs.

The Padaido Islands, which dot the sea southeast of Biak, are ringed with coral and offer fine snorkeling. Biak is also the home port of The *Tropical Princess,* a live-aboard boat that takes divers to perhaps the richest and most unspoiled reefs in all of Indonesia.

For secluded beaches and near-shore snorkling, head to nearby **Numfor**, a beautiful and lightly populated island. Thickly forested **Yapen**, looms just across the water south of Biak. If the weather is good, one can see it clearly from the Biak harbor. The island's forests host the beautiful birds of paradise, and the shores have numerous sandy coves fine for swimming and snorkeling.

Jayapura, Irian's capital and largest city, began its life as a Dutch port and administrative center. The city was placed here to mark the border with the German colony just a stone's throw away, and one can see into Papua New Guinea from the hills north of town. For many years, Hollandia was a small, back-water town, but it suddenly leaped onto the world stage during World War II as a staging point for General MacArthur's Pacific island hopping campaign.

Today, it is a thriving city of 170,000 with, in addition to Irianese, a mixed population of Javanese, Makassarese and Bugis Muslims, as well as many Ambonese and Manadonese Christians. Jayapura is one of the few places in Irian with paved roads and public transportation—including private taxis—and travel around the area is easy.

The **Cenderawasih University Museum**, in nearby Abepura, has a fine collection of artifacts from Irian, and another nearby museum, the Negeri, displays objects of material culture from Irian's various ethic groups. A visit to these two is a good way to get some background before heading to the highlands or the south coast.

From Jayapura, a short hop to **Yotefa Bay** offers the spectacle of scattered World War II relics—half-sunken ships, beached tanks and landing craft. Or your boatman can take you to nearby fishing villages that consist of huts mounted on a forest of stilts. At high tide, the water reaches a meter-and-a-half beneath the village; at low tide, a wide expanse of mud flats is revealed, which, in at least one area, becomes a makeshift soccer field.

Nearby **Lake Sentani**, dotted with islands offers a stunning panorama of velvet-green hills easing their way into the lake. A meal of crispy lake fish and even water-skiing are possible here.

If you want, you can also visit one of the several **crocodile farms** in the area, and have a look at these prehistoric animals up close.

Overleaf: *The popular "Base G" beach, just north of Jayapura, takes its name from a World War II Allied base. Although deserted here, it is a very popular site with Jayapurans on weekends.* **Opposite:** *A dancer from the island of Numfor, a short hop from Biak. Numfor is a beautiful, and rarely visited island.*

BIAK

Strategic Island to Irian's North

Despite Biak Island's relatively recent status as a major air stopover on Garuda, most passengers don't even bother to disembark here. This is a shame, because although Biak is not really developed for tourism, the island is rich in history and natural beauty.

Biak islanders are Melanesians, ethnically and culturally distinct from the majority of "mainland" Irianese. Unlike other parts of Irian, like the Baliem Valley, the traditional culture here has for the most part been wiped out by missionaries, and today everyone routinely dresses in western clothes.

But elements of the old lifestyle remain. Traditional drumming and dances, and firewalking displays, still take place—although today these activities are not common, and must be arranged specially for visitors.

The bride price, still widely used on Biak, consists of antique porcelain plates, silver bracelets made from old Dutch or American coins, and cash money. The average value is currently $350. The wedding feasts, where this exchange is made, are often lavish affairs. Other rites of passage—such as a child's first haircut—are also honored. Magic still plays a role in Biak, particularly in attracting abundant catches of fish.

During World War II, in fact, tiny Biak loomed large on the world map. After the war, the Dutch took over the American airfields and docks and, during the 1960s, the Indonesian government followed suit. Today Biak is the first Indonesian stop on Garuda's direct flights from the United States.

Geography and economy

Boot-shaped Biak Island, covering 1,834 square kilometers, extends 50 kilometers northwest to southeast, and averages 18 kilometers wide. The northernmost shore reaches within 60 kilometers of the equator, and the middle of the island lies at 1° south. It is hot and humid, sometimes uncomfortably so.

Supiori Island, northwest of Biak, is very nearly attached to Biak. It is split only by a tiny saltwater creek—Sorendidori—extending from Sorendidori Bay in the south to Sorendiweri Bay in the north. Just 100 kilometers west of Supiori is small Numfor Island.

Geologically, all these islands consist of uplifted coral limestone, with coastlines often ending in impressive cliffs as much as 60 meters from the waves below. The heavy rainfall has eroded the soft limestone into caves which on Biak Island in particular played a historic role in World War II as a hideout for Japanese soldiers. Inland, the terrain is generally flat, with occasional low hills, except in the northern part of Biak and in Supiori. Bonsupiori, the highest hill in the district, reaches 1,034 meters in southern Supiori.

Biak, Supiori, Numfor, and the Padaido islands form Kabupaten Biak Numfor, one of nine *kabupaten* or administrative districts in Irian Jaya. (Yapen is part of *kabupaten* Yapen-Waropen, which includes Yapen and the coastal Waropen area on Irian proper.)

The total population of the Biak district is a bit over 81,000, with about half of these living in Biak town and the surrounding area. Recent transmigrants, mostly Muslims from Java or Sulawesi and Christians from Ambon and Manado, have swelled the population of Biak town to an estimated 25,000. The island of Biak has 65,000 inhabitants; Supiori has 8,500 and Numfor 7,000. Eighty-five percent are Protestant Christians. The district's Catholics (1,600) and Muslims (8,700) live chiefly in Biak town.

Biak's economy looks to both the land and the sea. Taro is the staple crop, and manioc, sweet potatoes, soybeans and green vegetables are also grown. Copra, dried coconut meat, has long been the principal cash crop. Cacao, cloves and coffee are being developed.

Most gardens and plantations are located inland, behind the narrow coastal range. Chickens, and a few head of cattle and goats have been recently introduced to supplement the native pigs. Despite this diversity of livestock, most Biak islanders still get their protein from the seas.

During the past few years, Biak's economy has boomed thanks to timber and tuna fishing. A large sawmill, supplied with lumber from the north coast of Irian, churns out plywood. Large-scale cutting operations are also proceeding on Biak itself. Commercial tuna fishing, started by the French and now run

Opposite: *Boys paddle their small outrigger in a lagoon near Korem, in northern Biak.*

by Americans, are part of the Indonesian Van Camp Seafood Company. This operation produces up to 50,000 tons of locally canned tuna for export, along with frozen fish. Two other fleets of trawlers bring back to Biak chilled, sashimi-grade tuna. Boeing 727s, dedicated to this purpose, land several times a week at Biak to pick up 20-ton loads of this very valuable cargo.

Other sea products exported from Biak include *trepang* (dried sea cucumber) and sharks' fins, which end up in the Hong Kong and Taiwan markets.

The recent introduction of seaweed cultivation has given the economy of several coastal villages a welcome boost, and is beginning to displace fish bombing and other damaging ways of exploiting the island's coastal waters. The seaweed (*Eucheuma* spp.) is grown on rafts criss-crossed with ropes in the quiet, sunlit shallows. Once harvested and dried, the seaweed is shipped off to Java and then Holland to be processed into carrageenan, a valuable material used in cosmetics, toothpaste, pie filling, ice cream and cheese. Depending on quality, the raw seaweed can fetch $500 a ton in Surabaya.

The power of the ancestors

Biak islanders are a seafaring people, and even a few decades ago the men's houses in Biak were topped by boat-shaped roofs, and the bones of the dead were stored in boat-shaped coffins. Languages related to that spoken here are found as far away as Halmahera.

[Note: The name "Irian" is itself a Biak word, coined by Biak islander Frans Kaisiepo, a representative at the Malino conference in 1946. "Irian" originally referred not to all of western New Guinea, but only the part nearest Biak, now the Waropen district. The rough sense of the word was "hot climate."]

Biak's ancient animist religion emphasized the spiritual importance of ancestors, who were considered mediators of the wishes of *nanggi,* the central power of the universe. In times of scarcity, a ritual called *fan nanggi* ("feeding the sky") was performed with offerings that the ancestral spirits carried upward to the heavens, there interceding on behalf of their descendants. Some villages still maintain committees to record family genealogies.

Evidence of traditional beliefs can be found in the beautiful ancestral sculptures called *korwar.* These small figures, vessels containing the spiritual power of the deceased, were a tradition in Biak, Yapen and the Raja Empat islands. Before any important occasion, such as a war expedition or a fishing trip, a oracle would go into trance to consult the *korwar.* The figures were asked to keep away storms, bring favorable winds and protect the warriors or sailors against illness and evil spirits. *Korwar* became prized items in the collections of French surrealists André Breton and Paul Éluard.

Unfortunately, few of these sculptures escaped missionary burnings. Missionaries enjoyed some success in Biak in the early 1910s, shortly before the establishment of a Dutch outpost here, but an outbreak of smallpox wiped out their achievement. The disease was blamed on the ancestors' wrath at the people of Biak for abandoning their traditions. Despite this setback, the missionaries returned in 1929 and succeeded in destroying most of the physical manifestations of Biak's animist religion.

The Biak islanders are excellent sailors and traders, and have long maintained contacts with Irian and other Indonesian islands to the west. A war-loving people, they staged raids far into the Moluccas, even reaching Sulawesi and Java in their search for women, slaves and goods for ceremonial exchanges. These exchanges, the most important of which was the bride price, required goods of foreign origin, which could only be acquired by trading or raids. Today, as a result, the people of Biak share bloodlines with peoples of Seram, Ambon, the Sangihe Islands, the Kei Islands and Alor.

The Sultan of Tidore

The closest "foreign relations" were with the spice island of Tidore. Gurabesi, a culture hero from Biak, was supposed to have won the hand of a princess of Tidore, the daughter of Sultan Jamaludin. As part of the bride price, a light tribute had to be taken yearly from Biak to Tidore. In return, the aristocrats of Biak received prestigious titles from the rulers of Tidore.

The nobles who bore the tribute each year were also granted the privilege of touching the Sultan's big toe—this charged the supplicants with magic power, most useful in impressing the less fortunate classes back in Biak. Gurabesi and his Tidorese wife were the progenitors of Biak's leading clan, as well as the forebears of the rulers of the Raja Empat Islands west of Irian's Bird's Head.

Tidore's domination of Biak—as well as of other areas of Irian—was reinforced by periodic *hongi* expeditions of war canoes. The purpose of these raids was the collection of tribute, but they included thievery, pillage and rape as a matter of course, all made possible by firearms that the Sultan had obtained from Europeans. But internal strife and predatory expeditions between Biak and Irian were far worse than the Tidorese *hongi*. In the late 18th century, Prince Nuku, dispossessed pretender to the Tidorese throne,

recruited Biak warriors, who fought under his banner for 25 years. By 1861, the power of Tidore had waned, and the *hongi* ended.

In the course of their many wide-ranging trade and raiding expeditions, the men of Biak acquired techniques for forging metal. With iron from Halmahera and Gebe (which have myths and languages similar to those of Biak), metal implements were forged by shaman-smiths, who labored under the influence of supernatural power and knowledge. Metalwork, as well as trade, was under the control of the noble caste, the *manseren*, who sat on top of a social pyramid composed of commoners and slaves.

Men of the cloth

Missionaries began their labors on Biak after a Dutch government post was established in Manokwari in 1898. The first Protestant mission, on Supiori, was followed by a second at Bosnik, on Biak, in 1912. The Biak mission lasted just two years before a smallpox epidemic allowed the ancestral spirits to reestablish their spiritual authority.

This victory was, alas, temporary. The indigenous traditions of Biak, of which warfare was an essential element, were dealt a death blow in 1915. In that year Dutch forces under Lieutenant Feuilletau de Bruyn, "pacified" the other islands of Cenderawasih Bay. Fighting and head-hunting were banned, and the old system was left impotent, laying the groundwork for conversion to Christianity. Missionaries began proselytizing in earnest during the 1920s, picking up where they had left off in Bosnik.

As in other areas of Indonesia where the Protestants followed pacification programs, Christianity brought with it a program of western education. The schools of Biak have furnished many of Irian's civil servants and their numbers are disproportionate to their population—a product of the educational head start they receive in their overcrowded and not particularly fertile island.

World War II on Biak

The Japanese defense of Biak was, in the words of Lieutenant General Eichelberger "based on brilliant appreciation and use of the terrain." The commander of the Allied Hurricane Task Force describes the defenses

Opposite: *Dancers on the island of Biak. The drums, with elaborately carved handles, are unique to the island. The mantles worn by the men are made of cassowary feathers.*

of his enemy:

"A few aerial vertical photographs failed to show the terrain features dictating the enemy defenses: the network of caves. Within the terraces and cliffs are countless caves, many of which are connected and interconnected by fissures and tunnels. Stalactites and stalagmites add to the near impregnability of the caves as defensive positions, making the battlefields of Biak a military nightmare.

"The Japanese were free to chose the location of their position at will. During the night the enemy came out of their cave positions and made a series of harassing attacks. Mountain guns and mortars were brought out from the caves. Before morning they were returned to the caves, which caves, the infantrymen did not know. A form of warfare was encountered that required experimentation, trial and error, and all of our available weapons before the mission could be accomplished."

Initial Japanese opposition at the landing site of Bosnik, 16 kilometers from the airfields, was slight—but this, it turned out, was a ploy. Japanese Colonel Naoyuki Kuzume had purposely withheld his main forces until the U.S. troops had advanced to the rugged terrain beyond the beaches. Then, from the dominating cliffs and caves overlooking the moving Allied columns, the Japanese launched a savage counter-attack and succeeded in driving a wedge between the beach-head and the invading forces. That night, the Japanese brought in 1,000 more men from Manokwari.

The situation was critical until Allied reinforcements arrived. Even then, the fighting was tough. U.S. infantry units were bogged down, suffering from extremely unfriendly terrain, intense heat and a scarcity of water. A new form of warfare was encountered that required novel tactics and all available weapons, including flame-throwers. One product of American ingenuity was employed with deadly effectiveness: a cocktail of TNT and aviation fuel poured into the caves.

The immediate Allied objectives were the three airfields at Mokmer (one of which would later become today's Frans Kaisiepo Airport), Borokoe and Sorida.

Effective resistance on Biak was overcome by June 21, 1944. The final toll was 400 U.S. soldiers killed and 7,400 Japanese, many of whom committed ritual suicide when they realized their situation was hopeless. Only 220 Japanese surrendered or were captured.

The Allies quickly developed the captured airfields for their own use. An important heavy bomber base was constructed on Biak, and fighters and medium-sized bombers were stationed in Wakde, Numfor and at Sansapor on the northwestern tip of Irian. From these bases, the Far Eastern Air Force was to strike for the next weeks at Japanese positions in Seram, Sulawesi, Halmahera, Kalimantan, Java and the Palaus, in preparation for the assault against the Philippines.

VISITING BIAK

Caves, Fine Beaches and Fire-Walking

Biak is far from being a well-developed tourist destination, but it is relatively simple here to arrange transportation to a variety of interesting sites: the deep, muddy caves used by the Japanese in World War II; a blue-water pool in a cave behind Opiaref village; the Padaido Islands, surrounded by clear, coral-filled water; and fire-walking in the village of Adoki, a few kilometers from Biak town.

Touring the island: to the east

Paved roads radiate out from Biak town toward the north, east and west. Most are relatively short, with the 50-kilometer stretch to the Wardo market and bay to the west being the longest. On crowded public minibuses, it can take up to two hours (after waiting to leave) to arrive at any of the end points. It's much better to charter a minibus if you can.

To the east, it's 18 kilometers and a half-hour ride to Bosnik, where there are sandy beaches and near-shore reefs. On the way to Bosnik, some 5 kilometers from Biak town, you can stop at **Swapodibo Village** to see the work of the carver Ronsumbre. He carves drums, canoes, ancestral figures and panels, all featuring ancient motifs and designs. A sign outside his house reads: "Sanggar Kerajinan." The items for sale, carved from local hardwood, include drums ($25–$30), model canoes ($40–$45) and stylized human figures (~$1/inch of length). At the far end of Swapodibo, the **Amiekem Art Shop** sells a range of carvings produced by a cooperative of local craftsmen.

Continuing along the road, one soon comes upon the **Reptilindo Crocodile Farm** on the north side of the road. Here both saltwater and estuarial crocodiles are raised for their hides, which are tanned on the premises and shipped to Japan. The open pens hold beasts of various sizes, including a huge male, the prize stud bull.

A few kilometers past Reptilindo is a bird park and orchid garden. The bird park houses several dozen Irianese species in two wire mesh aviaries. On our visit we saw a single pair of lesser birds of paradise (and the male was not in his breeding plumage), but there were still plenty of interesting birds: cassowaries, a pair of hornbills, crown pigeons cockatoos, parrots, lories, and a variety of bright bee-eaters and other small specimens Two large eagles were confined to tiny, individual cages. It seems they had been in the main aviaries until someone noticed the stock was disappearing quickly.

Bosnik hosts a twice-weekly market (Wednesday and Saturday) and is a good place to hire boats to the Padaido Islands Panai Parai beach is here, and one passes limestone cliffs and a lovely brook fringed with sago palms on the way.

About two kilometers beyond Bosnik, narrow beach and picnic area abuts a sweep of raised coral. In the clear, shallow seas here one can see the rusting remains of American built World War II piers.

The paved road continues to **Opiare Village**. In back of the elementary school here is a beautiful and mysterious blue-water pool in the Goa Serumi cave. The path down to the pool is short, but slippery: wear tennis shoes and accept a helping hand.

For the best light, visit in the late afternoon, when the sun finds its way in the slant

Right: *A young fisherman displays his catch.*

d cave opening. And for an other-worldly experience, bring a mask and snorkel, and an underwater flashlight. A bit of snorkeling will reveal a series of deep pools, twisting down in the limestone formations. In places the bottom is suddenly 10 meters down, and in others it slopes downward to oblivion.

Huge, transparent prawns and strange, primitive-looking fish hover in the water. According to the people of Opiaref, a giant eel guards the pool, which provides drinking water for the village.

[Note: We discovered an unexploded World War II mortar here, deep under a submerged ledge. Never try to bring up such an item, as they can still be live. And don't tell the villagers, or the kids will try to find it, with potentially disastrous consequences.]

Opiaref is also noted for its woodcarvers. With sufficient notice (a day or two), you can see a dance performed here. Ask for the older dancers, not schoolchildren.

The paved road beyond Opiaref peters out just before reaching the next village, Saba. Just beyond a creek, Saba nestles into a bay with several miniature coral islands. Plans call for extending the road all the way to Biak's southeast extremity, Cape Barari.

Another paved road forks inland just before Saba, next to the **4-star hotel** building (ground was being cleared for it at the time of this writing) at Merau. A short ways inland, this road forks: the left branch heads back by an inland route to Biak town, and the right cuts east to a timber yard, reaching the sea at a deepwater port where the logs are loaded into ships for transport to the mills.

From the end of the road you can walk about two kilometers to a lagoon, on the far side of which is **Tanjung Barari**, where picturesque thatched huts perched on stilts. We suggest taking an outboard-powered canoe from Bosnik if you want to visit Tanjung Barari, however. The round trip (about an hour each way) should cost $30–$40.

The Padaido Islands

On market days in Bosnik, you can hop a motorized outrigger across to Owi Island for less than 30¢. **Owi Island** has a wide sand beach on its north shore, facing Biak. The best blacksmiths are said to live here, forging excellent *parang* blades and capable of making functional firearms. You might also ask around to see if any of the motorized canoes are heading for islands beyond Owi. Hop on and return on the next market day, or a week later. On non-market days, you can ask to be paddled across to Owi, about $1.50 each way.

The Padaido Islands are divided into two groups: Padaido Atas (Higher or Further Padaido) to the east and closer Padaido Bawah (Lower or Nearer Padaido), with Pakreki Island smack in the middle.

If time and finances permit, we suggest an overnight excursion to **Padaido Atas**, beauti-

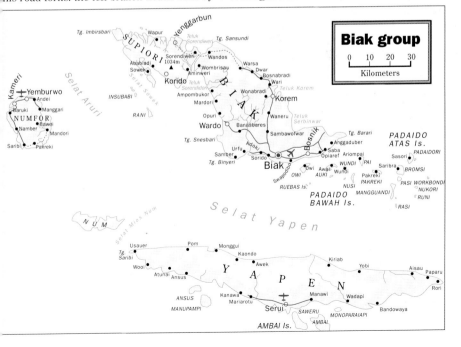

ful islands that rarely, if ever, see visitors. The diving off the easternmost islands of Padaido Atas—Runi, Nukori, Workbondi—is said to be excellent (according to divers working for Jacques Cousteau). Currently, the only diving available in the area is off the live-aboard *Tropical Princess* (see Biak Practicalities, page 78), which takes divers on package tours to Mapia Atoll and other tiny island groups far north and west of Biak.

The Padaido Bawah islands were of crucial importance during World War II. Five landing strips were laid down on Owi and a submarine base built off Nusi. The islands are all low-lying, with shores of white sand or raised coral. Huts line the larger islands. Men in tiny outrigger canoes, with patched-up sails, fish with hook and line.

One of the nicest spots for snorkeling is off two tiny islands—really just sandbars—off the western shore of Nusi Island. The seas around these islands, Urip and Mansurbabo, harbor a wide, shallow reef. In addition to lots of bright reef fish, we saw lobsters, a couple of small reef sharks, blue-spotted rays, a moray eel and a seasnake.

While you are swimming and snorkeling, your boatman will probably be fishing. With a bit of luck, a delicious grilled fish dinner will await you. If your boatman was unsuccessful, you can always buy fish from one of the little outriggers. Most of the boats to the Padaidos have a little shelter amidships, but don't forget to bring a hat, sunscreen, and a long sleeved shirt and long pants. Also, plenty of drinking water, and fruit and snacks.

The Japanese caves

Heading north from Biak town, just outside the urban area, a turnoff leads to the Goa Binsari, a complex of caves used by the Japanese as hideouts during World War II.

Before reaching the cave proper, a circular building houses a small museum of World War II memorabilia. One side is for Allied leftovers, the other for Japanese. The exhibit features a rusted-out jeep mounting a 50-caliber machine gun, some artillery shells, bombs and lots of odds and ends, including disintegrating army-issue footwear. In front of the museum, a fuel cell from an airplane juts up over what is said to be a Japanese skull and a few bones: a temporary monument until a more fitting one can be erected. More items are scheduled to be brought the the museum.

Past the museum are the caves themselves. The first thing one notices is a huge pit, overgrown with giant fig trees and creepers. This is where an American bomb landed directly on the cave. Down a stairway and along a moss-covered passageway, one can walk to either of the two original openings to the caves. Further exploration here or in any of the many other cave-labyrinths of Biak requires a trustworthy flashlight, a good guide and quite a bit of bravery.

Other than a few bits of rusting metal, nothing remains in these caves. The useable metal has been carted away as scrap, and the bodies of the dead have been laid to rest. The Americans took away their dead during and after the war, and the Japanese came in the late 1960s to cremate the remains of their countrymen. A simple monument has been erected on top of the cave to the Japanese soldiers who died here. Some of the soldiers' relatives come once a year, to pray at the cave's entrance and at the statue of the Goddess of Mercy, which stands in front of Hotel Irian.

Quite near the Goa Binsari cave is a strategic promontory that overlooks the airport. The Japanese bunkers, which blend into the landscape, and heavy shore batteries—made in Germany—attest to the tactical importance of this location. On a clear day, one can see as far as the island of Yapen, about 60 kilometers away. Before leaving the area, ask to see the anti-aircraft gun which, still in good shape, stands mute in back of a nearby house.

Fire-walking

This ancient custom, forbidden by the Dutch, was associated with traditional events such as weddings and feast given by powerful leaders. Men accused of adultery or corrupting unmarried girls could prove their innocence by walking over the hot stones.

Fire-walking is once more allowed. Some north coast villages occasionally perform it, but it is much easier to see in Adoki, a village at the end of a paved road some 11 kilometers west of Biak town. There is also a fine swimming beach just before the village entrance.

While the four families whose members can walk on the burning stones had not tried it since the early 1930s, at our prodding a couple of men gave it a go in 1990, just to show that their art was not lost.

Kindling and logs were laid down and coral rocks piled on top. The pyre burned for about an hour, until the coral rocks were blazing hot. Attendants removed any remaining smoldering wood and, using long sticks, pushed and pulled the heated stones into a flat bed of glowing rocks. Waves of heat rose from the surface.

The two men stood at the edge, prayed, then rubbed a bit of saliva on their soles. The oldest man started first, a bent-over octogenarian with a sense of humor. Full of confidence, he strode over the stones but about halfway across he started hopping and covered the remaining distance in record time, shouting that fire-walking was a dangerous business. Someone cracked a joke: the old man must have been fooling around with a

Opposite: *The cave at Goa Binsari, used by the Japanese in their World War II defenses.*
Below: *Fire-walking in Adoki village. The tradition had died out since being banned in Dutch times, but it is now making a comeback.*

girl. Everyone laughed except the chap with the singed feet, who was rubbing betel juice on his soles to relieve the pain.

His partner, evidently a more moral man, walked across the scorching stones several times and experienced no problems at all.

In spite of the burned feet, the people of Adoki village said that they would repeat the fire-walking with more participants, including women and children of ten years of age. Perhaps next time they may follow the old ritual with a feast of pork and manioc.

Korem and the north coast

On the main road heading north out of Biak town, villages and gardens set among low hills alternate with low vegetation vegetation. The asphalt greets the north coast at Korem, a nondescript little town on a wide, curving bay. Heavy breakers crash ashore during the west monsoon. At the eastern edge of the bay, an incredibly clear creek provides swimming and fishing for happy little boys. The western end of the bay receives a wide, sluggish river which can be crossed by canoe.

On the other side, work is proceeding on a paved road that will eventually reach Supiori Island. A bridge once spanned the narrow channel separating Biak from Supiori, but it collapsed and another is in the works. Once completed, the road will reach Wapur Village on Supiori, reputed to be the best in the area for swimming and snorkeling.

It's well worth the effort to travel to the west beyond Korem. Starting on the other side of the river, the paved road follows the palm-fringed shoreline past bays, coves, inlets stretches of white sand beach and raised coral. Bridges cross clear streams where locals bathe or wash laundry.

About five kilometers before the village of Warsa, a waterfall cascades down a mountainside several kilometers away. At Warsa another waterfall tumbles some 15 meters just by the main road. Children gleefully jump or dive off the top to entertain visitors. Although some houses have corrugated roofs and sawn timber walls, most of the beachside houses remain traditional: thatch roof, walls of *gaba-gaba* (the central spine of the sago palm leaf) with open porch, all raised on wooden piles a meter or so above the sand. And the people can always find a fresh coconut for a thirsty traveler.

The economy and subsistence of this stretch of the coast, as with much of the rest of Biak, centers around fishing and small-scale agriculture. Garden plots in generally poor soils, prepared by the slash-and-burn technique, yield tubers and vegetables. Coconuts are home-processed into copra and oil. Sago tree trunks provide edible starch. Occasional hunting of wild pigs with dogs and spears provides entertainment and protein. (Domestic pigs are killed only for festivals.) Pigs and other game are also caught in traps

set in the jungle.

Tiny fish are hunted in tidal pools with mini-bows and arrows, while lines trolled from outriggers land sharks up to 1.5 meters. Dried shark's fin fetches up to $18 a kilo. If you are traveling along this stretch in December, ask about a special rite performed prior to setting out to catch flying fish.

Wednesdays and Saturdays—market days in Korem—are best for travel along Biak's northwest coast. Public minibuses between Biak town and Korem are more frequent then. Korem functions as one of the district's three secondary markets (the other two are Wardo and Bosnik) and transportation hubs. All villagers on Biak's and Supiori's north coasts trade at Korem unless they are willing to make the longer journey to Biak town.

To the west: Wardo

The bay-side market of **Wardo** lies at the western end of a 50 kilometer paved road from Biak town. The hour-and-a-half ride is somewhat monotonous, although an occasional village appears against the deserted jungle backdrop, with waving kids. Much of the area is uninhabited. A couple of kilometers before reaching the market, a paved strip to the right leads to the **Wapsdori waterfall**.

From the end of the road, there is a steep downhill path to the top of the falls. But you can't see the falls very well from this position. For a good view, you have to somehow descend to the river at the bottom, which would be difficult even for mountain goats.

Instead of risking you life this way, we recommend hiring a little outrigger canoe ($3 and perhaps 1.5 hours) from the bay next to Wardo market, and gliding up the river through lush tropical vegetation for the several kilometers to the falls. This real-life jungle river-boat ride is worth the trip. If you are in a hurry you could hire a motorized outrigger, but the noise would spoil the fantasy.

The Wardo market, by a narrow, palm-ringed inlet, is the center of communications with the south coast of Supiori. Large outriggers with a central cabin and 40HP engines ensure a quick ride to Korido and other villages. On market days, these boats make regular trips to Supiori for $3–$4 a person, the trip taking 2–3 hours each way.

But Korido village, large but not very attractive, should not be your primary goat.

Head for **Sowek** village instead. The high hills of Supiori are often shrouded in grey and black clouds, forming an impressive backdrop to the sunny coast. The shallow reef approach to Sowek spreads long and wide, jutting a long ways into the sea before dropping off. The transparent waters provide ample work for local fishermen.

As you approach the entrance to Sowek through the open reef, a tree-crowned island with a spit of white sand beach could be a good spot for swimming and a picnic. Most of Sowek's houses are perched on stilts, lining the bay's inner shore. Very seldom visited by outsiders, the people are friendly and helpful.

The *camat* (head) of the south Supiori subdistrict lives in Sowek. A wide coral bed parallels the south coast of Supiori, just across the Sowek strait. The edges drop off steeply, and it is a fine site for snorkeling.

Insubabi is a tiny island on this coral bank, just across the strait from Sowek. The people are very friendly, and the reef just in front of the village is an excellent site for snorkeling. The recent introduction of commercial seaweed production provides needed cash income to the villagers.

South of Insubabi, shallow, sand-bottomed waters surround **Rani Island**. A long spit of white sand extends from the island's north side, another delightful swimming and picnic site. If you did not make plans to spend the night in this area, you will wish you had.

*Opposite: A coconut is deposited by the waves on a deserted beach near Korem. **Right:** The stunning waterfall at Wardo in western Biak.*

NUMFOR

A Quiet Island Paradise

A magical lagoon awaits visitors to the west coast of Numfor. The clear, tepid waters swarm with brightly colored fish. Occasional outrigger canoes squeeze under narrow coral overhangs. A tasty meal rewards every skillful throw of a fish-spear. Palms and mangroves ring the lovely lagoon, and bright red parrots squawk overhead. It is a peaceful, dream-like setting.

Laid-back Numfor Island remains largely undisturbed except for the occasional group of Japanese war veterans. Villages lie scattered all along the island's 70-odd kilometer circumference, where stands of mangrove trees alternate with white sand beaches. But paradise has its price: there are no hotels, and no English speakers.

A 50-kilometer road, built by the Americans during World War II, runs roughly parallel to the coast, encircling about two thirds of Numfor. With a bit of notice, you can hop on the back of a motorcycle to get around. Or better yet, hire a 40 Hp motorized outrigger, stopping along the way to snorkel and visit villages. This can be a bit expensive, as fuel costs are high, but is definitely worth doing, for at least several hours. Land travel is cheaper, but the roads seldom run within sight of the coast. Riding or hiking through the jungle can become tedious, as only the occasional plumage bird enlivens the scenery.

For the purposes of administration, Numfor is divided into two subdistricts, east and west. These are further split into village areas, each of which includes a primary school and several scattered hamlets. East Numfor has six villages with a total population of just over 4,100 while West Numfor has five villages, with some 3,800 inhabitants.

All households fish and farm for a living, which provides the basic necessities without a great deal of effort. Bits of metal left over from the war are forged and shaped into *parang*s (machetes), canoe-making adzes, and other implements.

The island does have several exports: delicious smoke-dried fish, seashells, green beans, coconuts and trepang. There are small stores stocking basics such as soap and batteries, but nothing requiring sizeable amounts of cash.

Small local motorboats, which shuttle passengers and goods between Biak and Manokwari, levy high charges, which discourages exports and doubles the cost of imported fuel. Plans are to build a pier at Manggari to accommodate larger and more cost-efficient boats. The government hopes that this will encourage people to produce more for export. But with plentiful fish and fertile soil, it is unlikely that the Numforese will jump on the consumer bandwagon.

Around the island by boat

During most of the year, motorcycles can take you around two thirds of the island, but boats are the only convenient way to reach picturesque coastal villages such as Bawei and Mandori, unless you are prepared for several hours of hiking. Bawei Village, less than an hour's canoe ride from Yenburwo, has a church built on a pile of raised coral.

Boat travel also allows for lots of snorkeling off the reefs which fringe Numfor, often too far from shore for easy access. Many of the coral formations are under one to ten meters of water, with a fair variety of colorful fish. On the edge of the reef between Ande nd Manggari villages, the remains of a U.S. ighter plane from World War II lies partially exposed to the waves.

On arrival in **Yenburwo**, next to the airstrip, check out the simple Japanese Shinto war memorial with a cross just in back of an enclosed space next to the main road. A local pastor helped to dedicate the monument, hence the cross. Near the memorial, the fuselage of a U.S. bomber served for many years as a family's home. Today, it is used for storage. The plane's serial number and seal can still be clearly seen on a sheet of metal. Another part of the fuselage, where the letters "U.S.A." are clearly visible, encloses a privy perched on stilts over the water.

Just two kilometers from Yenburwo, the village of **Andei** is home to a couple of small boats that make runs to Biak and Manokwari. From Andei, the road cuts inland through the jungle, with paths leading to small seaside settlements or inland gardens.

Manggari village contains the crumbling remains of a U.S.-built dock area, a small Japanese ship partially submerged in the sand, and the wrecks of a dozen amphibious landing vehicles. A bell, formerly used to call GIs to chow, has been hung in front of the church to call the faithful to prayer.

A shorter jaunt out of Yenburwo leads west some 5 kilometers to a beautiful long white sand beach at **Asaibori**, near a small village. A bridge, built over a wide creek during World War II, has now collapsed. As this was on the main road to the west, the currently used road, which cuts inland, misses this nice beach, favored by the local population for Sunday picnics.

The road along the western shore of Numfor reaches the village of Saribi, then peters out in the jungle before Pakreki. This last village remains accessible for motorcycles but to travel to Mandori, on the east central coast, you must go by boat or on foot.

Heading west from Yenburwo, you cross the boundary between Numfor Timor (East Numfor subdistrict) and Numfor Barat (West Numfor). Report to the West Numfor police, in the subdistrict capital of Kameri, just off the main road at the entrance to the village.

Offshore from Kameri, an American plane crash-landed in ten meters of water. South of Kameri, there are inland caves occupied by the Japanese during World War II. **Baruki**, the first village south of Kameri, lies at the end of a deep bay, fringed with white sand and protected by an island at the entrance. With sufficient notice, rousing song-and-

dance performances can be arranged here for visitors.

Namber, the next village down the coast, is the best place for an overnight stop. The scenery, especially the fish-filled bays, will easily occupy any spare time on your schedule. The village is split into two settlements, Namber Lama (Old Namber) and Namber Baru (New Namber). A short walk from the main road brings you to an exquisite spring-fed cove, whose waters flow through a narrow channel into a mangrove-lined bay.

A few huts perched on stilts form part of the village, most of which is located at a slight elevation. Here you can easily hop into a small outriggered canoe to explore the bay, the uninhabited island of Pulau Manem and a

delightful lagoon-bay called **Kasyom** a short way down the coast to the south.

Manem Island, a Japanese oupost during World War II, now hosts birds which flock to the mainland at dawn and return at dusk. Just south of Namber, at **Rumboi**, you can see the remains of a jetty built by the Americans. Another jetty was built near Saribi village. People at both Saribi and Pakreki say that there are weapons and other war artifacts inland. If you are willing to trek with them, they will be happy to show you the relics.

Opposite: *A young Numforese girl.* **Above:** *A spring-fed lagoon on the west coast of Numfor near Namber. A little corner of paradise.*

YAPEN

Coral Gardens and Birds of Paradise

Yapen island is a convenient distance from Biak and offers clear waters with excellent swimming, snorkeling and diving. Curious stilt-perched villages jut into the island's many small bays. A permit, necessary for a stay in Yapen, can be easily obtained at the Biak police station.

The island is long and thin, and reaches almost to the Irian Jaya "mainland." The interior is steeply mountainous with a blanket of multi-hued vegetation. Two small villages, located some 1,000 meters up in the tangle of forests and crags, grow some of the world's best cacao. Their problem is in marketing it—hiking the difficult route with big bags of cocoa beans. Local trekkers say it takes two to three days to cross Yapen from Serui to the north coast.

Together with a chunk of the mainland of Irian, Yapen forms the *kabupaten,* or district, of Yapen Waropen, with a total population of 60,000. About 10,000 of these live in Yapen one-fifth in Serui town. The district's 700 Muslims live in town. Everyone else on the island is Protestant.

Cacao and timber lead Yapen's cash economy, followed by fish, coffee, *trepang* and *massoi* bark (this last used in Javanese folk medicines). Locally, oil from *massoi* bark mixed with water, served in rites of purification, necessary after one had slain an enemy. After the oil-and-water bath, the deceased's spirit could not molest its conqueror.

Serui, a nondescript town if ever there was one, nestles at the bottom of a wide bay. The landing field spreads out at the edge of town. Merpati Airlines flies the 60 kilometers from Biak every day except Saturday for $28 round trip. Passengers, riding in 18-seat Twin Otters, spend 25 minutes in the air over the sea, as Yapen's steep, vegetation clad mountains rise into view. The plane banks over a turquoise bay dotted with stilted huts before landing at the town.

The best accommodations, at Losmen Merpati on Jalan Yos Sudarso, cost $15 a day for a fan-cooled room with attached ladle-type bath, sit-down toilet and three complete meals and snacks. Free rides to and from the airport are included. Two bare-bones accommodations, the Losmen Bersaudara and the Losmen Marena (the better of the two), run $5 a day without food.

Serui hosts a bustling early-morning market with vegetables and fish brought in by canoe. A paved road on the west side of the bay leads to two villages perched over the water: Pasir Hitam, a half hour's stroll, and Pasir Putih, which takes about an hour. If you prefer, entrepreneurs will paddle you there from Serui in a canoe for a pittance.

Yapen is heaven for serious bird watchers. A day's walk from Serui into the uninhabited mountainous interior reportedly affords glimpses of several species of birds of paradise and other shy and exotic forest denizens. The locals set noose traps for wild pigs and snare birds.

Unfortunately, they also hunt the protected birds of paradise. Live baby birds and the breeding plumes of adult birds fetch a high price in Jakarta. (As much as $75 for a live baby bird.) It is said that the hunters may even be using mist nets in Yapen, which is an extremely efficient way to collect the animals. As most of the hunting takes place near the more heavily inhabited southern coast, it is said that Yapen's north shore—easily accessible by boat from Biak—is now the best place to see them.

Shallow seas and bays, replete with coral gardens and fishing villages, are Yapen's main attraction. Sturdy bamboo outriggers can be hired for $20 to $30 a day, plus fuel. Petrol runs about $3-4 an hour at 10-12 knots. The canoes have a little cabin across the hull, and are powered by 40 HP Yamaha outboards. The boatman will stop for you at villages and diving spots, selected according to your mood and interest.

Hiring such a mini-yacht in paradise is highly recommended, but not during the season of heavy seas—September through January. If your Indonesian is up to it, bargain and charter one of these canoes. Otherwise, arrangements can be made through the Losmen Merpati or the Reverend Mesak Dawir, telephone 67.

Ambai Village makes the perfect destination for a half-day outrigger trip. The trip takes less than an hour from Serui, and passes sheltered bays with clear water and coral. Fish are more abundant outside the bays.

Ambai, perched on stilts on a small island facing Yapen, is huge by local standards— 3,000 people, including the "suburbs." Every Tuesday and Wednesday on a tiny island in the bay, people from Ambai bring fish to barter for vegetables brought from the facing "mainland" village. Long-established practices keep bargaining to a minimum. This picturesque market is strictly for early birds— 5:30 a.m. to 6:30 a.m.

Opposite: *A brightly colored traditional canoe slices through the water at Ansus, on the south coast of Yapen.* **Below:** *Although beautiful, the lionfish,* Pterois volitans, *should be treated with respect as its fin spines carry venom.*

Biak Practicalities

All prices in US$ (at press time approx. Rp1750 to US$1); Biak telephone code: 961

If arriving on the Garuda flight directly from the United States, immigration and customs formalities are taken care of at Biak airport. Since the flights (which continue on to Bali) come in quite early in the morning, you may have to wait a while until the officials show up.

Inside the airport or just outside, minibus and taxi drivers compete for your business. Town is just 2 kilometers away, and the rate varies according to your bargaining skills and command of Indonesian, usually settling around the rupiah equivalent of $3.

You can catch a public minibus to town on the main road just outside the airport for just Rp200. The three Titawaka hotels usually have a bus waiting at the airport for their guests. The Irian Hotel is about 100 meters from the terminal, and you can have one of the airport porters haul your luggage there for about $1.

ACCOMMODATIONS

Hotels and *losmen* here range from quite nice air-conditioned hotels to some very cheap digs for $3–$4 a night. For a very pleasant small hotel in town, try the **Wisma Titawaka**. A bit expensive, but it has a pretty view and a fair amount of art on display. The nearby **Titawaka Home** displays lots of art, along with birds. The **Hotel Irian**, before it is demolished, has a colonial charm and is near the airport.

The Titawaka hotels are all under the same management. For information and reservations Fax (961) 22372, or write to Titawaka Hotels P.O. Box 536, Biak, IRJA, Indonesia.

Wisma Titawaka. Jl. Selat Makassar 24 ✆ 21658. 24 rooms. On a little rise near the water. Nice staff and location. Has a display of traditional carvings with some items for sale $27 S, $42 D with all meals included.

Hotel Titawaka. Jl, Selat Makassar 3, ✆ 21835 and 22159 with 32 AC rooms, $27 S, $42 D with all meals included.

Titawaka Home. Jl. Monginsidi 14, P.O. Box 536, ✆ 21891. 10 rooms. Located right on the sea; crocodiles and birds, tasteful decorations. $26 S, AC w/ meals.

NOTE: Plans call for upgrading some of the rooms in the Titawaka chain, with hot water icebox and satellite dish reception. They are also planning on building the three-star, 60 room Titawaka Beach, which is planned to open in 1992. The location is on the beach near the Wisma Titawaka. Plans call for swimming pool glass-bottom boat, diving facilities. They also plan to build some 10 seaside bungalows just outside of Biak town, at Samao, between Biak town and Sorido.

Hotel Irian. Across from the airport. Jl. M Yamin, P.O. Box 137, ✆ 21939, 21839. 55 rooms, 31 with AC. This hotel is scheduled to be demolished sometime in the mid-1990s. In the mean time, it is a charming, if somewhat

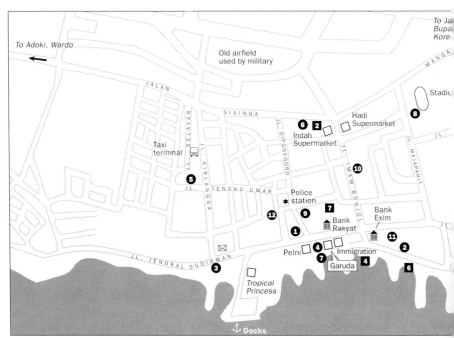

n-down, Dutch-built hotel. It retains a leisurely
eel in its lobby and dining area. The bar is the
nly decent one in town. Nice view over a wide
wn to the sea, but watch the sea urchins if you
o swimming. Shrine for Japanese war dead on
ont lawn. Fan-cooled $12 S, $21 D; AC $21 S,
35 D; VIP $29 S, $41 D.

otel Mapia. Jl. A. Yani, ℰ 21383. 23 rooms.
ll rooms with ladle bath. Large traditional
anoe in front. Economy $6 S, $10 D; fan-cooled
11 S, $14 D; AC $14 S, $17 D; all w/breakfast.

osmen Maju. Jl. Imam Bonjol 45, ℰ 21841.
9 rooms with basic attached toilets. $5–$8
er person; AC $13/person; all w/breakfast.

osmen Solo. Just off the seashore, run-down,
n cooled, shared toilets $4 per person.

inar Kayu. Jl. Selayar, ℰ 21613, at the edge
f town. 24 rooms. Fan-cooled only, toilets out-
de rooms. $3.

LOCAL TRANSPORTATION

Minibus/taxis. Within Biak itself, minibuses
re abundant and make frequent runs to the
nds of the paved roads. But first they wait at
e terminal, next to the Inpres Market, until
ey overflow with passengers. The public
inibuses charge Rp250 around town.
hartered taxis in town are $3/hr. To Bosnik by
ublic transportation is Rp200–Rp300. Round-
ip charter to Bosnik, including waiting time,
out $10. Public transportation to Korem,
p500; round-trip charter, including waiting
me, $20. Minibuses run much less frequently
fter dark, so unless you return to Bosnik,
orem or Wardo before 6 pm, you might have a
–3 hour wait—or sleep there.

Local boat travel. The double outriggered, outboard-powered canoes are locally called
"Johnson," although the engines are all
Yamahas today. Cheapest if you go as one of
many paying passengers. Most frequent on
market days, Wednesday and Saturday. To the
Padaido Islands from Bosnik, to north Biak and
north Supiori from Korem, to south Supiori from
Wardo. Motorized canoes from various villages
arrive either the afternoon before or on the
morning of market days to return home that day
or the following morning. Prices, depending on
distance, vary from $2 to $6. Some boats have
a little roofed cabin, others don't, so be prepared for hot sun or rain. You can probably
return on the next market day.

Some of these boats can also be chartered,
with prices depending on distance and your bargaining skills in Indonesian. Anywhere from $30
to $175 for a round trip. Plan on staying
overnight to take full advantage of your trip and
not to have to hurry back.

Outrigger canoes can also be rented from
the fishermen's cooperative in Biak town. Ask
someone with some English to take you there
and arrange things. Chartering to visitors is
new, so it could take a day or two to arrange. Of
course, travel agencies can set up everything,
albeit at a higher cost. (See below).

DINING

The restaurants in Biak serve basic Indonesian
and Chinese dishes, all quite tasty and moder-
ately priced. The better hotels all serve meals.
Beer is sold where available at just over $1 for
a small bottle.

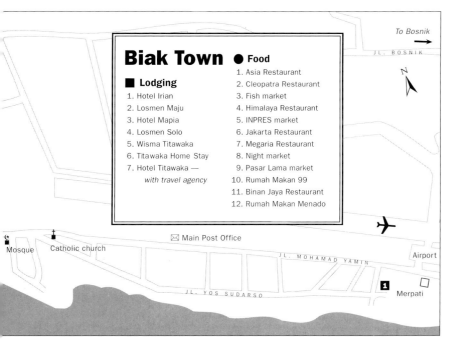

To Bosnik

Biak Town ● Food

■ Lodging

1. Hotel Irian
2. Losmen Maju
3. Hotel Mapia
4. Losmen Solo
5. Wisma Titawaka
6. Titawaka Home Stay
7. Hotel Titawaka —
   with travel agency

1. Asia Restaurant
2. Cleopatra Restaurant
3. Fish market
4. Himalaya Restaurant
5. INPRES market
6. Jakarta Restaurant
7. Megaria Restaurant
8. Night market
9. Pasar Lama market
10. Rumah Makan 99
11. Binan Jaya Restaurant
12. Rumah Makan Menado

JL. BOSNIK

✉ Main Post Office

Mosque   Catholic church

JL. MOHAMAD YAMIN

JL. YOS SUDARSO

Airport

Merpati

For a wide range of Indonesian cooking, try the **Puja Sera**, located diagonally across the intersection from the Bank Exim, with 14 stands under one roof. We recommend the **Pojok**, serving chicken or goat *saté* at $1.75 for ten brochettes, with soup.

There is a night market alongside the stadium, just off Jl. Majapahit. Try the grilled fish, available in several stands. Don't expect fresh fish daily—but the food is cheap.

The adventurous should try the spicy-hot dog meat (called R.W. and pronounced "air-vay") at the none-too-clean **R.M. Menado.** No sign for the restaurant, see map for location and ask around in the vicinity. $1 will get you a lot of bony chunks of dog.

Asia. Jl. Sudirman. Varied menu, cheaper than other restaurants. More spacious, but darker and less business-like than the others.

Cleopatra. Jl. A. Yani. Pleasant in good weather, with outdoor tables under umbrellas. Inexpensive chicken dishes, $3; shrimp $3.50; fish $3. Less varied menu than other restaurants.

Himalaya. Jl. Sudirman. Hard liquor $10 a bottle or $1.50 a shot. Chicken, pigeon, shrimp, beef, pork, crab, frog or squid, fish $2-$6.

Jakarta. Jl. Imam Bonjol 58, ✆21969. Simple Indonesian dishes $1–$1.25; crab $3; squid $2.50; beef $2.50; large fish $4; shrimp $3. The only place in town serving *trepang*, $3.

Megaria. Jl. Sudirman. Asparagus soup, chicken, crab, beef, pigeon (imported frozen), fish, squid, $3–$8.

Minang Jaya. Jl. A. Yani, ✆21591. Typical Pandang-style. Eat your fill for $2–$5.

New Garden. Jl. Imam Bonjol 12, ✆21972, 22222. A nice new place with AC, wide variety of Chinese-style dishes, most in the $2–$5 range. For parties of four, try their *sabu-sabu*, lots of goodies on a burner on your table, $16.

R.M. Binan Jaya. Jl. A. Yani 8, ✆21591. Pandang style food, $2–$3 (10% higher in the AC room), usually recently prepared dishes.

Restaurant 99. Jl. Imam Bonjol. Small, Chinese-style. Typical Chinese dishes $2–$5. Open in front with AC rooms at side and back. Mastercard and Visa accepted.

Banks and money-changing

The **Expor-Impor Bank** on Jl. A. Yani will change Amex, Mastercard, Visa Citicorp, Bank of America, Barkleys and Thomas Cook travelers' checks in $US, $A, £, ¥, D.M. and guilders at good rates. They will also take cash (if in perfect condition) of the above currencies as well as $Singapore. The **Bank Rakyat** down the street changes B of A, AmEx, Visa and Citicorp traveler's checks in $US, at an awful rate. Banks open 8am–1pm (to 10am Sat.)

Post Office

The main office is on Jl. A. Yani, towards the airport. There is a branch office on Jl. Sudirman, in town. Both are open 8 am–5 pm.

Medical

The hospital is Rumah Sakit Umum, on Jl. Sriwijaya Ridge 1, ✆21294. Some of the doctors speak passable English. Pharmacies include Apotik Cenderawasih, Jl. Imam Bonjol 34, ✆21754, and Apotik Gandawati. Jl. A. Yani.

Bookstore

Pojok Buku. Jl. Mongonsidi 18, ✆21425, 21498. Some English language books, including the best missionary literature on Irian.

Shopping and souvenirs

There are a few souvenir stores in town, including at the Pasar Lama market, and all the Titawaka hotels sell some handicrafts. You can also buy items at the airport. Bargain everywhere, except at the airport. Most of the items for sale are stone axes (which quickly fall apart), penis gourds and string bags from Wamena, some bad Asmat carvings, and quite nice strings of glass and ceramic beads. Occasionally you find a nice piece, but Biak is not really the place to shop for handicrafts.

Markets

There is not much excitement in Biak town, but a walk through the markets can always reveal strange produce, new smells and surprises. There is an early morning and (sometimes) afternoon open air fish market just off Jl. Sudirman, past the branch post office, toward the sea. There are two other markets: Pasar Inpres on Jalan Teuku Umar, next to the "terminal" or central taxi station. Here you can find fresh food and some dry goods. The Pasar Lama market, on Jl. Selat Makassar, sells bird-of-paradise skins, live cockatoos (about $40 for a young, healthy one that can say: "Selamat Pagi!" with some skill), Chinese ceramics, dry goods, clothes and household items. (Of course, don't even think about buying the live birds or illegal paradise bird plumes.)

AGENCY TOURS

P.T. Titawaka Indah Tour and Travel. Jl. Mongonsidi 7, P.O. Box 127 ✆21794, Fax 22372. Mr. Joop Tetelepta, who speaks English and Dutch, runs day tours of Biak island. Various buses are available, for $4–$13/hour depending on size of group. Mr. Tetelepta's daily guide fee is $40. For a visit to the Japanese cave, add $5, and for the bird park add $2. Fire walking $100; traditional dances $90, plus $65 for local traditional singing. The agency can set up a bird-watching tour to Yos on Yapen Island for $150–$390.

Sentosa Tosiga. Jl. A. Yani 36, ✆21398, 21956. As elsewhere, tours are expensive for just one or two clients, but the per-person price drops dramatically for a large group. City tour including the caves and beach, run $17–$3 for two, $52–$80 if a dance is included. A tour

Korem beach costs $22; to the Padaido Islands (Urip, Mansubabo and Nusi) $90. Tour Owi and Auki, $85.

AREA TRANSPORTATION

Biak is well served by both Garuda Indonesia and Merpati Airlines. Always check with the airlines for current schedules and prices.

Garuda. District Manager © 21331; Station Manager © 21199. Ticket office: Jl. Sudirman, © 21416. The flight to Los Angeles leaves from Biak on Tuesday, Wednesday, Friday and Sunday nights. Some other Garuda flights:

Denpasar	Tu,W,Th,F, S,Sun	$210
Jakarta	Tu,W,Th,F,Sa,Su	$305
Jayapura	W,Sa	$53
Ujung Pandang	W,Sa	$111

Merpati. Jl. M. Yamin 1, opposite the airport, 21213, 21386, 21416. Telex: 76186 MNA A. Some local flights:

Bintuni	M,W (via Manokwari)	$49
Enarotali	M,W,F,Su (via Nabire)	$61
Fakfak	M,W,Th (via Nabire)	$82
Jayapura	T times daily	$59
Kaimana	M,W,Th (via Nabire)	$75
Manokwari	M,Tu,W,Th,F	$42
Nabire	Daily	$44
Numfoor	Tu,Th	$26
Serui	Daily	$18
Sorong	M (also W,F,Sa via Manok.)	$71
Timika	Tu,W,Th,F,Sa,Su	$47

Also: Merauke ($143), Mindiptanah ($189), Moanamani ($64), Ransiki ($42), Sarmi ($57), Serminabuan ($92), Waghete ($64)

Some national flights:

Ambon	M,Tu,Th,F,Su	$104
Denpasar	Daily (via Ambon or U.P.)	$244
Jakarta	Twice daily (via U.P.)	$311
Manado	W,F (via Manokwari)	$159
Surabaya	Daily (via Ujung Pandang)	$279
Ujung Pandang	1–2 times daily	$188

Pelni. Jl. Sudirman 27. © 21065, 21593; Fax: 22225; Tlx: 76158 PELNI IA. Pelni boats (deck passage only) run to Jayapura and Sorong every 10 days or so. They have two ships doing circle routes, Jayapura–Sorong, calling at Sarmi, Serui, Biak, Nabire and Manokwari. Four days to Jayapura and 3 days to Sorong, deck passage, no food provided, $10.

Weather

Yearly rainfall is a bit under 3,000 millimeters in Biak during some 170 days. The rainy season here is unpredictable, but runs approximately December to March. It seldom rains more than a few days at a time, however. The dry season is July to September.

DIVING

The *Tropical Princess* is a live-aboard dive boat operating out of Biak harbor. One-week and 10-day tours are offered to Mapia atoll, and a number of other sites north of Biak Island.

According to very experienced divers, the diving off this boat is superb. The *Princess* runs year-round, but the best diving is March to November (July–September is the very best.) Avoid December and January.

The boat is being heavily booked, so make your arrangements early. The 10-day cruise runs $2650, and round-trip by Garuda airlines from Los Angeles to Biak costs $1050. Agents: **P.T. Prima Marindo Paradise.** Jl. Pintu Masuk Pelabuhan, Biak, IRJA, Indonesia. © (961) 21008 Fax: 21804
Hotel Borobudur. 3rd flr, shop 34, Jl Lapangan Banteng Selatan 1, Jakarta 10110. © (21) 380555 ext 7602 or 7604; Fax: 3803567
Poseidon Ventures Tours. © 800/854-9334 or 714/644-5344 (Southern California).
Sea Safaris. © 800/821-6670 or 213/546-2464 (Southern California).
Tropical Adventures Travel. © 800 / 247-3483 or 206 / 441-3483 (Washington state).

Numfor Island

Merpati flies the short distance to the landing strip at Yemburwo from Biak (Tu,F; $26) and Manokwari (F; $19), and boats also make the run once or twice a week: from Biak (8–9 hrs, $6); from Manokwari (5 hrs, $4.50). The plane from Biak arrives early in the morning, so once you have settled in at the *camat* and taken your passport and *surat jalan* to the police, there's still a good half-day left to explore.

If you can afford it, hire a motorized canoe and spend two or three days motoring around the island, sleeping in villages along the way. While actual travel time is only some 10 hours, stopping at various villages and exploring the deep inlet at Bawei will make this journey much more memorable than a quick zip around. Much of the island is fronted by wide tidal flats, and you can only travel close to shore at high tide. Plan on spending one night at Namber, the most beautiful part of Numfor.

Boat rental costs $12 per hour of actual motoring time. It takes about 10 hours to completely circle Numfor. Hiring or riding on the back of a motorcycle is an alternate way to explore the island. Motorcycle rental (with driver) is $4.50 half day; $7.50 full day. Guide/porter costs $6 a day.

The *camat* (government head) at Yemburwo, whose house is next to the landing strip, has spare bedrooms and his wife prepares good meals. Elsewhere, you could stay with the other *camat* at Kameri, a village head, a schoolteacher, or anyone else with some extra space. Count on paying $4–$5/day.

Market days at Yemburwo are Wednesday and Saturday (5:30 am–7 am). Electricity is found only in Yemburwo, from 6 pm to midnight. Bring snorkeling gear, hat, sunscreen and umbrella, air mattress, pillow and bedsheet,

JAYAPURA

Irian's Bustling and Modern Capital City

Jayapura began its life as Hollandia in 1910, became Kota Baru after Irian's integration into Indonesia, and again changed briefly to Sukarnopura before assuming its current name. The bustling city of almost 170,000 spreads in back of what used to be known as Humboldt Bay, now Teluk Yos Sudarso.

The best view of the town and harbor sweeps out from the base of the tall red-and-white communications tower. A paved road leads to the top of the steep hill but no public transportation climbs up there. Still, Jayapurans occasionally find a way up to take in the panorama, especially when the Indonesian national passenger line's huge *Umsini* is expected to call.

Founding the city

In 1858, the Dutch war-steamer *Etna* cruised Irian's north coast on its journey of colonial exploration. The *Etna* visited Humboldt Ba and a landing party scouted the immediat surroundings. On its way back to Ternate the Dutch team called at Dore (near presen day Manokwari) where the ship's officer gave Sir Alfred Wallace, the great British na uralist, an account of their findings. Wallac writes: "They had stayed at Humboldt Ba several days, and found it a much more beau tiful and interesting place than Dorey, as we as a better harbour."

The Dutch were finally prodded int founding Hollandia by German claims on th northern coast of New Guinea. The 141° eas longitude line had been settled upon as a bor der, and by positioning their capital just 2 kilometers from the line, the Dutch thoug they would make it easier for the Germans t respect the border. Civil servants formed th nucleus of Hollandia's tiny community unt World War II broke out. The Japanese quickl swept aside the Dutch defenders and bui Hollandia into an important base.

Allied units under General Dougla MacArthur captured Hollandia after a amphibious landing and made it into a gigar tic forward staging area from which to wag the Pacific campaign. The Japanese-built ai field at Sentani, enlarged and improved became the home base for a wing o Superfortress bombers and swarms of figh ers. At the height of the Allied push Hollandia's population reached a quarter mi

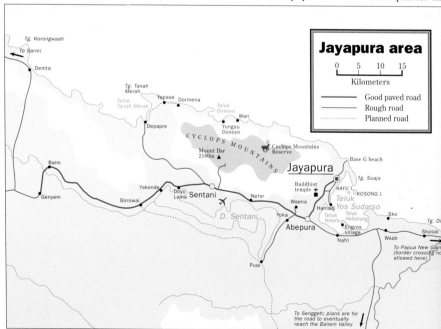

on. (See "World War II," page 38.)

After the war and Indonesian independence, the Dutch clung to Irian as their last remaining possession in the East Indies. In 1955, Hollandia's population of 16,700 was made up chiefly of those fleeing from the Sukarno regime. But in 1963, Irian and Hollandia were integrated into Indonesia. In 1971, the capital's population reached 35,000 and thereafter increased steadily to today's 70,000. Many Javanese, Makassarese and Bugis Muslims, as well as Ambonese and Manadonese Christians, have migrated to Jayapura, where, because of a "frontier" economy heavily subsidized by Jakarta, jobs are more readily available.

Hamadi: beachside suburb

The beachside suburb of Hamadi, located off the main road to Sentani about 4 kilometers out of town, has the only souvenir stalls in the area. Don't expect any real antiques or masterpieces—just souvenirs, reasonably priced, consisting of crude Asmat and local carvings, and penis gourds and other goods from the highlands. On the outskirts of Hamadi, a couple of World War II vintage tanks and landing craft rust peacefully, sinking slowly into the sand along the beach.

One can swim here, but it is no great joy. The best beach in the area is 7 kilometers in the opposite direction from Jayapura, at the old Allied "Base G." The sand is clean and the water clear. Jayapurans go there in hordes on Sundays, the only day public transportation makes the run.

Short jaunts out of town

The stilt-perched village of **Engros** on Yotefa Bay in front of Hamadi, is fun to visit, and one can even stay overnight in a *losmen* over the water. There are no luxuries here, but Engros offers an introduction at the coastal lifestyle. At low tide, the bay bottom next to the village turns into an animated soccer field. This is probably the only place in the world where the tides interrupt the matches.

There are several beaches a bit out of town yet still within striking distance. About 45 kilometers from Jayapura, an hour or so past Sentani town, a paved road reaches Tanah Merah Bay at **Depapre** village. There is some coral here, particularly in the eastern part of the bay, but the long beach between Dormena and Dosoyo Bay, and the beach at Yangsa Dosoyo, are said to be much nicer.

Holtekang Bay, just east of Jayapura, has a good sandy beach, and is quiet even on weekends. There is no coral here, so forget snorkeling, but several interesting species of birds are known to inhabit the vicinity. Another good birding spot, the lighthouse a

Overleaf: *Beautiful Yos Sudarso Bay. The heart of Jayapura city is at left.* **Below:** *A village in front of Kayu Island in Yotefa Bay.*

half hour's climb from Base G, also offers spectacular dawn views of Jayapura. Below the lighthouse, big waves crash around the rock formations. Another superb little bay, locally called **Pasir Enam**, can be reached either by boat from Jayapura or by an hour's stroll along a footpath beginning at the expat enclave of Angkasa II. The isolated beach here offers good snorkeling.

A half-day excursion out of Jayapura (or Sentani) covers several points of interest between the airport and the capital. The **University of Cenderawasih Museum** in Abepura boasts quite a good collection of Irianese artifacts and a souvenir stand offering recent carvings and craft items. Ask for Nico Tanto, who works here and also has an excellent crafts shop in his house. A few kilometers further out of town, the **Museum Negeri** offers exhibits on the natural history and material culture of several Irianese ethnic groups. Both museums are open from 8 a.m. to 1 p.m., Monday through Friday.

There are two floors to the Museum Negeri's main building, housing a variety of artifacts from all districts of Irian. Some are labelled in English and there are plans for more thorough descriptions. The collection of the University of Cenderawasih is the best of the two aesthetically, but the Museum Negeri gives you a better idea of the material culture of several Irianese groups. There are miniature huts showing regional variations in living quarters, including a 1:4 scale front of a Asmat *jeu,* or men's house, and a Dani *hona* Particularly fascinating are two Asmat troph or ancestral skulls, skillfully decorated. On display is of traditional bride price item another has musical instruments. Upstair the Summer Institute of Linguistics has liste 245 languages and dialects of Irian, keyed to large map. Historical trade contacts with th island are documented with Chinese Japanese and Dutch porcelain and othe exchange items.

Lake Sentani

Just out of Sentani, a paved road wind upward for 6 kilometers and climbs to **Mou Ifar** in the Cyclops Mountains. At Ifar stand a monument to General MacArthur, whos headquarters were here. The site overlook the humid lowlands and offers a splendi view of the lake. Local lore states that whi gazing out over island-strewn Lake Sentan MacArthur conceived his famous island-ho ping strategy in the Pacific.

At several places on the shores of **Lak Sentani**, you can arrange to rent an ou board-powered dugout ($10–$15 per hour) visit the island villages or just ride around th lake. While there are regular services, it better to charter one of these outboard-pov ered canoes, if you can afford it. Some ar magnificent craft, hollowed out from a singl huge trunk. Many have painted or carve

notifs in the old Sentani style, formerly one of Irian's great art centers. One of the canoes, with a raised human figure in a stylized background, should belong to a museum.

If you rent a boat, ask to be taken to **Apayo Island**, where craftsmen make bark cloth paintings and sculptures in the traditional style. Or just ride around for an hour or two and take pictures of the hills disappearing into the water at the foot of the Cyclops Mountains. It is safe to swim in the lake. If there are any crocodiles left, they are concentrated around the more remote shores where there are no buzzing motors.

Women do most of the fishing here, and the men work the sago palm and fish only occasionally. The men's canoes are more rounded than the women's and more difficult to balance in. Don't take your camera if you want to try one of the canoes by yourself.

Occasionally one of the boys from the **Yougga Restaurant** on the shores of the lake uses scuba equipment to spear fish here. The lake is said to reach depths of over 100 meters. One diver said that visibility is so bad that you have to be almost touching the fish before spearing them. He also tells of some men with *ilmu*, or "esoteric knowledge," who live without any equipment, stay underwater or three days and bring back a huge catch.

Crocodile farms

Four crocodile farms raise the critters in the vicinity of Jayapura. If you want to visit one, we suggest c.v. **Bintang Mas**. There is no road sign for the croc farm, but it is about halfway between the 6 and 7 kilometer markers on the road from Jayapura to Sentani. Watch on the right-hand side for Klinik Pantai Nirmala. A dirt road to Bintang Mas runs right next to the clinic. In about a half kilometer you will see the roadside pens.

At the farm, crocodiles of different sizes are carefully segregated to prevent the smaller ones from getting gobbled up by their older siblings. Feeding time—fish and shrimp—is around 3 p.m.

Thanks to the farms, you can buy crocodile meat around Jayapura for $3 per kilo, less than one third of the price in Hong Kong or Singapore—where much of the frozen meat ends up. The Chinese say crocodile meat cures asthma and other ills.

Of course, the crocs are chiefly raised for their valuable skins. Most of the 15 farms in Irian raise the animals for 3-4 years, when their length reaches 1.5 meters. At this size, a croc produces 15 kilos of saleable meat and

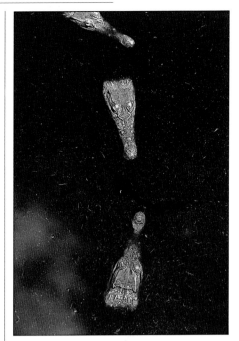

the crucial 30-40 centimeter width of belly skin. At this size, the skin is tough, yet still pliable. The belly skins end up in Paris or Tokyo, and the rest of the hides get worked into local souvenirs.

Breeding crocodiles in captivity is a very tricky affair. The eggs react to minute changes of temperature and humidity and unless conditions are perfect the embryos turn out to be all males—or all females, or they all even die. (In a natural setting the mother crocs pull together a heap of vegetation, and the heat of decomposition incubates the eggs.) Rather than trying to hatch eggs, the crocodile farms find it much easier to buy small, month-old crocodile babies. These are purchased from the people who live near the animals' natural nesting grounds.

Conservationists approve of this method, because it involves the local community in the crocodile's welfare—the people don't eat the eggs or kill the reptiles, and the economic motive gives them an incentive to keep out poachers. In addition, the egg collectors' cash payment is sometimes supplemented by chicken eggs so that the old source of protein will not be missed.

Opposite: *The traditional means of transport on Lake Sentani is by small dugout canoe.*
Above: *Crocodiles in a pond near Jayapura. Crocodile skins are a valuable export, with the best going to Tokyo and Paris.*

Jayapura Practicalities

All prices in US$; Jayapura telephone code 967

All flights land at Sentani Airport, 32 kilometers from Jayapura. Outside the airport, minibuses wait to take you to town for $5–$10. If you have little luggage and a tight budget, walk the 200 meters from the airport complex to the main road. The trip to town by public minibus consists of two legs: to Abepura (40¢), change buses and then to Jayapura (40¢).

If your visit to Jayapura is just a hurdle on the way to the Baliem valley, you may want to just drop your gear at one of the *losmen* in Sentani and zip to town for your Merpati ticket (leaving 7 am the next day) and *surat jalan.* Count on 3–5 hours for the trip including waiting for the *surat jalan* and ticket.

The bulk of Jayapura nestles in a short valley running straight inland, and most government offices are along the shoreline. Commercial activity centers on Jalan Ahmad Yani, which slices through town with a constant flow of traffic unchecked by stoplights. The police station, needed for the essential *surat jalan,* and the Expor-Impor Bank, the best in town for money exchange, Jl. A. Yani.

SURAT JALAN

The police station, next to the Hotel Matoa, issues the essential *surat jalan,* the travel permit required for the interior. Bring your passport and four photos—usually only two are enough, but you never know. A half-hour should do the trick, unless the man who controls the stamps is out. Merpati, the only scheduled airline flying to the Baliem, has its main office on the other side of the Matoa. (See "Travel Advisory" page 186 for more information on the important *surat jalan.*)

ACCOMMODATIONS

Jayapura is well provided with a number of air-conditioned hotels, as well as *losmen* catering to the budget traveler. But there are no accommodations as cheap as one could find in Java and Sumatra, for example.

Matoa. Jl. Ahmad Yani 14; ✆ 31633; Fax: 31437; Telex: 76208 Matoa IA. Two stars; the only international standard hotel in town. All rooms with central AC; dining room/bar; helpful staff; elevator; taxis in front. All rooms with color TV/video, mini-bar. $45 S, $60 D, $100 Suite with continental breakfast.

Triton. Jl. Ahmad Yani 52; P.O. Box 33, ✆21218 or 21171. 24 rooms. Free airport taxi; color TV/video, all rooms AC. Next to the Rasa Sayang Restaurant (steak, occasionally venison). $13 S; $19–$32 D w/breakfast.

Irian Plaza. Jl. Setiapura 11; ✆ 22649. 39 rooms. Meeting room, phones in rooms. Fan cooled $11 S; AC $18–$23 S, $21–$27 D w/ light breakfast.

Dafonsoro. Jl. Percetakan Negara 20/24 ✆ 31695, 31696. 27 rooms, all AC. Restaurant. $20 S, $23 D w/ simple breakfast.

Numbai. Jl. Trikora 1, about 5 km from down town, close to the bemo route Dock 5. ✆21394 22185. Meals available ($2.50) if ordered ahead. AC $10 S, $13 D; $3 less if fan-cooled All w/ simple breakfast.

Hotel Sederhana. Jl. Halmahera 2; ✆ 22157 20 rooms, some AC, some fan-cooled, some with attached bath. With fan and outside bath $6–$7 S and $11–$13 D; with AC and attached bath $9–$12 S and $16–$19 D w/ simple breakfast.

Losmen Lawu. Jl. Sulawesi 22, about 4 km from downtown, ✆ 21937. 15 rooms, 4 with AC. AC $8 S, $14 D; Fan-cooled $4.50 S, $8 D all w/ simple breakfast. Meals from food stalls $1 to $3.

Losmen Kartini. Jl. Perintis 2, ✆ 22371. 12 rooms, quite clean. With outside bath $5 S $9 D; with attached bath, $12 D. All w/ simple breakfast.

Losmen Jayapura. Jl. Olahraga 4, ✆ 21216 Dingy. $4 S, $6 D w/outside bath; $5 S, $7.50 D w/ attached bath.

Losmen in Sentani

All include simple breakfast, police for *surat jalan,* and transportation to the airport.

Mansapur Rani Guest House. 200 meters from the terminal, Jl. Jaboso 113, 20 rooms. $7 per person w/ light breakfast.

Minang Jaya. In the town of Sentani, just of the main road to Jayapura, past airport turnoff 25 rooms. $9 S, $15 D w/fan and attached bath; $15 S, $18 D w/AC.

Sentani Inn. 3 km from the airport on the main road to Jayapura. Clean, friendly staff Breakfast included. 16 rooms. $9 S, $16 D w/fan; $12 S, $16 D w/ AC.

LOCAL TRANSPORTATION

Jayapura is compact and you can walk around most of the town, but to reach Sentani and the beaches, you need transport. The hub of the public transport system (minibus) is the taxi terminal across the road from the post office Drivers wait for at least a partial load before leaving and most swing through town before setting off, shouting to raise additional passengers. Prices are 15¢–40¢ to nearby destinations (Base G, Abepura, etc.).

Renting a minibus with driver locally runs $3–$5/hr, with a day rate of about $40, or $50–$60 if further away than Lake Sentani. Be sure you notify your hotel ahead of time if you will need a taxi. There may not be one available for spur of the moment excursions.

DINING

For a seafood orgy, sitting in comfort, try the **Porasco**, located near the harbor, next to the big church. The food is great, but not cheap—up to $15 per person, including cold beer. Jayapura also boasts numerous sit-down restaurants serving tasty Indonesian and Chinese dishes based on chicken, pork, shrimp, squid, beef and fish for a moderate $2 to $6. A few places serve western food, not very good and pricey.

Dhanita Corner. Just a bit out of town heading north, on the bay. Nice place to have an after-noon coffee. Often reserved for private karaoke parties on Saturdays. Open 9am–3pm and 7pm–10pm. Indonesian dishes and seafood, $1–$4.

Hawaii. Next to the movie house, just off the park down-town—good box lunches, shrimp, chicken dishes; reasonably priced, good ser-vice, air conditioning.

Himalaya. Jl. Matahari, half block from the main drag, Jl. A. Yani. Cold beer. Chicken, cut-tlefish, pigeon, frog, shrimp, beef $4–$6; sim-ple, filling Chinese dishes $1.50–$2.

Jaya Grill. Jl. Koti #5, ✆ 22783. On the water, towards the main docks, enclosed and AC. 10:30 am–2:30 pm and 6:30 pm–10:30 pm. Shrimp, seafood cocktail, crab, shrimp, squid, chicken, frog, pork, $5–$6; steaks (from Jakarta) $8–$10; abalone $15; simple Chinese or Indonesian dishes $1.50–$2.50; wide vari-ety of booze; hard stuff, $1.50–$5, cold beer. Although the service is horrible, the restaurant is the most frequented by local expats.

Kebon Sirih. Jl. Seitapura 10, ✆ 31261, in front of the Irian Plaza Hotel. Specializes in grilled sea food, which you pick out front, before going in. Often crowded, but can run out of fish. Moderate prices: $3 plate of shrimp; $2 squid, $5 average fish.

Matoa Restaurant. In the Matoa Hotel. Pleasant, modern dining room (at last check, still waiting for cook who can prepare European food). Bloody Mary, Singapore Sling $2.20, fish dishes $6–$15, squid $6, chicken $5–$10, beef $4–$15, soups $8–$19, crab dishes $9, shrimp $6, abalone $32, pigeon $9, frog $6; also, a few cheaper Indonesian/Chinese dish-es; juices, canned drinks $1.10; beer $1.25; imported liquors $5.

Nirwana. Jl. Ahmad Yani 40, on the main drag. Good selection of Padang style food (choice of dishes, what you eat is what you pay for). AC. About $3–$4 for a meal; grilled *ikan mas* (gold-fish) available.

Padang Simpang Tiga. Jl. Percetakan 92. Large, clean, Padang style restaurant. reason-able prices.

Porasco. On the bay, next to the church. This open-sided restaurant is open only from 6 pm to 11 pm. Before you enter, you look over the vari-ety of fish, squid, lobster and choose what you want (ask the price at this stage, as it can get quite expensive). Then the cook grills your choice. Cold beer. Simple fish fillet $4–$6 depending on variety and size.

Queen. Behind the Expor-Impor Bank. Best for a big table with lots of people: steamboat or other large dishes for parties; whole pig $75; huge dishes for four people $15 simple

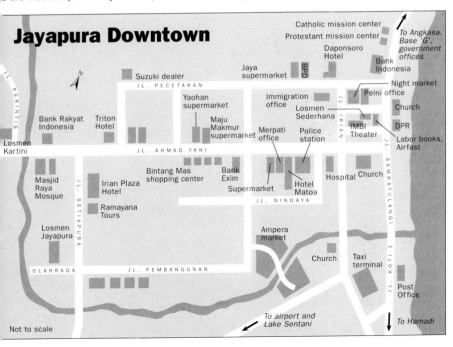

Jayapura Downtown

Not to scale

Chinese dishes $1.50–$2; private dining room available; soups, chicken, shrimp, crab, squid, much more in many varieties of preparation.

Rabina Coffee House. Jl. Angkasa/Trikora, 5 km from downtown, ✆ 21490. Run by a very pleasant woman, Nyona Meles. Mostly frequented at night by the younger set, under the Nyona Meles' watchful eye. *Bakso* soup 75¢, soft ice cream 75¢, sundaes $1.50; other meals have to be ordered one day ahead, even the hamburgers ($1.30).

Rasa Sayang. Part of the Hotel Triton, Jl. Ahmad Yani 52, ✆ 21171. Crab, pigeon, frog, shrimp, pork, fish, cuttlefish, sate $4–$5; abalone $10, steaks $6–$10; venison (average availability: twice a month) $12.

Yotefa. Jl. Percetakan 64. A new place, nicely decorated; European and Indonesian food, cold beer. Chicken, shrimp, squid dishes, $2–$3; fish, to $5 depending on size; rice and noodle dishes $1–$2.

Warungs and food stalls

Lively night market in front of the Pelni office, serving *bakso, soto madura, bubur,* and lots of fried bananas and other tasty snacks. A bit further, towards the harbor, on Jl. Halmahera, you can cloth-draped stalls serving delicious, inexpensive grilled fish and squid—big fish steaks 75¢, whole fish $2. Good ambiance. Other stalls line Jl. A. Yani up near the mosque, including an excellent fried noodle and fried rice stall just across from the Triton Hotel.

Banks and money exchange

The best exchange rate is found at the Expor-Impor Bank on Jl. Ahmad Yani. 8 am–1 pm. Quick, pleasant service. They change US$, $A, £, ¥, D.M., Swiss Francs and guilders at good rates. Travelers' checks exchanged: American Express, Bank of America, Bank of Credit and Commerce, Barclays, and Citicorp (in US$); Sumitomo (in ¥); and Cooks (in US$, £, and Swiss Francs).

Medical

Puskesmas. (hospital) Jl. Ahmad Yani. Dr. Toni Pranato is the malaria and dengue specialist.

Dr. Oey. Jl. Kesehatan, just below the hospital, ✆ 21789. Dr. Oey speaks English and German.

Dr. Manapa. Jl. Irian (near the cinema), ✆ 22463 (office), 21473 (home). Dr. Manapa peaks English.

Newspapers

Newsweek, Time and the Jakarta Post are sometimes available at **Toko Buku Labor** (✆ 21173) on Jl. Sam Ratulangi next door to the Airfast shipping office.

Shopping and Souvenirs

Store hours in Jayapura generally run from 8 am–12 m, and then again from 5 pm–9 pm. Souvenirs can be found at the Hotel Matoa

shop, at the shop attached to the museum a Cendrawasih University (and the Neger Museum mentioned in the text above) and a the Perindustrian office in Abepura. In Hamac are several stalls selling penis gourds (75¢ t $1), net bags ($2–$3), and stone axes ($2–$3 from the highlands and small Asmat carving ($15–$20). Bargaining is expected.

EXCURSIONS

The folks at your hotel can help you design you own tour around the Jayapura–Sentani area Some suggestions:

Boating in the harbor. Rent a catamaran (40 H motor, around $15/hr) and cruise Yos Sudars Bay to Kayu Island with its church and Koson Island with its mosque. There is a beache World War II amphibious assault tank on Det Island in Yotefa Bay.

Visit Lake Sentani. Nearby, island-dotted Lak Sentani makes a pleasant day's diversion Motorized dugout canoes rent for $10–$15 pe hour; paddled canoes, negotiable. There ar only two certain places to rent, Jahim and th Yougga Restaurant.

Jahim, which is the "market harbor" o *pelabuhan pasar,* is at the end of a side roa that runs by the Sentani town market, endin after a couple of kilometers at the lake. Ther are usually at least half a dozen dugout canoe stationed here, waiting for passengers to ferr to the islands of shoreside villages.

Yougga Restaurant, 22 kilometers fron Jayapura, is right next to the main road an Lake Sentani. Motorboats rent for $16/h There is also a 10-room *losmen* at this prett little lakeside setting ($14 S, $20 D w/break fast). The restaurant specializes in *ikan ma* (literally "goldfish," but bigger than the orna mental variety and as tasty as perch) and local variety called *mujahir*, served grilled c fried ($2–$10, depending on size). The place i quiet on weekdays and busy on weekends.

Visit Engros village. Engros is a fishing villag perched on stilts off Abe beach. There is a *lo men* of sorts here, too. Get a permit at th YPMD office (Yayasan Pembangan Masyaraka Desa, or Rural People's Development Founda tion). Their office is just across from the PISG church on the main road to Sentani. When yo get your permit you pay $3 a night for as mar nights as you wish to stay in Engros village Then you catch another minibus from Abepur to Abe beach (15¢) whence you can be paddle to Engros for $1.

Once you get there, a nice old man will se up mattresses in the "losmen" for you and an fill the "bath"; if you want to eat fresh grille fish, ask for it ahead of time; it will cos $1.50–$6 depending on size. For about $5C you can commission a dance. 20 to 30 me wearing old beads, traditional decorations, an loin cloths. At low tide, watch the soccer matc es next to the village. At high tide, the villag perches above some 1.5 meters of water. This is a typical fishing village, with friendly people and few tourists.

REGIONAL TRANSPORTATION

Jayapura is well connected by air to the rest of Indonesia. Within the province, Merpati connects the main towns, and many of the smaller villages, while missionary planes land on even more remote grass strips. Sea transportation, to Jakarta or less distant points, is also available. Merpati has a disconcerting tendency to be overbooked, so CHECK, DOUBLE-CHECK, AND RECONFIRM YOUR RESERVATIONS! This cannot be overemphasized. Below are some of the flights available at press time, but check with the airline offices for current schedules.

Merpati Jl. A. Yani 15 Lantai I/21, next to the Hotel Matoa. © 21327, 21913, 21810, 21111. Mon–Thurs, 8 am–3 pm, Fri to 12 m, Sat to 1:30 pm, Sun 10 am–12 m. The Merpati hub is Biak, so relatively few flights leave out of Sentani; the most important are the several daily flights to Wamena, which leave from 7 am–10:30 am and are usually in the relatively large Fokker F-27's.

Biak	Twice daily	$59
Ewer (Agats)	M, also, unreliably, F (via Wamena)	$70
Lereh	W,Su	$30
Manokwari	Tu,W,F,Sa (Tu via Biak)	$101
Merauke	M,Tu,Th,Su (M via Tanahmerah)	$85
Nabire	M,W,F	$71
Sarmi	Su	$45
Senggeh	M	$20
Serui	F,Su	$77
Sorong	M,Tu,W,F,Sa (M via Biak; Tu,F via Manokwari)	$127
Tanahmerah	M	$65
Timika	Tu,W,Th,F,S,Su	$63
Wamena	3–6 times daily	$34
Also: Arso ($15), Genyem ($15)		

Some national flights, mostly milk runs:

Ambon	Daily (via Timika, Biak)	$159
Denpasar	Daily (3–4 stops)	$299
Jakarta	2–3 daily (2–4 stops)	$344
Manado	W,Sa (3 stops)	$189
Surabaya	Daily (via Biak, Ujung Pandang)	$339
Ujung Pandang	Twice daily (via Biak)	$249

MAF. The Missionary Aviation Fellowship office (a Protestant support airline) is next to the Sentani air terminal; no commercial flights to where either Garuda or Merpati flies. Officer: Wally Wiley, © 171 (Sentani, by day), © 178 (evenings). For charters, they can be contacted through the Missionary Fellowship office in Jayapura, located a bit past the Bank of Indonesia on the harbor road, P.O. Box 38, Jayapura, © 21264, Telex: 76142.

MAF's schedule is set according to the church's requirements, and they take into account the weights of passengers, including their luggage, with missionaries having first priority. For a special chartered flight, contact them several months ahead of time. Then confirm, 2 weeks prior. (See also "Highlands Practicalities," page 154, for more information on flights in the interior.)

AMA. Associated Mission Aviation is the Roman Catholic equivalent of MAF. Officer: Bosco Fernandez, whose office is close to the Sentani airport, next to MAF, © 26. Planes are Cessna 185s (4–5 passengers). Charters run $180/hr. AMA can be contacted through Airfast (a cargo outfit, but they also charter Hawker Siddeley 748's at $1,100 per hour) at Telex 76122 AIRFAST, or Jl. Sam Ratulangi 3, P.O. Box 1234, Jayapura. © 21925.

Sea transportation

Pelni. Jl. Halmahera 1, © 21270, Fax: 21370. P.T. Pelayaran Nasional Indonesia's huge passenger ship *Umsini* calls at Jayapura every 15 days. Up to 2,400 passengers can travel on this German-built ship from Jayapura to Jakarta, via Ternate and Sulawesi. There are five classes of cabins (the cheapest is dormitory style but still clean). Some prices:

Jakarta	1st class $224/dormitory $63	
Surabaya	$204/$55	
Ujung Pandang	$146/$46	
Bitung, Sulawesi	$106/$30	
Ternate	$92/$26	
Sorong	$58/$17	

The *Umsini* takes a week to Jakarta. It is not a cruise ship, but the food is good and it's an excellent alternative to flying if one has a bit of time to spare. Book your passage as early as possible. Pelni has other ships where deck passage is available, for example to Biak about twice a month for $5–$10, to Sorong for $10 . It takes about a week to get there with several calls on the way.

Yotefa shipping lines. Jl. Percetakan 90A, © 31687, Telex: 76148 YAKJ. They have 200-ton coasters that take up to 75 deck passengers from Jayapura to Sorong (and points between) about once a month; from Merauke to Fakfak and to Aru, about every six weeks. These are "trampers."

Route #1: Jayapura Sarmi Serui Biak Nabire Manokwari Sorong Manokwari Biak Nabire Serui Sarmi Jayapura on the Jayapura-based *Dayala Nusantara*. 14-day cycle, 26 voyages a year, total distance: 1,826 nautical miles.

Route #2: Jayapura Sarmi Trimurus Bagusa Kasanaweja Bagusa Trimurus Puwai Kaipuri Dawai Ambai Serui Waren Waipoga Napan Nabire Biak Korido Jeggerbun Ransiki Windesi Waior Nabire Biak Ansus Serui Dawai Waren Serui Kaipuri Sarmi Jayapura on the Jayapura-based *Nyala Perintis*. 28-day cycle, 13 voyages a year; 1,804 nautical miles.

PART III

The Bird's Head Peninsula

The Bird's Head Peninsula, Kepala Burung in Indonesian, and Vogelkop in Dutch, is so-called because on the map it looks like the head of a huge westward-flying bird. Although the first European settlement on Irian was here, it is today considerably less well-known than the coastal regions and highlands to the west. Considerable mission-ry activity takes place here, and in areas here are settlements of transmigrant rice farmers from western Indonesia, but almost no tourists visit.

Any exploration of the Bird's Head proper must begin at the main coastal towns of Manokwari and Sorong. The point of entry to the Bomberai Peninsula south of Berau Bay—included in this section for the purposes of this book—is Fakfak, a small town on the south coast of the Onin Peninsula.

At least a basic working knowledge of Indonesian and plenty of patience and initiative are essential for visiting this area, though the towns are all served by scheduled flights and occasional steamers.

Because there is almost no tourist infrastructure in the interior of the Bird's Head, tourists may not be free to travel just anywhere in the region. You may have to negotiate with the police to get a *surat jalan* to the more remote inland areas.

Physically, the bird's head is one of the most beautiful parts of Irian. Although the peaks are not as high as those in the central cordillera, it is mountainous in the north, with broad lowland swamps and plains in the south. The Anggi Lakes, south and inland from Manokwari, are known particularly for the natural beauty of their scenery.

Manokwari is one of the main missionary centers for American evangelical sects on Irian, and the hub of a rapidly-growing network of transmigration settlements, logging concerns and plantations. It sits at Dore Bay, site of Captain John Hayes' first ill-fated settlement in 1793. (See "Europeans," page 36.)

Naturalist Alfred Russel Wallace had visited earlier, in 1858, but his collections were disrupted by an infected foot, and infestations of ants that sometimes literally carried away his specimens.

The oil-town of **Sorong** at the western tip of Irian is the jumping-off point for visits to the Raja Empat Islands to the west, reportedly the best place to witness the birds of paradise in their natural habitat.

Sorong itself is a somewhat faded town, as the oil yield has fallen off. Timber harvesting, nickel mines, and transmigration settlements keep the town going. Still, it is not a very attractive or inherently interesting place for tourists. Think of it as a place from which to plan a trip to nearby Salawati or Waigeo, or to Ayamaru Lake in the interior.

The district capital of **Fakfak**, which controls the lower coast of the peninsula, may be reached by air from Sorong and Manokwari. The town is on a hill facing the harbor, and the scenery in the area is spectacular.

Lining the north coast of the Onin Peninsula are rock paintings similar to those produced by aboriginal Australians. The paintings grace niches cut by waves into sea-facing limestone cliffs, and must be viewed from a boat. Similar rock art is found near **Kaimana** on Kamrau Bay to the south.

A canoe trip from either of these pretty little towns to the rock art sites is a fine excursion, and one that very few outsiders have ever made. The waters are clear and blue, offering a stunning setting for the red and black paintings set into the chalky rock. The coral growth, particularly in Triton Bay south of Kaimana, is rich and undisturbed.

Overleaf: *The snow fields surrounding Puncak Jaya, at 4,884 meters the tallest peak between the Himalayas and the Andes. Photo by Kal Muller.* **Opposite:** *The strange and moody cassowary, the largest native land animal in Irian Jaya. Photo by Alain Compost.*

MANOKWARI

Hub of the Bird's Head Peninsula

This small town on the north-east tip of the Bird's Head takes pride in having hosted the first permanent Christian mission in New Guinea. On February 5, 1852, after sailing for 25 days out of Batavia, the capital of the Dutch East Indies (now Jakarta), German missionaries Johann Geissler and C.W. Ottow landed on Mansinam Island in Dore Bay.

For many years, the mission achieved little success, but nevertheless laid the groundwork for the district's current Christian majority. The fact that the pale white missionaries bore an uncanny resemblance to the locals' conception of ghosts did not help to attract converts. The graves of these pioneer missionaries now lie under an elaborate monument—a traditional hut with lots of pop art, just outside of town.

Missionary efforts were renewed after World War II, mostly by well-organized and financed American fundamentalists. Two of them, Walter Erikson and Edward Tritt, were slain by their porters when they tried to penetrate the Kabar district west of the town.

A theological seminary, located in the suburb of Sowi (past the airport), has been named after the two martyrs. Forty-eight students were enrolled here in 1990. Missionaries and the Summer Institute of Linguistics have a strong presence in Manokwari. If you want to meet the missionaries, go to Pasir Putih beach on a Saturday afternoon. White skin and blond hair obviously no longer excite the curiosity of the local Irianese.

Visiting naturalists

Shortly after Ottow and Geissler established their Christian beachhead on Mansinam, the great naturalist Alfred Russel Wallace spent several months at Dore Bay (often spelled Dorey or Dorei in old texts). A couple of decades later, in 1872, Italian naturalists Luigi D'Albertis and Odouardo Beccari landed here and trekked into the Arfak Mountains where they discovered many new bird and insect species. They also had a brush with local warfare.

Because it has a well protected harbor, the Dutch set up the administrative post for Irian's north coast at Manokwari. The area later lost much of its importance when Hollandia became the capital of Dutch New Guinea. During World War II, the Japanese established a military base here, bombed and bypassed by the Allies. After the war, the Dutch returned to prepare Irian for independence. After Irian was handed over to Indonesia, some rebels in the hills resisted the new administration, but the fighting essentially ended in the 1960s.

While linguists classify the peoples of the Manokwari region into over 30 separate language groups, the government has simply divided the district into three ethnic groups: the Wamesa in the south, the Arfak in the Arfak mountains, and the Doreri, belonging to the Biak language group, along the coast. The latter arrived from Numfor and settled around Manokwari as well as on Leman and Mansinam islands, centuries before the arrival of the first Europeans. A majority of the district's 120,000 inhabitants (67 percent) are Protestants, with Muslim (20 percent) and Catholic (8 percent) minorities. The population density is very low—just under 3 per square kilometer.

The economy of the Manokwari district is quite diverse. The Bintuni subdistrict produces oil, and Koreans are now logging mangroves as well. The inner reaches of Bintuni Bay is thought to hold the most extensive stand of mangroves in the world. The soils in the region are among the best in Irian, and an agricultural station was set up by the Dutch. This is now being followed up by a branch of the University of Cenderawasih.

Cash crops include cacao, grown on British-run estate at Ransiki, palm oil from processing plant in the Warmeri district, cloves from around Manokwari and coconut everywhere along the coast. Major exports also include sea products such as smoked and dried fish, shark's fins, seashells and turtle shells harvested from the rich waters of Cenderawasih Bay.

Sights of Manokwari

The town of Manokwari, stretching around Dore Bay, lies in an attractive setting of low hills dominated by the Arfak Mountains to the south. Indonesian-Chinese–owned shop

Opposite: *A palm-lined beach near Manokwari.*

re well stocked with all the essentials and a air number of luxuries. The main shopping area is Jalan Merdeka, near the Hotel Mokwam. A newer shopping complex has gone up near the Hotel Mutiara.

For the best overview of town, hike up to the **Japanese War Memorial**, about 2 kilometers from the Hotel Arfak. You start off on paved road, then a wide earthed path climbs up a sweat-inducing slope before leveling off for a pleasant jungle stroll in the **Gunung Meja Park**. The simple, enclosed monument is complemented by a concrete and wood replica of a traditional native hut set on piles. The panorama, a bit hemmed in by trees, looks over much of the town, Dore Bay, and a chunk of the Arfak Mountains. Continuing on the same path for some 4 kilometers brings you to a campus of Cenderawasih University.

Heading out of town past the hospital and the police station towards Pasir Putih, you soon reach **Gereja Koawi**. The monument to the first missionaries, built over some of their graves, is located just behind the church. Two angels trumpet over the entrance. A large traditional native house sits on piles over the graves with local warrior statues guarding the sides. A long panel in the back, colorful if not particularly well-executed, shows life in the region before and after the arrival of Christianity. The same bayside road continues on to **Pasir Putih**, "White Sand" beach. There is good swimming here, and a shallow coral bank offers decent snorkeling. Continuing on the seaside road, you reach a lighthouse, where many birds flock.

Manokwari's central market spreads out along the west side of Dore harbor. A series of high-roofed buildings shelter mini-stores, the occasional butcher and scattered piles of fresh vegetables. Try not to walk on the harbor side at low tide as the market's accumulated garbage takes the charm out of any stroll. The taxi terminal is next to the market.

While the central market operates all day, the fish market just to the south starts at dawn and lasts until about 9 a.m. There might be a huge spotted grouper for sale, or barracuda, red snappers and many other species. Motorized outriggers depart from here later in the day in various directions, pulling up next to the fish market to wait for passengers.

If the weather is clear, take a boat out to **Leman and Mansinam Islands**. Motorized outrigger canoes can occasionally be found at the main dock but your chances of finding one are better next to the fish market, by the central market. The right light brings out shades of the sea ranging from clear white to turquoise to deep blue, depending on the depths. The waters of Dore Bay, lined with wooden houses perched on stilts and fronted by a variety of boats, remain surprisingly clean—but don't look too close to the shoreline, especially near the market at low tide.

After a tour of the harbor, head to small

Leman Island, its few huts and white sand beaches standing out against the backdrop of the Arfak Mountains. Just offshore to the north of Mansinam Island, facing Manokwari, a large white cross commemorates the pioneering work of missionaries. This was where Ottow and Geissler landed to set up the first mission outpost in Irian. An old church and well sit just inland from the cross.

The eastern side of Mansinam presents stretches of coral raised to the tree line, alternating with short stretches of white sand beach, inviting for a secluded dip. A tangle of jungle reaches the sea here. As you approach the island's southern shore, look for birds and trees full of the large fruit bats called flying foxes, which sometimes erupt from the trees by the thousands. A semi-circular bay on the far south side of the island faces coral formations making up the area's best underwater scenery.

About three quarters of the way down the west coast, ask your boatman to stop by a large Japanese ship sunk during World War II. The ship lies on its side in seven to ten meters of clear water, easily visible from the surface. A good view of the craft, home to fish and sprouting coral formations here and there, can be had by snorkelers. While you can easily reach the top side of the ship, peering inside takes unusual lung capacity. Local fishermen maintain there have been no shark sightings, so swimming and snorkeling should be safe.

South from town

The paved road south of Manokwari now extends past the transmigration settlements at Prafi, about 60 kilometers away, and reaches past Ransiki. This road heads south past the airport and hugs the shore of **Lake Kabori**, oval in shape and barely separated from the sea. An old dirt road runs between the lake and the sea, but fallen logs and a washed-out bridge prevent vehicles from following this more picturesque route.

From the main road, there's only one viewing spot affording a clear panorama of the lake, but unfortunately this is next to a garbage dump. The paved road runs above the lake, cutting through limestone hills, before crossing a bridge at **Maruni**, 29 kilometers from Manokwari. Just ahead, a 6-kilometer side road leads to the seaside village of **Momi**. Just beyond this turnoff, the road swings inland, climbing steeply. If the weather is clear, Numfor Island is visible across the sea. Dropping down from the hills, the road

enters a wide, fertile valley containing som of Irian's best soils. A private company own huge palm oil and cacao plantations here. small town, **Warmeri**, is the sub-district cap tal, 40 kilometers from Manokwari.

Beyond the town another dozen kilome ters of pavement cut across rivers, creeks an oil palms, reaching the oil processing plan and eight transmigrant settlements a **Prafi**—the largest in the Manokwari distric The 15,000-odd transmigrants are mainly ric farmers from Java, with some also fron Timor and Flores. About 5,000 Irianese hav also resettled here. Each family has bee given two hectares by the government as we as a small house, agricultural implement seeds and a year's supply of food. A smalle Javanese community of 280 families had se tled in the vicinity of **Oransbari** on the coa south of Manokwari.

The Anggi Lakes

The best side trip from Manokwari is to th Anggi Lakes in the Arfak mountains. Bac packers can cover the distance in four day (lop off two days by hopping on a minibus a far as Warmeri), but we suggest flying ir Before entering the Arfak mountains, plane has to fly in a wide circle over th Warmeri valley to gain the necessary altitud Then it's densely wooded, steep-walled va leys, tree tops looking like a blanket of bro coli and huts in the middle of nowhere wit cleared patches on impossible slopes.

The tallest peak in the Arfaks, Gunun Umsini, reaches 2,926 meters and five othe mountains top 2,000 meters. The flight pat crosses the village and landing strip a Manyembow before more mountain scener then the flat, swampy, bog-like terrain exten ing out from one end of Anggi Giji. A tiny ou rigger or two might be on the lake to add t the spectacular effect of swooping down ove the water just in time for a turn to land on th dirt strip at **Sureri Village**. The scenery o the flight is itself worth the price of the ticke

From paths above the lake, the panoram sweeps over steep slopes covered with ferr or forest tipping into the smooth waters, wit the only ripples coming from paddled outri ger canoes. Sunlight, fog or clouds each cr ate a different setting and mood, so spend few days to experience the shifts of atmo phere. Walking trails connect the villages.

With a bit of luck, you can see the larg Arfak butterflies, found only in this region-

Opposite: *One of the beautiful Anggi Lakes.*

with wings beautifully marked by iridescent green patterns. Or accompany bow and arrow hunters stalking wild pigs, the marsupial cuscus or a variety of birds. Delicate, colorful orchids also enliven a forest stroll. Anggi Giji, considered the male lake, covers 2,900 hectares while Anggi Gita, the female lake, spreads over 2,500 hectares.

This lake district and the 12,000-strong Sougb ethnic group living in the area were opened to the outside world by the opening of an airstrip and an American evangelical post at the village of Sureri in 1955. The current missionary, a tall, blue-eyed German chap with 21 years' residence there, has recently completed the translation of the New Testament into the Sougb language.

He has also successfully introduced high-protein hybrid corn to supplement the staple diet of starchy sweet potatoes. Other vegetables, now airlifted to Manokwari thanks to special rates by the Missionary Aviation Fellowship, include garlic, onions, carrots, white potatoes, celery and cabbage.

Cash is also earned through the sale of the Arfak butterflies, orchids and an occasional sack of smoked fish. While the lakes had originally contained only native fish, the carp and goldfish have been introduced, ecologically not necessarily a good thing. Some of the goldfish now grow bigger than a man's thigh. The fish are caught from canoes with hook and line. Cattle did not fare so well—

they went wild, then had to be exterminated.

The Sougb people, now Christians, maintain some of their native traditions. A bride price—ancient beads, store-bought cloth, *ikat* cloth from Flores or Timor, pigs and seashell bracelets—is still required to wed.

All diseases, including the common cold, are believed to result from black magic. Toy pistols are now loaded with potent powder and fired from a hidden position at one's intended victim. The missionary thinks it will take a couple more generations before belief in the efficacy of black magic begins to wane.

Traditional dances are still occasionally performed and can be put on for visitors if given sufficient advance notice. The men dress in red loincloths while the ladies wear black. There are two basic dances, a conga-type affair, single file around the huts, and a linked-arms dance. The missionary does not object to these if a certain decorum is maintained, but some unavoidable lewdness invariably creeps into the proceedings.

Most of the Sougb huts are built in the traditional manner, raised a meter or so on stilts, with wood floor, bark walls and thatched roof. Those who can afford it cover their houses with sheets of corrugated metal—not very aesthetic but it ends the chore of replacing the thatching every three or four years. Inside these family huts, the men sleep in bunks on one side while on the other side each woman has an enclosed mini-apartment.

SORONG

Old Oil Town on Irian's Western Tip

The town of Sorong is a fading oil center, with rusting tin roofs that stretch along eight kilometers of seashore at the westernmost tip of the Bird's Head. There is no town center—its one long main street runs past government buildings, shops, banks, oil installations and the harbor. Nearby are transmigration settlements, rice farms run by Javanese.

The oilfields off Sorong, one of the reasons the Dutch hung on to Irian after being forced to grant independence to the rest of Indonesia, were first tapped in 1932. While the relative importance of oil has declined in Sorong (just over 10 million barrels were pumped in 1987), the state oil company, Pertamina, maintains major installations in town: storage tanks, a port with docks for tankers and the town's best private homes, on a hill called Kuda Laut ("seahorse").

The numerous foreign oilies who used to carouse in Sorong have dwindled to a handful. The foreign community today consist only of a few priests and a few expats working for the timber companies. But there are plenty of guest workers, from other parts of Irian and Indonesia. Sorong's prosperity shows in new bank buildings, shops and a modern shopping center. The town's population is evenly divided between Muslims and Christians. There is a Catholic cathedral, mosque and several Protestant churches.

Until 1965, Sorong was located on nearby Doom Island (pronounced "Dom"). When the town grew too large for the island, it shifted to the mainland. Today, some 45,000 people live in the urban area.

Although the relative importance of the oil industry has declined—it used to be the only source of employment—Pertamina still dominates the local economy. But the timber industry is now a close second. The lumber companies used to ship out entire logs (over 3 million cubic meters) to be processed overseas. But new government regulations require that milling and processing take place locally, and a plywood factory is being built in Sorong, promising many new jobs.

The mining industry, which has extracted nickel ore from the nearby Raja Empat Islands, has suffered a number of ups and downs. The mines on Waigeo and Gebe have been shut down but the one on Gag Island remains alive and well.

The seas around Sorong provide lots of fish for local consumption as well as tuna and shrimp for export to the United States and Japan. Frozen shrimp exports run $25 million a year, and tuna accounts for about $2.5 million. The Japanese send home cultured pearls from a farm they manage on Kabra Island. Shark's fins and trepang, shipped chiefly to Hong Kong, are also valuable exports—as are, unfortunately, illegally hunted bird of paradise skins.

Visiting Sorong

Sorong is definitely not a tourist town. While the disco nightlife can be lively, daylight activities are strictly business. Still, the markets are interesting, there are local beaches and reefs, and Sorong is the place from which to visit the Raja Empat Islands, though this is not particularly convenient or cheap.

Mount to the roof balcony of the **Kohoin disco** and sports (weights and squash) complex to get a view of the islands in the sea to the west—Salawati, Batanta and Waigeo shimmer just on the horizon while the closer, Buaya ("crocodile") and Sop Islands are visible in the blue-green seas. Little boats paddle around, far and near. The road around the Pertamina housing complex on **Kuda Laut** will offers a better view of the city itself.

The **Pasar Boswesen** fish market offers a bewildering assortment of local varieties, but you have to get there around 7 o'clock in the morning. Later in the day, have a look in the **Pasar Sentral** at the other end of town. This turns into a typical night market after dark with many *warung*-type food stalls.

The best nearby beach lies about 10 kilometers from Pasar Boswesen, on a decrepit road, at **Tanjung Kasuari**. After a rain, the road is impassable, but it is scheduled for improvements. The large, white-sand beach is favored by locals on weekends and holidays, when food and drinks are sold. Nearby coral reefs offer good snorkeling. On the way to the beach there is a small obelisk erected as a monument to the Japanese who died here in World War II.

A more famous war memorial is in town, on Jalan Arfak, a short ways up the hill near the Cenderawasih Hotel. Most drivers should be able to take you to **"Tugu Arfak."** To reach this monument to the Japanese war dead, you have to cross the backyard of the local police chief. Some drivers are scared of the chief, others are scared of the chief's dog. Both are harmless, but you have to take the initiative. The house is usually open, so just peer in and ask: "Boleh ke tugu?" (Can I go to the monument?). The answer is invariably affirmative. The monument complex includes an obelisk, a bronze Shinto deity and long,

Opposite: *Doom Island. Sorong began on Doom, but oil-stimulated growth in the '60s drove the urban center to the mainland.*

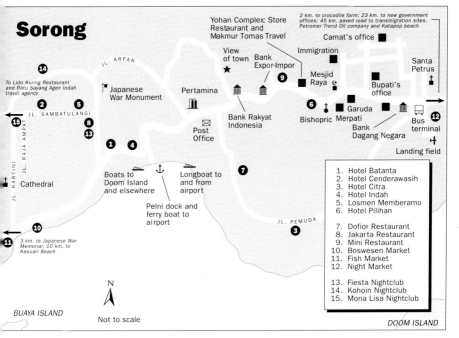

Sorong

Yohan Complex: Store
Restaurant and
Makmur Tomas Travel

2 km. to crocodile farm; 23 km. to new government
offices; 45 km. paved road to transmigration sites,
Petromer Trend Oil company and Katapop beach

Camat's office ■

JL. ARFAK

View of town ★
Bank Expor-Impor

Immigration

Santa Petrus ✝

To Lido Kuring Restaurant
and Ratu Sayang Agen Indah
travel agency

⑭

Japanese
War Monument

Pertamina 🏛

Mesjid
Raya ☪

Bupati's
office ■

⑮ ② ⑤
JL. SAMBATULANGI ⑧
⑬

Bank Rakyat
Indonesia 🏛

⑥ ✝

Garuda ■

Bishopric Merpati

JL. RAJA AMPAT

① ④

Post
Office ✉

Bank
Dagang Negara

Bus ■ ⑫
terminal

Landing field ✈

JL. KARTINI

Cathedral

Boats to
Doom Island
and elsewhere

⚓

Longboat to
and from
airport ⚓

⑦

Pelni dock and
ferry boat to
airport

JL. PEMUDA

③

⑩

⑪ 3 km. to Japanese War
Memorial; 10 km. to
Kasuari Beach

1. Hotel Batanta
2. Hotel Cenderawasih
3. Hotel Citra
4. Hotel Indah
5. Losmen Memberamo
6. Hotel Pilihan

7. Dofior Restaurant
8. Jakarta Restaurant
9. Mini Restaurant
10. Boswesen Market
11. Fish Market
12. Night Market

13. Fiesta Nightclub
14. Kohoin Nightclub
15. Mona Lisa Nightclub

N
Λ

BUAYA ISLAND

Not to scale

DOOM ISLAND

thin memorial plaques.

The World War II relics in the area are concentrated on Jefman Island, the site of the current airfield (originally built by the Japanese). There is said to be a large, intact shore battery, some bombed-out anti-aircraft guns and lots of bunkers. The Allies never invaded here—they just bombed the airfield and sank all the ships, then bypassed Sorong on their way to Morotai.

Doom Island

This is a pleasant little island, close to Sorong, and little outboard-powered boats make the run frequently. Today, the island is one village, with houses hugging the entire shoreline and continuing into the interior wherever the low hills allow them to.

Catch a boat from the beach next to the Pelni dock (20¢ one-way when one of the boats fills, or $1 charter) and in 5–10 minutes you land at a scruffy beach on Doom, next to the big sheet-tin warehouse which functions as a market. The islands' shops are mostly concentrated in this area and a couple of *warung*s serve *nasi campur*—but forget getting a cold beer. Also forget about walking around the beach, which serves as the island's garbage dump. Instead, make a slow loop around the perimeter road, which will take an easy hour. About halfway around the island, there's a large cemetery, with Christians buried on one side and Muslims

on the other. Just behind the graves are some "Japanese" caves, used in the war, which locals say have not been visited for years. If you speak Indonesian, try to find an old man living near the graves. The pleasant old chap remembers World War II like it was yesterday, the nearby seas covered with Japanese ships and the huge bombing raid from Sausapor which sank them all. Bodies floated ashore on Doom for days, he said.

The Sorong region

The nearby islands in the Raja Empat group are hard to reach. There are no convenient regular boats to Batanta, Salawati, Waigeo or any of the further islands.

The only possibility for a quick look around Sorong seems to be a full-day tour arranged by the local Makmur Thomas travel agency. Their jaunt takes you to Doom Island then to Pulau Buaya (Crocodile Island) for swimming off a fine sandy beach. (Don't worry about the crocs. The island takes its name from its general shape, not from an abundance of the critters.) On the way back to Sorong, you can visit other small islands and, if the opportunity presents itself, join some local fishermen.

A more extensive tour takes you to **Kabra Island** to visit a pearl farm under Japanese ownership and supervision. Statistics show that some 20 kilos of pearls are exported from here each year, worth close to half a million dollars. From Kabra you continue to **Maton Island** with its white sand beach, for a swim and lunch. With notice, the organization might be able to find scuba gear for rent.

The same travel agency can set up a trip to see birds of paradise and other birds on **Waigeo Island**. This involves some five to six hours of motoring and about four to five days of scouting for the bird perches on the island. You bring a tent or sleep either in local huts. Somewhat closer and cheaper, **Batanta Island** (three to four hours' motoring) has birds of paradise and other colorful endemics, but they are somewhat more difficult to see here than on Waigeo. The best time to see the birds—as well to travel in a small boat on the open seas—is from August to February. The rainy season here runs from March to July.

Above: *The bronze Shinto diety at Tugu Arfak, a monument to Japanese World War II dead that stands on a hill overlooking Sorong town.*
Opposite: *A limestone rock painting gallery along the coast of Bisyari Bay near Kaimana.*

BOMBERAI

Rock Art and Crystal Clear Bays

The Bomberai Peninsula is one of the most beautiful parts of Irian Jaya, if not all of Indonesia. Cut off from the Bird's Head by Berau Gulf, the MacCluer Gulf of the past, the coastline of the peninsula is dotted with numerous large and small islands, indented by inlets and bays, and walled in by a continuous chain of mountain ranges.

This region is far off the tourist circuit. It is visited by only a few Europeans, chiefly missionaries trying to make inroads into what was for several centuries the domain of the Sultan of Ternate. This is a journey for the adventurous.

It is also a destination for the increasing number of people seeking the enigmatic images of the distant past, the rock paintings of the original inhabitants of this vast island. Although rock art sites are found in a number of scattered localities throughout New Guinea, the two most important and extensive site complexes of rock paintings are found here: on the south coast of Berau Gulf, and along the shores of Bitsyari Bay.

The visitor begins in Fakfak or Kaimana, both attractive little towns that can be reached by air from Manokwari and Sorong, or even Jayapura, via Nabire. The journey to the rock painting sites is by dugout canoe, somewhat precarious-looking vehicles as in this region they do not carry outriggers. The best time for sea travel, and thus for a visit to the region, is September and October.

Beauty and tradition

The scenery is spellbinding. Pristine rainforest descends the mountain chain from cloud-embracing peaks to the jagged coastline. The limestone rock occasionally shows through the dark green veil as white scars caused by landslides. Some mountain spurs jut out far to sea. Over eons the sea has worn passages and wide channels in these promontories, or undermined their cliffs, causing them to collapse into rugged boulders.

This coast has produced hundreds of peaceful coves, some graced with tiny islands surrounded by a crescent of white sand. Inland, the jungle growth is held at bay by tall, slender coconut palms, stretching their crowns over the beach. Villages have grown up in some of the larger coves, with clustered beachfront dwellings on stilts. Dugout canoes

GEORGE CHALOUPKA

of all sizes are moored to the posts. Some of these vessels are 13 meters long.

The local people—members of dozens of language and ethnic groups—often undertake one or two hundred kilometer journeys along the coast or across the open sea. Everything along this coast seems to be done on a grander scale.

The area is also known for a very special bride price. In most parts of Irian Jaya where the bride price is still paid, it now consists of jewelry, money, and perhaps some old porcelain. In the Fakfak area, the most treasured component of the bride price are *lela*, antique bronze cannon, usually of Portuguese origin. These three or four hundred year old pieces remain priceless family possessions.

Fakfak town

Fakfak, nestled against the side of a steep slope on the south coast of the Onin Peninsula, is the administrative center of this region. The airstrip is literally hewn out of the side of a mountain, and only craft with short take off and landing capability (such as the De Havilland Twin Otter) can call here. The town itself extends from the water right up the steep slopes and gullies. It is a maze of winding and narrow roads, and is quite a picturesque place to stay for a day or two.

The main reason for coming here, however, is to hire a boat and travel along the coast north to Berau Gulf to see the rock paintings, or to explore the coastline south to Telul Sebakor. (See map page 105.) Along this coast are numerous villages, secluded beaches, coral reefs and at the bottom of Sebako Bay, an amazing, two-kilometer stretch of massed orchids.

Here too are stunted trees which would appeal to bonsai lovers, and further inland rare butterflies, birds of paradise and ground and tree kangaroos. But the best coral reefs are still further south, along the coast where the Kitikiti waterfall cascades down sheer cliffs of the Kumafa Range into the sea.

On a calm day, the journey by dugout to the first of the rock carving sites takes about five hours, but high waves can increase this to seven hours. At the time of our visit, this was the only way to reach Kokas, although by now the road from Fakfak may be completed.

The rock paintings

The sites are located along the coast and on nearby islands between Kokas and Goras, a distance of about 30 kilometers. The paintings, mostly in shades of red, are found on the back walls of horizontal wave cuttings and water worn caverns in the limestone cliffs lining the south shore of the bay. They stand some 5 meters or more above sea level. Some of the small offshore islands look like giant mushrooms, the relentless action of the waves eroding their base. Older surf galleries higher up are decorated with paintings. (See

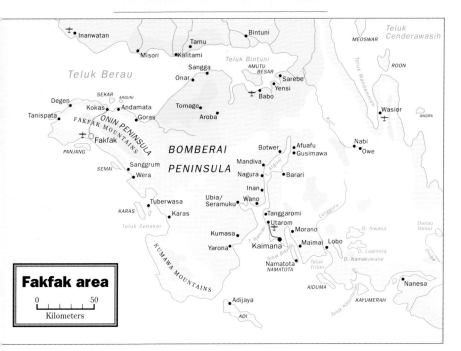

Fakfak area

0 — — — 50
Kilometers

Rock Paintings" page 107.)

In the past, most of the painted galleries served as burial grounds, where wooden coffins were placed and surrounded by gravesite goods such as antique pottery, carvings and beads. Although scattered bones and pieces of timber document this funerary custom, collectors and dealers have long since scavenged these gifts.

Some of the painted galleries are quite extensive; others, on sheer cliffs high above the sea, may have simply a few hands stenciled in red against a white background. Hand stencils are the most common subject, but there are also stencils of human feet, fish, and of angled boomerangs and clubs. Paintings of fish are common, as are *matutus*, part human and part animal figures who are said to be the great ancestors of the current population. There are also abstract designs whose meaning can at this point only be guessed at.

The most mysterious gallery is a large cave located in the mountains, two days walk from Kokas. There are so many designs covering its walls that it is said you can always find your own name among the sprawling and superimposed lines.

Kaimana: paintings and sunsets

Another complex of rock paintings is accessible by boat from Kaimana, a small town 45 minutes by plane from Fakfak. Despite its remote location, and that it sees almost no visitors, Kaimana is well-known in Indonesia. It features in a very popular song, which describes the beauty of the sunsets there. The town and the adjoining villages encircle a bay with a backdrop of dark, forested mountains, cut with deep gorges.

The first rock carving site is on the western shore of Bitsyari Bay, just half an hour from Kaimana by outboard-powered canoe. Here three wide-eyed anthropomorphic figures executed high up on a now inaccessible wall stare across the water to sites on the eastern coast of the bay. Our canoe continued, gently floating past sculpted cliffs, coves and islands, with painted galleries and niches at their surf-worn waists, over a clear sea full of coral and colorful fish.

The largest site, some 4 kilometers long and containing a hundred or more individual paintings, is adjacent to Maimai village. From here, one enters the passage between the mainland and Namatota Island, passes by more rock art sites, and then the waves begin to rise and toss the canoe. If you are brave you should carry on. For once you get through the passage and pass a cape where the sea boils, you enter Triton Bay — and then you are in paradise.

—*George Chaloupka*

Opposite: *Returning in a long outboard-powered dugout from Arguni Island in Berau Gulf.*

ROCK ART

The Painted Sea Cliffs of Bomberai

Throughout the world, early hunter-gatherer societies documented their existence with rock paintings, and Irian Jaya is no exception. Caves and shelters with engraved images, or yellow, white and black paintings can be found on Waigeo Island, crude scratched images can be found in scattered highlands caves, and one can find engraved fish, lizards and turtles on the slopes above Lake Sentani, a few kilometers from the airport.

But the two largest and most interesting complexes of rock art are found on exposed rock sea walls along the southern shores of Teluk Berau, just across the peninsula from Fakfak town, and just south of this area, in the region of Kaimana.

The Berau Gulf paintings

Although the western coast of New Guinea was exceedingly remote, European adventurers first discovered the paintings here in 1678, more than two centuries before Altamira, the first decorated cave discovered on the European continent, was found.

The first rock art site found in New Guinea is just south of the current administrative center of Fakfak. In 1878, a second major complex of sites was discovered along the southern coast of Teluk Berau, formerly the MacCluer Gulf. (See map page 105).

The Teluk Berau sites lie extend some 30 kilometers, between the villages of Kokas and Goras. These paintings were first studied by Josef Röder, a member of a 1937–38 expedition to the Moluccas and Dutch New Guinea sponsored by the Frobenius Institute. Artist J. Hahn recorded the paintings, and his plates and Röder's analysis of 34 sites were later published in *Felsbilder und Vorgeschichte des MacCluer-Golfes West-Neuguinea*.

Röder identified a number of styles which he placed in chronological sequence, noting the order of superimposition. The exact age of the paintings has not yet been determined. The first four art styles in this sequence were executed in red pigment. These were followed by a phase of black paintings. The most recent were figures executed in white pigment. One of the white paintings, a representation of a hornbill, was previously recorded by a 19th century visitor, which suggests that even the white paintings are not new. The rock art styles were named after the localities of their type sites—places where there are large numbers of similar motifs.

Hand stencils

The earliest, Tabulinetin style paintings are from a site on the western side of an island of the same name. It is also represented in numerous works at Cape Abba and at other sites. The style is characterized by a large number of stencils, and paintings of animal motifs depicted as full silhouettes.

The stencils were created by placing an object against the rock surface, and blowing pigment around it. The majority of stencils are of hands, which at both Tabulinetin and the Abba site densely cover the available surface. The sprayed pigment from layers of stenciled hands stained the rock with varying tones of red ocher. Hand stencils are interspersed with those of feet, fish and a range of artifacts. The most interesting of these are stencils of angled boomerang-like objects.

Hand stencils have their origin in a local myth. People here say that long ago their ancestors, a man and two women, came from the direction of the rising sun, or emerged out of the sun itself. They were blind, and as they moved along the rocks feeling their way they left imprints of their hands and feet. The stencils found now in the shelters are said to bear witness to this ancestral journey. Paintings executed in this style are found in superimposition and variably weathered, suggesting that the style was extant for a considerable period of time.

Paintings of fish, humans, and anthropomorphs are also common motifs in this style. The human figures are shown frontally with bent legs and raised arms. Some are lizard-human forms, with pointed heads and a long curved tails. These are said to represent the Matutuo spirits associated with fishing.

The Manga style

The Tabulinetin style was succeeded by the Manga style, typified by elaborate, decorative designs. These were essentially non-figurative, although the ambiguous human-lizard

Opposite: *Rock paintings near Kaimana.*

GEORGE CHALOUPKA

figures and fish continue to appear. The range of symmetrical designs extends from simple concentric circles to mazes of interlocking spirals and scrolls. They are painted in bold, clear outlines in which red pigment may be combined with yellow.

Fish, lizards and anthropomorphs become stylized and are often portrayed with a "lifeline" and interior patterns which may represent x-ray features. In one instance a pair of fish are symbolically represented by abstract skeletons, much like the famous paintings of the aboriginal Australians.

Stencils of objects which may represent Dongson bronze axes are currently placed within this stylistic period. Dongson bronzes were produced in what is now northern Vietnam from 400 B.C. to A.D. 100, and were trade items throughout Indonesia. The bronze axe stencils and the decorative elements—which share an affinity with those on Dongson drums—may give a hint of the period in which the Manga paintings were executed.

Other styles

Chronologically following the Manga style is the Ota I style, in which some subjects are rendered at a considerably larger scale, in stylized and rather crude forms. The first boat motifs occur in this style, and later become characteristic of the Ota II style, which is the black painting phase.

The black figures are less numerous than those encountered in the red periods. The pigment is charcoal, and they remain as thin, sketchy and often fuzzy lines, although some designs have broader strokes. Simple human figures, lizards, fish, boats and non-figurative designs are common.

Some of the images identified as boats consist only of a long curving line rising to a hook at one or both ends, suggesting a decorated stern and prow. This motif, often with a series of lines suggesting passengers, are elements in the "ship of the dead" or "soul boat"

motif that is prevalent in Indonesian art. This also has a Dongson origin.

White figures are restricted in their occurrence, and Röder did not accord them a classification. They are sketches in thick bold lines or silhouettes, and are considered the most recent examples of Berau Gulf art.

Kaimana area styles

The rock art of Kaimana, when fully recorded, will prove to be as extensive as that of MacCluer Gulf. Although there are some

common elements and motifs, expressed in similar techniques, the Kaimana region art is on the whole rather distinct.

The majority of paintings are in red ocher varying from dark brown to orange-red. Yellow pigment is also used, and the most recent designs are in white. There is little evidence of drawings in charcoal. A number of superimpositions are identifiable, but these will not be classified as styles until larger samples of each layer can be analyzed.

Painted images predominate. Stencils of hands, or hands and arms are present, but there are few feet or object stencils. However lines and blown patches of bright yellow and red are common, and are in some instances associated with painted motifs in compositions. The human form is the major motif, followed by lizards and anthropomorphs.

A frequently found motif is that of a male figure in an oval enclosure. Over time the human form has been abstracted into a central column with outwardly curved lines, and finally into a vertical line with two dots representing arms and legs. The task of recording Kaimana's rock art in sufficient detail to allow analysis lies ahead.

—*George Chaloupka*

Above, left: *A rock engraving or scratching at Lake Sentani, near Jayapura.* **Above, right:** *A Tabulinetin style painting at Tabulinetin, a small island between Sekar and the coast.*

Bird's Head Practicalities

Manokwari

Manokwari telephone code: 962

At press time Merpati scheduled flights to Manokwari from Biak on Monday, Tuesday, Wednesday, Thursday and Friday (6:30am, 8:10am; $42), and from Jayapura on Tuesday, Wednesday, Friday and Saturday (7am, $101).

SURAT JALAN

You can easily obtain a travel permit for Manokwari in Jayapura, Sorong or Biak. If you plan to spend the night outside of Manokwari, check with the police to find out if you need an endorsement, then report to the local police on arrival. (For more on the *surat jalan,* see "Travel Advisory," page 188.)

ACCOMMODATIONS

The Mutiara Hotel, owned by Merpati Airlines, and another new hotel (not yet named) are planned to open sometime soon. Neither was operating at presstime. The owners are planning them to be the best in town.

Hotel Arfak. Jl. Brawijaya, © 21293, 21195. 13 rooms. This former Dutch officers' mess rates is a best buy: quiet, inexpensive with a good view over the bay and the Arfak Mountains. AC $18S, $27D; standard (fan and attached bath/toilet) $15S, $24D; economy $12S, $21D. All meals and service charges included.

Hotel Mokwam. Jl. Merdeka. 12 large, clean rooms. An attached restaurant serves Indonesian and Chinese dishes, ($2.50–$4). $30–$36S, $36–$43D.

Losmen/Mess Pelabuhan. Jl. Siliwangi. 3 rooms, $3.50–$6.

Losmen/Mess Fasharkan. Jl. Sudarso. 7 rooms, $10–$15 w/ meals.

Losmen/Mess Binhar. Jl. Sudarso. 7 rooms. The Ekaria Restaurant is attached. $4–$18.

Losmen Apose. Jl. Kotabaru, in front of the Merpati office. 9 rooms. $3.50–$7S, $9–$12D.

Losmen Sederhana. Jl. Bandung. 11 rooms, no attached facilities. Fan-cooled, $4S, $6D.

Losmen Beringin. Jl. Sudirman. 8 rooms and 5 non-attached toilet/baths. Attached restaurant has simple rice-based meals (50¢ to $1.20). AC room, $9; fan-cooled $4.50.

DINING

Ekaria. Jl. Sudarso. New, clean place with a wide variety of Cantonese dishes of frog, crab, squid, pigeon, chicken, pork, beef, rice and noodles, $2–$5.

Hawai. Jl. Sudirman. International and Chinese dishes $1–$3. One dining room is AC and one is fan-cooled.

Evaria. Jl. Merdeka. Across from the Hotel Mokwam, Chinese cooking, $2–$3.50.

Kebun Sirih. Jl. Sudirman. roasted fish of several kinds, $2–$4.50 depending on size and species; also serves squid and shrimp.

Simpang Raya. Jl. Percetakan. Padang style cooking, $1–$2 per plate.

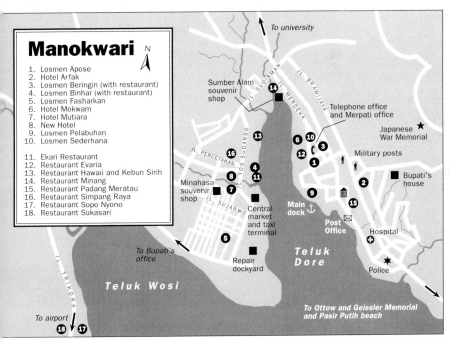

Minang, on Jl. Sudirman, and **Padang Merantau**, on Jl. Merdeka serve Padang food, $1–$2.The **Suponyono** and the **Sukasari** are both on Jl. Trikora, across the road from each other, a couple of kilometers from the airport. Both serve Indonesian meals for 50¢ to $1.25.

Banks and money changing

Bank Expor-Impor. Jl. Jogyakarta 1. Open Mon–Thurs from 8 am to 12:30 pm, on Fridays till 11 am and Saturdays till 10:30 am. US$, A$, Can$, £, ¥, D.M., and French and Swiss Francs. Travelers checks from Visa, Thomas Cook, American Express, Citicorp, and the Commonwealth Bank of Australia are accepted.

Souvenir Shops

Toko Sumber Alam. Jl. Sudirman 47. Has lots of porcelain plates (some quite old), along with beads still used as bride price, some mounted butterflies, awful Asmat carvings and still worse penis gourds.

Toko Souvenir Minahasa. Jl. Pahlawan. Also has a fair selection of porcelain (Chinese, Japanese and Dutch) along with bride price items such as woven *ikat* cloths from Timor and Flores, beads and silver bracelets from Biak. There are also stone axes, bows and arrows.

For **butterflies**, see Mr. Simandjuntak whose office is on Jl. Sudarso 59, ✆ 21677, 21045. (Home: Jl. Kotaraja 14, ✆ 21139.) All butterflies are carefully wrapped for export. He knows his prices on the international market.

EXCURSIONS

Prafi village. Collective minibuses from Manokwari make several round trips each day to Prafi, charging $2.50 per person. Chartering your own minibus for the round trip costs about $45. If you decide to spend the night in this area, you have to report to the police at Warmari with your passport and *surat jalan*. There are no commercial accommodations, so it's either local hospitality or sleeping out.

Mansinam Island. When there are passengers, some craft paddle out to Mansinam Island, but we suggest hiring your own motorized canoe for a two-to-four hour jaunt, allowing plenty of time for swimming and snorkeling. The boats hold 10 to 15 passengers. Charter prices are negotiable, between $18 and $30 for the ride.

Anggi Lakes. Merpati has two scheduled flights each week to Anggi (W,F, $20) on a De Havilland Twin Otter. MAF (Missionary Aviation Fellowship) may also have space available, for about the same price. While there are no accommodations in the district, either the police, the *camat* or a village chief will help you find a place to sleep. Bring a sleeping bag, sweater and jacket as it can get chilly at night up there at elevations over 1,800 meters. Although some food is available locally, bring a few tins for supplement.

A little store in Iray stocks basics, but air-freight makes prices higher than in Manokwar Market days on Iray are Monday and Thursday from 7 am to 8 am. The same hours also for th weekly Friday market at Sureri.

REGIONAL TRANSPORTATION

Merpati. Jalan Kota Baru 39, ✆ 21133, 21153 At the airport, ✆ 21004. Merpati offers a num ber of scheduled flights to the interior of th Bird's Head and elsewhere in Irian:

Anggi	W,F	$20
Babo	W,Sa	$35
Biak	M,W,Th,F,Sa,Su	$42
Bintuni	M,Th	$22
Fakfak	Sa	$40
Jayapura	Tu,Th,F,Su	$101
Kebar	M,Th	$30
Merdey	Tu,F	$30
Numfor	F	$19
Sorong	Tu,W,F,Sa,Su	$66
Timika	W,F (via Biak)	$82
Wasior	W	$42

Also: Nabire ($86)

Some national flights:

Ambon	F (via Biak, Numfor)	$120
Manado	W,Sa	$152
Ujung Pandang	F (3 stops)	$195

MAF. Mission Aviation Fellowship flies a Cessn 185 to many remote strips in the interior. The take passengers on a space available basi$ MAF's hangar and operations are located o the far side of the airport, ✆ 21155.

Sea transportation

Mixed freight/deck passage coastal steamer stop at Manokwari every week or two on the run along Irian's north coast. Pelni Lines' larg passenger boat *Umsini* calls at Manokwa every four weeks on its way from Jakarta t Jayapura. (See "Jayapura Practicalties" pag 88 for more details on Pelni Lines.)

Weather

Unpredictable. Temperatures range from 26° to 32°C, and an average of 2,700 mm of ra falls each year, on 124 days.

Sorong

Sorong city code: 951

Sorong's main airport is on Jefman Island, 2 kilometers east of town. You have no choic from Jefman but to get in a public "longboa for the $3 trip to Sorong, or pay $23 to chart a boat yourself. Taxis at the landing site charg $3 to just about any destination in town, but you are traveling light, a public minibus on th nearby main road is 15¢.

To return to the airport from town, your ta (chartered or public) lets you off at the Pel dock. You need a ticket (6¢) to enter the do area. A ferry usually motors to Jefman Island the early morning and again in the late afte noon. The one-hour ride costs 85¢ and ge ou there in time for your plane. If you miss the erry, you have to charter a boat ($23).

ACCOMMODATION

Hotel Batanta. Jl. Barito, ℂ 21569. 24 rooms. $9–$15 S, $12–$19 D. Better rooms with AC. Small dining room only, billiard hall.

Hotel Cenderawasih. Jl. Sam Ratulangi 54, ℂ 21740, 21966, Fax: 21966, Telex: 77127. With 20 rooms, all AC. Favored by the few expats around. Large dining room, full menu, various dishes from $1.25 to $4. Singing entertainment on Mon., Wed. and Sat. evenings in the dining room and well-stocked bar. Central to the three discos. $21 S, $24 D w/ breakfast.

Hotel Citra. Jl. Pemuda, ℂ 21246. 14 rooms. All with AC, with dining room, full menu, dishes from $1.50 to $3. $12–$25 S, $15–$28 D.

Hotel Indah. Jl. Yos Sudarso, ℂ 21514. With 33 rooms. Morning and afternoon snack included. Restaurant and car rental. This white tiled, 3-story hotel has an enclosed top balcony which offers a good view of the area. Try to get a room on the third floor. $12 (AC and TV) to $4.50 (bare-bones).

Losmen Memberamo. Jl. Sam Ratulangi, ℂ 21564. 10 rooms. All AC. Pleasant dining room with rattan furniture, fair variety of dishes from $1.25 to $3. $17–$20S; $21–$22D.

Hotel Pilihan. Jl. A. Yani, ℂ 21366. 15 rooms. Better rooms with AC, otherwise fan-cooled. Kitsch figures in entrance yard to amuse guests. $10–$11S, $16–$18D.

DINING

Pofior. Jl. Pemuda. Chinese, Indonesian food or $3.50 to $7 per dish. A view of the sea; considered by some to be the best in town.

Lido Kuring. Pertokoan Lido, Jl. Yos Sudarso. Fish and other seafood $2–$4, other dishes similarly priced. The specialty is grilled fish.

Mini. Kompleks Pertokoan Yohan, Jl. A. Yani. Mostly Chinese food and seafood; $1–$7 for the various dishes.

Mona Lisa. (Next to the Mona Lisa disco.) Jl. Sam Ratulangi. Japanese food, $9–$12 per dish; international cuisine, same price.

Money Exchange

Bank Dagang Negara; Bank Expor-Impor.

EXCURSIONS

P.T. Makmur Thomas. Kompleks Pertokoan Yohan A15, Jl. A. Yani, Sorong, IRJA 98414. ℂ 21183, 21953, 21594. Fax: 21897. Telex: 77123 MTSON IA. This agent, linked with Setia Tours, can arrange regional tours, guides and car service. English-speaking guides, $9 a day. Car rental, from $2.50 per hour.

Doom Island, Pulau Buaya. $30 per person, min. 2 people. Doom Island tour, swimming off a fine sandy beach on Buaya, visit to some of the smaller islands.

Jabra Island. $60 per person, min. 4 people. A visit to the Japanese cultured pearl farm.

Waigeo Island. Approx. $500 per person. This is a trip to see birds of paradise on Waigeo Island. It includes almost a full day at sea, and 4–5 days scouting. The price varies widely depending on the number in your group.

Batanta Island, other Raja Empat islands. (Variable.) Easier to get to than Waigeo, but the birds are somewhat more difficult to see here.

REGIONAL TRANSPORTATION

Merpati. Jl. A. Yani HBM No. 81, ℂ 21344. (also: STN Mopah, Jl. PGT, ℂ 21182.) Merpati offers a number of scheduled flights:

Ayawasi	Tu,Th	$22
Biak	M,Tu,Th,Su	$71
Fakfak	M,Tu,W,F,Sa	$46
Inanwatan	Su	$29
Jayapura	M,Tu,Th,F,Su (via Biak)	$127
Kambuaya (Ayamaru)	Th,Su	$28
Manokwari	Tu,Th,F,Su	$66
Teminabuan	Tu,Su	$21

Some national flights:

Ambon	Daily	$56
Denpasar	Daily (via Ambon, U.P.)	$197
Jakarta	Daily (via Ambon, U.P.)	$247
Manado	M,Tu,W,F,Sa,Su	$92
Ternate	M,Tu,W,F,Sa,Su (via Ambon)	$78
Ujung Pandang	Daily (via Ambon)	$147

Fakfak

One can fly to Fakfak on Merpati from Jayapura ($135) or Biak ($82) via Nabire, or from Manokwari ($40) or Sorong ($46) direct. Of Fakfak's three *losmen,* **Losmen Sulinah** is preferred, as its owner can arrange the rental of motorized canoes. It sits on the bay, so the hired boat arrives to pick up its passengers at the doorstep. The front of the building faces one of the main roads, and is conveniently located just opposite the police station, where one obtains the necessary *surat jalan.*

Losmen Sulinah. Jl. Tambaruni 79. Room rate includes three meals and morning and afternoon coffee or tea. $12 S. Dugout canoe rental. $50–$70 a day, with driver and assistant.

Kaimana

One can fly to Kaimana from Biak ($75) or Jayapura ($127) via Nabire, or from Fakfak ($36). The **Losmen Diana** ($12 S) is right on the main street, and the rooms look out over the sea and Kaimana's famous sunsets. All meals are included.

The owner can arrange the rental of an outboard-powered canoe to Bisyari Bay. The biggest and most stable canoe in town is the *Waikiki,* which rents for $63–$86 per day, including driver. Unfortunately, it carries only a 15 HP motor, but the nearby rock paintings can still be easily reached.

PART IV

The Baliem Highlands

The Grand Valley of the Baliem River, green and fertile, nestles incongruously in Irian's cordillera of rocky peaks. Coursing down its center is the silt-rich Baliem River, a branching stripe of cafe au lait against the valley's green floor. The Grand Valley is mild and beautiful: the soil is covered with trees and grass, and everywhere, tidy plots of sweet potatoes. Looming on all sides, shrouded by mist and clouds, is the mountain wall.

Author Robert Mitton called it "the only place in the world where man has improved on nature." Not normally given to such overstatement, he also calls the valley: "as close to Paradise as one can get."

The Grand Valley is home to the Dani, the most populous of Irian's highlanders. Most famous for their ritual warfare and sartorial habits—in particular, the *horim,* or penis gourd—the Dani are also first-rate farmers, the key to the valley's high population.

The Dani's numbers are increasing even today, rising from some 50,000 in the early 1960s to currently more than 100,000 in the valley itself. There are also 129,000 Western Dani or Lani, who speak a slightly different language and live west of the Grand Valley.

The Indonesian government and four decades of Christian missionaries have brought considerable changes to the Dani lifestyle, but many traditions remain. The grunts of the beloved family pigs can be heard around the thatch-covered hut compounds and the valley landscape is cross-hatched with rectangular mounds of purple-green sweet potato vines.

Although shorts and T-shirts are common in Wamena, a town of about 8,000 that is the capital of the Grand Valley, outside of town most men continue to wear penis gourds, and the married women their low-slung fiber skirts. Weddings and other ceremonies mark the changes in Dani life, and continue to be celebrated in much the same way. But the stone axe, 25 years after the first steel axe was seen in the valley, is now a tourist item.

Ritual warfare is not quite forgotten, although it has been 20 years since the last great battles were held. Feuds still develop over land, women and pig stealing, and old rivalries. Such disagreements, now settled on the sly, claim dozens of lives each year..

The traditional Dani bride price has felt the effects of inflation. Today, the bride's family expects the following: 5 fiber skirts, 10–20 strands of shell money, 30 or so net bags and 10 pigs. But not just any pigs. At least two or three have to be big ones, which cost about $300 each. The others, medium-sized critters, can still cost $100 to $200 a head.

The Grand Valley is 1,600 meters high, 60 kilometers long and 15 kilometers wide, and is surrounded on all sides by 2,500–3,000 meter peaks. The Baliem River flows into the valley from the north from two sources: the East Baliem, which begins near Gunung Trikora, and the West Baliem, which begins in the Ilaga-Tiom valley system. These two rivers join, then briefly disappear underground in the Baliem Swallet, just southwest of Tiom. The waters join the North Baliem, and then drop to the floor of the Grand Valley, where they become a slow brown river.

After leaving the valley, the river gains speed and rushes south, pouring through the only break in the mountain chain, the earthquake-prone Baliem Gorge. First dropping 1,500 meters in a series of spectacular cataracts, the Baliem then becomes the Siretsj, a wide, muddy tidal river that slowly empties into the Arafura Sea.

Overleaf: *The Uwe (or Wamena) River at dawn.*
Opposite: *A Dani man decked out in feathers and hat. In the Baliem valley, long thin penis gourds (or* horim*) like this one are preferred, while the Western Dani outside the valley wear much fatter and shorter gourds. But these are just general styles. Men are very particular and individualistic about their gourds.*

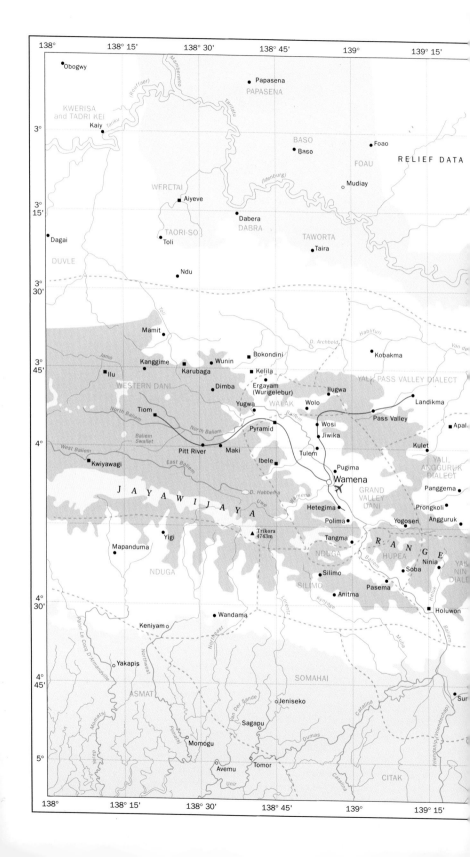

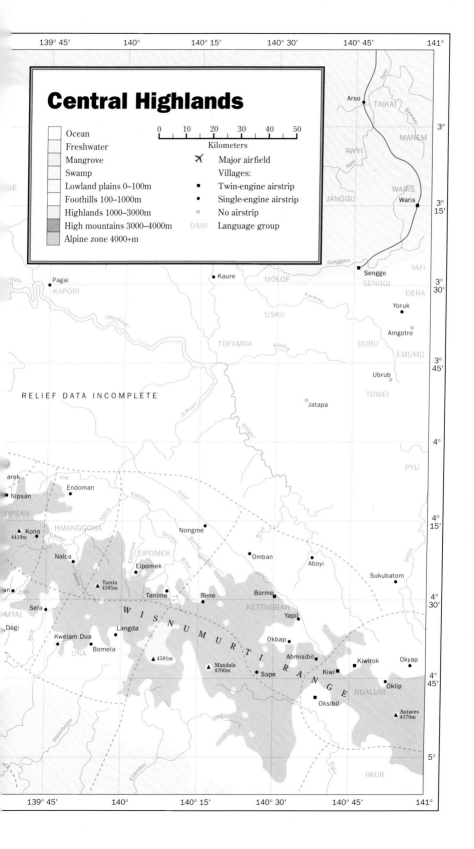

ARCHBOLD EXPEDITION

An American Adventurer in the Highlands

American Richard Archbold, scouting his third expedition to New Guinea, was the first outsider to lay eyes on the magnificent Grand Valley of the Baliem. As he peered out of the window of his seaplane on June 23, 1938, the terraced green fields of the valley appeared from among the rocky peaks like a mirage.

The 14-month highlands expedition was Archbold's third in New Guinea (the other two were in eastern New Guinea), all under the auspices of the American Museum of Natural History. Archbold was a mammalogist and explorer, as well as a millionaire.

At first, the bureaucrats in Batavia (now Jakarta) were reluctant to produce the needed permits, but then the Dutch colonial government decided to co-sponsor the trip. Soon, dozens of men and tons of matériel were heading for Hollandia (now Jayapura), the population of which at the time was barely 200: government personnel, their servants, Indonesian artisans and Chinese traders.

The area chosen for exploration was the northern face of the Snow Mountain Range—the largest remaining blank on the map of New Guinea at the time. Previous expeditions had explored the southern slope of this impressive range, returning with important biological collections. And though the 1921–1922 Kremer expedition had succeeded in reaching the north slope of the Snow Mountains, Kremer had to abandon his precious collections to the jungle on the exhausting trek back to the coast.

The Guba

The key to the Archbold expedition's success was a huge Catalina flying boat called the *Guba*. The craft was a Consolidated PBY 2, the standard U.S. long-range patrol bomber that had been specially modified by Howard Hughes for salmon fishing expeditions to Alaska and then subsequently sold. Experts considered it the most air- and seaworthy aircraft in existence at the time. Lift was provided by a 31.7 meter wing which supported a 20.4 meter fuselage. The plane was powered by two 1,000 HP Pratt and Whitney Twin Wasp engines fed from a 1,750 gallon fuel cell and holding 110 gallons of oil in the crankcases. The Guba could lift three tons at sea level and cruise for a distance of 800 kilometers, but when taking off from 3,225-meter-high

Lake Habbema, the payload had to be restricted to just one ton of cargo and a standard crew of four men.

It was during one of the exploratory flights of the *Guba* that Archbold first sighted the Baliem Valley. Immediately, he realized the importance of his discovery. He was looking at the largest highland valley in New Guinea, as well as the most densely populated. Of course, he did not suspect that the Dani inhabitants were also the highland's most feared warriors. Archbold saw the Dani's watchtowers, but did not guess that their purpose was to keep an eye out for enemy ambush parties.

Getting underway

Archbold and the Dutch military members of the expedition decided to set up two camps in the interior of Irian: a high one on Lake Habbema at 3,225 meters and a low one in the Meervlakte (the "Lakes Plains" region north of the mountains), 50 meters above sea level. The area to be studied was bounded by Mount Wilhelmina (now Gunung Trikora) on the south, and the Idenburg River (now Taritatu) on the north.

The military arm of the expedition, under the command of Captain Teerink and Lieutenant Van Areken, consisted of 56 officers and men. The porters included 73 Dayaks (the mountainous terrain of their homeland, Borneo, equipped them well for Irian's rugged landscape) and 30 convicts.

The Dutch authorities did not want to lose American lives, and the military men ordered that precautions be taken. Foremost in their minds was an emergency retreat route, should the *Guba* for some reason be unable to pick up the party at Lake Habbema. So men, equipment and supplies were flown up to the Idenburg River, which offered relatively easy river access to Irian's north coast.

Aerial reconnaissance was crucial in determining the best route (about 100 kilometers in a straight line) between Lake Habbema and the Idenburg camp. The military patrols were to leave from each of the two staging areas and meet up in the Baliem Valley. Shortly after Lt. Van Areken's patrol cut upwards from the Idenburg River, the group experienced a pleasant surprise: a large, heavily populated valley and, best of all, a lake, immediately dubbed "Lake Archbold." Located about one kilometer from the Habifluri River (which flows into the Van de Wal), Lake Archbold measures 1,000 by 800 meters, at an altitude of 700 meters.

Once the Dayaks chopped down some

Opposite: *A group of Dani men at the Baliem River camp. One man has adopted a waste fruit can lid as an ornament.* **Below:** The Guba *on Lake Archbold. This reliable plane was the key to Archbold's success. Photos courtesy the American Museum of Natural History.*

trees for the approach, the *Guba* could land on the lake to bring in supplies. From Lake Archbold, the going really got tough—steep climbing through forest, and no trails.

Once the party began to approach the Baliem Valley, the local highlanders became numerous and friendly. Too friendly, in fact. In several villages, Lt. Van Areken was welcomed with food, but the tribesmen did not want the party to leave. Only the "utmost determination" kept the group moving, according to the expedition journal. One day, after a friendly reception, the party found their path blocked by a barricade of warriors with spears. The journal laconically states: "Here occurred the one incident where more than a show of force was necessary."

A later missionary account states that two Dani were shot and killed before the party could proceed into the Grand Valley.

The expedition journal says nothing about why the Dani had turned hostile, but it seems that the warriors were trying to block the expedition from moving into enemy territory. Seeing the expedition's resources of valuable cowrie shells (the highland currency), steel axes and knives—all liberally traded for food or offered as gifts—the natives wanted to continue profiting from the strangers' largess, and to keep their enemies from doing so.

Exploring the Lake Habbema area

A total of 105 people had by this time been flown to Lake Habbema in the Guba, along with tons of supplies. The military team under Capt. Teerink trekked down from the lake through the Ibele Valley and on to the Baliem Valley. They experienced very friendly receptions, but there were no more killings. It was time to set up camp in the valley.

After exchanging locations by radio, Lt. Van Areken and Capt. Teerink rendezvoused in the Baliem. They calculated that an emergency retreat from Lake Habbema to the Idenburg camp would take 14 to 16 days, now that paths had been cut. The two parties exchanged a number of Dayaks before returning to their respective points of departure so that some men would be familiar with the entire route between Lake Habbema and the Idenburg River.

The men at the Habbema camp got used to sunburn, freezing cold, cracked lips, altitude sickness and thin air. Lake Habbema is in an area of alpine grassland, consisting mostly of limestone bedrock with some large sandstone outcroppings. The lake lies on a 9 kilometer wide upland shelf. The northern edge of these uplands forms the rim of the Baliem Valley, and from the southern edge rises Gunung Trikora and the Sudirman Mountains.

The scientists noted that the lake was rich in birds, and the locals hunted ducks there with bows and arrows. The 20-centimeter long crayfish discovered in the lake provided a welcome addition to the explorers' tinned diet. The explorers found a path rising to 3,800 meters, in some places worn shoulder deep by local foot traffic. This communications link was used for both trade and social calls between the people of the Baliem Valley and those living in the foothills south of the mountain ranges.

Once the Lake Habbema region had been explored, the upland party shifted to the Baliem Valley. When the expedition set up camp in the lower Baliem, they were given a huge feast by their hosts. Pigs were killed and both the Dani elders and expedition leaders ate the animals' livers in a bonding ritual. Speeches were delivered and the pigs' blood was sprinkled on the foreigners.

New introductions

Agricultural practices in the heavily populated valley were highly-developed: the steep valley walls were terraced using stone and timber retaining walls, and erosion control and crop rotation were extensively employed.

The sweet potato was the staple, but in addition, the expedition journal notes, the Dani grew bananas, tobacco, taro, sugar cane, cucumbers, gourds, spinach and beans. Peanuts, introduced by the Archbold expedition, soon caught on and are today very popular in the valley.

Whenever sweet potatoes, vegetables or pigs were required by the expedition, cowrie shells were used to barter for them. The Dani wanted only the smaller shells, preferably with the back, or convex part removed. Quality—and purchasing power—was determined by the shell's shape, size, ribbing and luster. An average cowrie purchased 10 kilos of sweet potatoes; 6–10 good ones fetched a small pig.

The expedition lasted 14 months, and produced a body of important scientific work as well as a *National Geographic* article that was to pique further scientific and missionary interest in the region.

Opposite: *The Baliem Valley in 1938, as seen from the window of the* Guba. *Photo courtesy the American Museum of Natural History.*

THE DANI

Irian Jaya's Famous Highlanders

The sun had climbed over the valley, and its light flashed on breastplates of white shells, on white headdresses, on ivory boars' tusks inserted through nostrils, on wands of white egret feathers twirled like batons. The alarums and excursions fluttered and died while warriors came in across the fields. The shouted war was increasing in ferocity, and several men from each side would dance out and feign attacks, whirling and prancing to display their splendor. They were jeered and admired by both sides and were not shot at, for display and panoply were part of war, which was less war than ceremonial sport, a wild, fierce, festival.

Peter Matthiessen
Under the Mountain Wall, 1962

Since explorer Richard Archbold's first glimpse of this beautiful oasis of green, dotted with smoking huts and laced with tidy mounds of purple-green sweet potato vines, the Grand Valley Dani have captivated the writers, photographers and anthropologists who have had the good fortune to visit the highlands of Irian Jaya.

The Dani are most famous for their glorious battles, where hundreds of warriors, shining with pig grease and determination, faced off in a very dangerous "sport." But more important than warfare in their success—the Dani and Western Dani taken together are Irian's largest ethnic group by far—are the Dani's skills at farming.

Although large scale warfare has ended, the Dani retain a very strong sense of cultural identity. Despite missionary and government efforts to change the belief structures and lifestyles of the highlands—Christian doctrine instead of traditional beliefs based on ancestors and spirits, pants instead of penis

Right: *Two men at Daelah village, west of the valley on the way to Habbema.* **Opposite:** *The men of Wunin village whoop it up during a pig feast and mock battle organized by the author.*

gourds, concrete block houses instead of straw and wood *honai*—the majority of the Dani, particularly in the Grand Valley, have yet to be convinced that their ways are not those best suited to life in the Baliem Valley.

The first whites arrive

The Grand Valley went unnoticed during the early phases of Irian's explorations, but encounters between Dutch teams and the Dani had occurred six times, beginning with the 1909–1910 Lorentz expedition. J.H.G. Kremer crossed the Baliem River's headwaters in 1921 en route to Mt. Wilhelmina (Gunung Trikora), but missed the valley by several kilometers.

The sight and news of fair-skinned men begot a legend among the Dani people. Whites and Dani used to live together in a cave called Huwainmo. The whites, with clothes and guns, emerged first, but went far away. The Dani left the cave later, wore penis gourds, and settled nearby.

During World War II, Allied planes flew over the Baliem, looking for possible airfield sites. American pilot Major Myron J. Grimes, American pilot first glimpsed the Baliem (he did not know about Archbold), which he called "Hidden Valley." He noted the watch towers and sweet potato mounds, which he later described as "laid out in checkerboard squares as perfectly formed as farmlands of the Snake Valley in Idaho."

As Hollandia grew as a staging area for the Pacific war, pleasure flights over the Baliem Valley became a common activity for pilots and servicemen. Two war correspondents, George Lait and Harry Patterson, dubbed the valley "Shangri-la" after being flown over it in 1944, and the name stuck.

In May 1945, one of these flights, with 24 people aboard, crashed in the valley. Sergeant Kenneth Decker, Lieutenant John McCollom, 20-year-old W.A.C. Corporal Margaret Hastings survived the crash, and an air patrol eventually spotted them near the wreck. Since there was as yet no way to land, a funeral service for the victims was conducted in an aircraft circling overhead, and a Roman Catholic priest, a Rabbi and a Protestant minister read funerary rites over the radio.

Supplies were dropped to the survivors, and paratroopers landed. They built a glider strip and, 47 days after the crash, whisked everybody out in gliders hooked back into the air by a snatch plane.

'Mandate from heaven'

The next white face seen by the Dani belonged to Lloyd Van Stone, a tall young Texan missionary from the U.S.-based Christian and Missionary Alliance, who was dropped off by hydroplane on April 20, 1954. After the war ended, the CMA had begun vigorously pursuing its evangelical work in the highlands, claiming "a mandate from heaven to invade the Baliem."

The first mission station, established at Hetegima, was built to American standards using flown-in materials. In the words of one author, the station was "a transplant of American comfort in Cannibal Valley." It took seven months to build the first airstrip. Later, missionaries discovered an ideal site for a landing field next to what was to become the Dutch government post of Wamena in 1958.

Evangelical work among the Dani proved slow going. One of the missionaries, with experience in other highland tribes, called them the "toughest nuts to crack." Among the many difficulties was the Danis' strong distaste for the whites' body odor. When walking with the Dani, the missionaries were always asked to keep downwind.

The Dani were a proud and confident group, and numerous petty insults by the missionaries, and more serious grievances — such as the two men killed by the Archbold expedition, for which the white "tribe" as a whole was held responsible — made converting them harder still.

Linguist Myron Bromley arrived in the valley shortly after Van Stone. His work advanced slowly, but he eventually determined that the Baliem Dani could be divided into three dialect groups: north, central and south. While the central speakers could understand the two others, the north and south languages were mutually unintelligible.

A high point of early evangelical work was reached on February 14, 1960. Thanks to sermons by "witness men," who were converted Christians from the Ilaga area of the highlands, a huge fetish-burning took place at Pyramid, at the northern end of the valley. A pyre of fetishes over 200 meters long, more than a meter wide and 60 centimeters high went up in a tremendous blaze. According to one missionary account, 5,000 Dani participated in that particular burn-in. (However, the same account states that 25,000 Dani—the total population was then just 75,000—flocked to hear the "witness men.")

Many obstacles to the whole-hearted acceptance of Christianity remained. Some Dani groups saw the missions as a threat to their political power, Sunday services occasionally faced attacks. And another challenge to the American Protestants was the arrival in the valley in 1958 of Catholic missionaries of the Franciscan order.

Ancestral beliefs remain strong among the Grand Valley Dani. Conversion to a poorly understood Christianity when it did take place was largely pro forma. The missions as well as the government schools and economic projects continue to be much more successful among the Western Dani.

The Dani practice of polygamy, which is still widespread, illustrates the quandary religious leaders find themselves in. One Catholic missionary had no objection to this practice, saying that this way every woman no matter how old or crippled, is part of household. Dynamic, hard-working men, wh can raise the $500 bride price, take extr brides. The priest also says that, according t Catholic hospital birth records, girls outnum ber boys three to two.

Arguments against the practice state th many young men can't find spouses becaus the girls are "bought" by older men with ple ty of pigs available for the bride price. Sinc the men cannot always sexually satisfy a their wives, this leads to extramarital rel tions. A man caught in an illicit affair, he ha to pay a pig-fine to the woman's husband– who uses the animals to buy still more wives

Harvard-Peabody Expedition

Modern anthropological work in the valle began only in 1961, with the arrival of th Harvard-Peabody Expedition, including a fil crew led by Robert Gardner, still photogr phers (among whom was Michael Clar Rockefeller), anthropologist Carl G. Heide and novelist-explorer Peter Matthiessen.

The expedition spent half a year amon the Kurelu Dani, named for the war chief c *kain* Kurelu, who lived on the easternmos part of the valley, near Wuperainma an Dukum. (Thanks to the expedition, Kurelu who died a few years ago, became quite celebrity, and was regularly visited by trave ers and journalists.) The crew shot a beautifu

ocumentary film of the Dani entitled *Dead irds,* and produced a superb book of photographs, *Gardens of War.* Matthiessen's ccount, *Under the Mountain Wall,* is a oignant and informative blend of novel and hnography.

Anthropologist Carl Heider stayed on after e rest of the expedition left, spending a total f 21 months completing research for what ould become *The Dugum Dani,* his careful nd well-written description of the Grand alley Dani. It was a culture "trembling on e edge of change," he writes.

At the time the Harvard-Peabody expedion arrived, the only signs of outside influnce among the Kurelu Dani were a few steel xes. Just two weeks after the expedition left, August of 1961, the Dutch colonial governent "pacified" the southern Kurelu.

[The expedition faced considerable conoversy, particularly after Michael Rockeller disappeared in the Asmat region in ovember 1961, triggering a highly publized search and bringing considerable interational embarrassment to the Dutch governent of western New Guinea. Some unscruplous journalists accused the expedition of citing the warfare they filmed and recordd, which seems patently absurd. Although t mentioned by Gardner or Heider, at least e source has said that the expedition paid ompensation to the families of those killed.]

Ritual warfare

he Dani of the valley are divided into some) clans (or sibs) organized into political its that Heider terms "confederations." The ani believe that men and birds once lived gether in harmony, not realizing they were fferent. As a result of this former relationip, each clan has developed an affinity with particular species of birds, which are themlves considered clan members.

Leadership, of a highly informal variety, as traditionally provided by so-called "Big

Men" or *kain*s—charismatic individuals who rose to a position of power through strength and success in war, the pigs and shells they gave away, and the number of wives they could afford. *Kain*s acquired their positions through their skill in manipulating the economic system, but emerged and faded with changing circumstances.

The Danis' ritual warfare, well depicted in the film *Dead Birds,* was a far cry from our usual definition of war. Conflicts, according to Heider, were mostly over pigs and women, with land rights coming in a distant third. On a metaphysical level, warfare was waged to placate ghosts who lived nearby and who controlled death, human illness and pig diseases.

Some ghosts were associated with geographical features, others were ancestors or tribesmen recently fallen in battle. These latter in particular had to be quickly avenged or they would create great mischief. Thus an individual's woman or pig problem—usually theft—was reinforced by the need to stay on the good side of the local spirits. To win back their favor, kills had to be made in battle.

Once a confederation decided to wage war, it would seek support from its allies. These confederation-based alliances (of which there were six in the Baliem in 1961) were unstable and subject to kaleidoscopic shifts in composition. Hostilities usually persisted for long periods, but were characterized by very sporadic fighting. A major battle every 10 to 20 years usually led to new alliances being formed, with warfare continuing along new frontiers.

Warfare consisted of formal battles in designated areas as well as surprise raids. Tall watchtowers, constructed of strong poles lashed together with vines, dotted the valley to guard against sneak attacks. Most encounters were bloody, but fatalities were rare. The sense of victor and vanquished was at best ambiguous. A handful of wounded warriors was the typical result of a day's fighting.

To the Dani, "a day of war is dangerous and splendid" writes Peter Matthiessen. Formal battles had many of the elements of a pleasure outing. The men rubbed their hair and bodies with pig grease and wore fancy headdresses of cuscus or tree kangaroo fur and feathers of all kinds, necklaces and bibs of cowrie shells or large, spoon-shaped

Opposite: *A Dani compound near Kurima, with sweet potato gardens and the mountain wall behind.* **Above:** *The women of Wunin prepare sweet potatoes and greens for steam baking.*

mikak, pieces from baler shells. The weapons employed were long spears, measuring up to 4.5 meters, and bows and arrows. Women watched from a safe distance, bringing food whenever the men wanted to take a break from the fighting.

Before the action started, insults were traded. These were often humorous, highlighting the opponents' sexual or other inadequacy. Clashes brought the enemy within arrow range, sometimes spear range. Actual fighting seldom lasted more than 10 or 15 minutes and the battle usually involved fewer than 200 men on each side, though many spectators were always present.

Retreating groups were pursued only a short distance, as reinforcements would be standing by. Some 10 to 20 of these clashes made up a full day's battle—which could always be postponed when it rained. (The warriors were very loath to spoil their fine feathers and furs.)

Dani warfare emphasized competence and what Heider calls "exuberant exhibitionism." There was always the possibility of being killed or wounded, but an alert warrior dodged incoming spears and arrows. Maximum arrow range was 90 meters, but to reach further that 10 or 20 meters the arrows had to be lobbed in a high arc. Except when launched from very short distances, the arrows wobbled and were easy to see. There was no firing of coordinated volleys.

Heider characterizes Dani battle as aggressive behavior without aggressive emotions. Antagonists were seldom mad at each other. They just wanted to show off. The wounded who could not walk were carried behind the line of battle by friends, there to have the arrows painfully dug out of their flesh. The shaft of the arrows was weakened bout 10 centimeters back from the tip to insure the tip would break off in the victim.

Deaths usually came later from infection. When a battlefield death did occur, the body was carried back to the warrior's home compound amid much wailing. A kill touched off two days of dancing, not so much to celebrate the victory but to call forth the spirits.

A kill also triggered a cycle of revenge. The enemy now plotted to even the score. If deaths could not be avenged in formal battle, sneak raids would be conducted, without the fun and glory. Children and women were fair game on these raids, and women's digging sticks carried both a blunt point for weeding and a sharp one for defense. Even after ritual warfare ceased under government pressure,

these secret raids continue to be used to eve scores between feuding communities.

Spirits and death rites

Dani religion, like warfare, is based on spir placation. These spirits are either associate with particular features of the landscape c ancestors. Staying on the good side of th spirits was crucial for survival and prosperit All ceremonies and pig killings were directe at winning their favor. Sacred objects, calle *ganekhe,* which included stones, can b manipulated to prevent the approach of spi its. Enclosures for ghosts, with bundles c grass representing the deceased, are locate far from the villages.

Funerals once were the most importa Dani rite. They lasted several years, startin with a cremation to drive the ghost from th living area. Elaborate rituals were held fc important men and those killed by the enem The ghosts of these men were especially po erful and dangerous. They could be induce to "pre-kill" an enemy, after which his actu death was then sure to occur in battle.

Sometimes the desiccated corpses c important Big Men were not cremated bu kept for supernatural reasons. These ar today's "mummies," which tourists can se and photograph (for a small fee). Apart fro the mummies, the Dani show little interest genealogy. Descent is patrilinial and includ no territorial rights. Nuclear family ties a generally unimportant when compared wider kinship relations.

One of the adjuncts to the cremation cer mony was the cutting off of a girls' finger Anesthetic was crude at best. The finge (usually the outer two of the left hand) we tied off with string a half-hour before the ce emony, and just before the ax fell, the gir were slapped hard in the upper arm to kill th sensation. The wound was staunched wit leaves. The fingers were left to dry, burne and the ashes were buried in a special place.

In Heider's time, every female older tha 10 had lost four to six fingers to impress th spirits. Although this is no longer practice one can still see many middle-aged or olde women with missing fingers. During funeral Big Men distributed pigs and shell ban among their relatives, reinforcing ties.

Occasionally—every four or five years— the most important man of an alliance wou

Opposite: *This women has smeared her face and body with yellow clay in mourning for a los relative. Jiwika, in the eastern Baliem Valley.*

initiate the Ebe Akho. This alliance-wide bash was principally directed at the spirits of the deceased. Formal mass marriages, sometimes more than 200 at once, also took place at this time. The main event was a huge pig killing and feast. The more pigs, the more prestige for the Big Men.

The sweet potato

Roasted or steamed, the sweet potato, here called *hepere,* constitutes 90 percent of the Dani diet. More than 70 varieties are cultivated, but four or five are commonly identified. The most common variety has light yellow, almost white flesh, and tastes like a cross between the orange sweet potato common in the west and an Irish potato. Taro and yams, as well as bananas, various greens, ginger, tobacco and cucumbers are also grown.

The high-yield gardens are sustained by sophisticated irrigation works that cover 20 percent of the area. Rich mud from the ditch bottoms is periodically scooped out to fertilize the soil of the raised rectangular mounds where the sweet potato vines grow.

The Dani never form large villages, but prefer to live in scattered compounds near their gardens. Clusters of compounds, each holding two to five families, form settlements bound by clan ties. Each roughly rectangular compound is surrounded by a fence and at one end stands a domed men's hut, which serves as the focus of much clan-based ceremonial activity. Several round women's huts, each a scaled-down version of the men's hut, line another side of the compound. On yet another side stands a long, rectangular cooking shed and covered pig stalls.

Men and women sleep separately. Sexual intercourse is considered dangerous and weakening. Taboos prohibit sexual relations after about the fourth month of pregnancy and can last three to four years after birth. Only after a child can walk well and take care of itself do the parents resume relations. This keeps the mother from being burdened with several young children at the same time.

Daily life

The men's work consists of cooperative digging and maintenance of the irrigation network and fences, and occasional hut construction and repair. They have plenty of leisure time, spent chatting with their fellows. The men also tend the gourds which they "train" to grow according to the shape of the penis sheaths they wish to wear. They also weave armbands and braid brides' skirts.

Though unimportant today, in the past one of the chief duties of the men was to stand watch and protect women working the fields from marauding war parties. Women's work is long, tedious and can often be lonely: planting, weeding, cooking, and tending the pigs and children.

Domestic animals include dogs and pigs,

crucial to all rituals. These have the run of the land, crashing into any garden unprotected by a stout fence. A large, locally common spider, which is encouraged to weave on prepared frames, almost qualifies as a third domestic animal. The matted webbing spun by this creature is worked into fabric used for men's caps and magical strips suspended from the neck. The latter protect against spirits, which usually attack at the throat.

The chief item of men's clothing is the penis sheath, called *horim,* and men keep gourds of various shapes and sizes. Married women wear skirts of strong plant fibers. These subtly colored skirts, called *youngal,* are short and slung so low on the hips that they look certain to fall off at any minute.

String bags, called *noken,* are an ever-present part of the women's apparel. The bags are loosely knit, like nets, and are filled with sweet potatoes, wood, a child, a piglet—anything that needs carrying. The bags are supported by the forehead like a tumpline and when empty, help keep the early morning chill off the women's backs. The bags are knit from bark fibers that are rolled on the thigh into string. The coloring comes from clay, orchid tubers and small ferns.

Stone tools

Some 30 years ago the only tools used were stone axes and adzes, stone and boars' tusk scrapers, knives made from sharpened bamboo, and wooden spears and digging sticks. The wooden implements were readily available, but the stones had to be brought from the bed of the Yalime River, about 150 kilometers northwest of the Baliem in the Nogolo Basin. In 1962, the Austrian explorer Heinrich Harer was the first white man to visit this site. The stone was "quarried" on the river bank, he writes, by building fires on the large outcroppings. The heat would then split small chunks off the larger mass.

Three types of stone were taken from the Yalime, of which the greenish *andiba* was most prized. It has a hardness of 6–7 on Moh's scale. A bluish stone, called *wang-kot me* was used for small chisels and adzes. Also used was a black flint called *ka-lu,* although this was not of a high quality. All of these stones formed part of the bride price.

Trade and economics

The current system of weekly markets around the valley, as well as the permanent one in Wamena, has eased the Dani into

monetary economy, providing steel axes and luxuries like candles, matches, cigarettes and clothing. The traditional long-range trade networks died out a generation ago.

The traditional medium of exchange was seashells (though the Dani possessed no notion of the sea), with the cowrie as the basic unit. Imported items included stone for axe heads, furs, feathers, fibers and decorative shells. Traders left the valley with salt from brine springs, pigs and cowries.

Status-seeking leaders conspicuously gave pigs and cowries to their followers on ritual occasions. Women were (and still are) paid for with pigs, cowries and other traditional items. But the shells, sewn on fiber strips of varying lengths for display, are now more often sold to tourists. Pigs, however, remain a valued medium of exchange.

In 1938, the Archbold expedition purchased 10 kilos of sweet potatoes for one cowrie shell. Six to ten good ones would buy a pig. When the Harvard-Peabody team arrived, 24 years later, a shell was worth a potato or two, and no number of cowries could convince an owner to part with a pig.

Above, left: *This man, preparing to participate in a mock battle, has shined his face, hair and chest with a mixture of pig grease and soot.*
Above, right: *The staged battle begins.*
Opposite: *A "wounded" warrior is hustled off the battlefield by his amused comrades. Wunin*

The Dani today

The Indonesian government has come under considerable (and justified) criticism for its treatment of the Irianese, today the government shows a great deal of tolerance. Initiatives like "Operasi Koteka" (*koteka* is an Ekari-derived word for penis gourd) in the 1970s, which was run like a military campaign and failed miserably in its goal of getting the Dani to dress like Javanese, have been abandoned.

The government has also tried to get the Dani to move from their huts (the thick smoke inside is considered a health risk) into concrete block houses. The houses, it turned out, were too hot during the day and too cold at night. The Dani's thatched roofs and double outer walls keep out the heat during the day, and keep it in at night. The smoke keeps insects away. (Some Dani have used the new government houses for their pigs, building Dani-style huts nearby for themselves.)

The government has successfully poured money and effort into the Baliem Valley. There are schools everywhere, and roads to several population centers and hospitals. Goats, sheep, and fish have been introduced, as well as new crops. Cargo flights are subsidized so most items cost about the same as they do elsewhere in Indonesia. The subsidized items include gasoline, cloth, cooking oil, salt, sugar and other foodstuffs, as well as tinned food and biscuits.

The vast majority of the Dani, however, are still subsistence farmers, growing the staple sweet potato for local consumption. Introduced vegetables—carrots, cucumbers, cabbage, onions and tomatoes—all grow well in the rich highlands soil, and the Dani willingly bring them to market. The Baliem is one of the few places in outer Indonesia where vegetables are plentiful and inexpensive.

The problem is that Wamena and the villages of the valley can absorb only so much produce. The natural market for the surplus would be Jayapura, but the capital receives its vegetables from Javanese transmigrant settlements nearby. A partial solution has been found in subsidized flights shipping vegetables to the mine at Tembagapura.

The government is also making an effort to introduce rice cultivation as a cash crop to supply local needs, thus eliminating rice imports to Wamena. Dani farmers have created some 80 hectares of rice paddies, with a government goal of 150 hectares. A variety of rice from the highlands of Sulawesi seems best suited to the soils and Torajan school teachers, stationed in the valley, impart their technical skill in cultivating the grain. The rice is inter-cropped with soy beans to replenish soil nutrients. Dani farmers can also raise cash by growing high value coffee beans and collecting the highlands' excellent honey, already selling for $6 a bottle in Jayapura.

GROWING UP MONI

A Childhood in the Highlands

The 25,000 Moni live in the highlands east of the Paniai Lakes and Enarotali, which was the first Dutch post in the central highlands. Despite this proximity and that the Moni are one of the highlands' largest groups, little has been written about them.

Unlike the Ekari around the Paniai Lakes, the Moni have proudly resisted assimilation. Western encounters with the group seem always to produce strong reactions: "sarcastic," "a tribe of all chiefs and no Indians," and even "treacherous," are often heard. Other observers find much to admire: "they have such gentle features," and "they have inherited all the good points of the tribes around them and blended them into one."

Having grown up with the Moni, I can only say that none of these is accurate. Or perhaps, they all are.

First contacts

The first documented meeting between a European and the Moni took place in 1937, when Dr. J.W. Cator, the Assistant Resident at Fakfak, flew from the coast to Lake Paniai and trekked to the village of Kugapa. In 1939, Controleur Dr. Jean Victor de Bruijn mounted an expedition to Kugapa and continued on into the heart of Moni country to the village of Sanepa in the Kemandoga Valley. His first impressions were condescending (in the habit of the time), but positive:

"The Miganis [Monis] are a superior race and are very conscious of being so. Not only are they superior in warfare, but ordinarily conduct themselves with better manners and greater dignity. They are a proud people, more reserved, and unlike the Ekaris, will never ask or beg."

De Bruijn spent the better part of five years learning about the Moni and living in their villages while supplying information to the Netherlands Forces Intelligence Service on Japanese troop movements in west New Guinea. To this day legends abound among the Moni about "Kontolull" (Controleur) whose men floated to the ground on "clouds and shot their enemies with "rain fire arrows. (Presumably tracer bullets.)

After the war ended, several missionary families landed on Lake Paniai in amphibiou aircraft and began the treacherous walk into the highlands east of Enarotali.

One of these pioneer couples was Bil Cutts and his wife Grace. They had heard o the Moni tribe and were prepared to face bone-wearying elements and unpredictable encounters in order to win a place in the hearts of the Moni. Days blurred into weeks and weeks into months as they grappled with Moni idiom and syntax, the Moni's fear and suspicion of the "bleached white spirits," and the logistical nightmare of establishing a bas a day's walk from the end of the earth.

The little white spirit

Into this already complicated situation cam the "little white spirit," later to be named Zar Mala by the Moni. This was their best effor at saying "Johnny," which is difficult whe your language has no "J" sound. The nam has stuck to this day.

While the missionary couple struggle eight hours a day trying to comprehend thi unwritten language, Zani Mala was bein tutored by villagers, who were themselve quite curious about the strange people wh blew their noses into a piece of cloth an saved it, and performed many other abnorma rituals. The elder Cuttses began to find ou that the shifting and decentralized Mor social structure made their work of prosely tizing more difficult.

The younger Cutts, however, was found t be very impressionable and overly talkative thus challenging these Moni to expose Zar Mala to their customs and traditions. It migh even be possible to transform this outside into a no-nonsense Moni chief.

The scene was set for major conflic between the elder Cuttses, who felt it wa their duty to "civilize" Johnny during the fe remaining hours left after a grueling day con jugating Moni verbs, and the Moni, wh monopolized Zani Mala from dawn till dusk.

No easy task

I found out that being a Moni son was no eas task. The "how to make" category was en

Opposite: *John Cutts as a child in the highlands, with his friends Alice and Abe, two orphans adopted by Bill and Gracie Cutts.*

ess, and included bows, arrows, various raps, bird blinds, huts, fences, bark string, ets, woven bracelets, and fire starting sticks. Bows could only be made from four types of rees, which I had to learn to identify. Mineral prings attracted birds, and I had to learn to ind these. I had to learn to see the evidence f faint animal trails, so I would know where o set traps.

There is also no place for a Moni with a weak stomach. The Moni's "what you can at" list would make the average person reak into a cold sweat: certain species of spiers, several types of beetles, a type of wild ockroach, praying mantis egg cases, and nany types of worms and grubs.

A special treat were colonies of *zigi* orms, an indigenous species of silk worm. Certain trees would become infested with the aterpillars, which would strip off all the eaves and spin a large silk nest. Discovering ne of these moving, pulsating colonies in a are tree not only assured us of a feast for all, ut the silk shroud made a fine head ornanent. Stacking branches at the base of the ilk tree was the Moni way of saying "Mbai Maia" (No Trespassing). Thus the worms ould be allowed to mature, and still be harested by the one who first discovered them.

The horrified looks on the faces of Mom nd Dad when witnessing a worm feast rought squeals of delight from the Moni, ho loved shocking these finicky eaters.

Not wanting to be outdone by my mentors, I too introduced a new type of shock treatment. An electric fence had been installed to keep pigs off the grass runway. I would hold onto the fence (wearing rubber boots) and beckon some poor, unsuspecting man just back from the forest to come greet me. Imagine his total bewilderment when his body began to tingle unexplainably from top to toenail. To add insult to injury, the whole village was spread out on the grass in fits of uncontrollable laughter.

Natural resources

We youngsters were also kept busy learning the identifying features and uses of various plants and other natural products. The leaves of the *zumba* tree produced suds when pounded with water, and served as a kind of soap, even removing grease. The bark from the *domo* and *migi* trees made the best roofs for huts, while that of the *zembelo* and *butala* were more suited to making carrying nets, skirts and string. The fibrous core of the *dago togo* tree was perfect for soaking up the brine in the famous Moni salt wells. *Mese,* a plant with an abrasive leaf, is the medicine of choice for aches, pains, and general external discomfort. The leaf is rubbed on the aching spot and welts appear immediately.

The Moni are well tuned to the resources of their land, and the list of useful plants is endless. I found this information fascinating.

BILL CUTS

After daily classes and field trips of this kind, it is no wonder that boarding school at age six seemed like prison camp.

Leadership and cowrie shells

The term *sonowi* in Moni means chief, and growing up among these people meant daily reinforcement of the absolute necessity of becoming a chief, and outlining of the steps that could bring about this coveted status.

Chief Isasabo, in particular, went out of his way to include me in his *muna dia* sessions (a kind of negotiation that precedes a business deal) so I could learn about money, which among the Moni was based on pigs and cowrie shells. One cannot barter or trade successfully without understanding the six grades of cowrie shells and their worth.

Cowrie shells take years to travel from the coastal areas where they are collected to the highlands, passing through many hands en route. The Moni are well-known for their skill with cowrie shells.

According to the Moni legend, they and their neighbors all came out of an area near the Wose caves called Mbubumbaba. The Moni were given the job of naming all the shells and setting up a monetary system. The Dani were given special skills in breeding pigs and were given the ability to work tirelessly, but no talent in dealing cowrie shells.

The value of the shells varies widely: *sae,* about 50¢; *munga,* from $10 to $20; *kubawi,* from $40 to $75; *indo lagupa,* from $50 to $100; *hondo,* from $200 to $1,500; and *indo,* from $250 to $2,500. Within each grade, value is determined by color, the number of bumps, and the style in which the back was cut off. Shells of the top three grades are all given names, and accompanied by a detailed history of every transaction in which they were involved. Over time, this history also adds value to the shell.

Sitting around the fire of a men's hut, I was offered a key strategy to becoming a successful chief: "A real chief will build his hut on a major crossroads. He will thus have many visitors, who will be indebted to him for his hospitality. Weary travelers will spread his fame by word of mouth."

A boy wanting to become a chief could begin with clearing a patch of jungle and planting sweet potatoes. The sale of this crop, together with the sale of bows and arrows he made or salt he collected, could yield enough shells to buy a baby female pig. Fattening the pig will result in more pigs to be raised and sold. Eventually, with the help of family mem-

bers, he may accumulate enough pigs an[d] shells to buy a wife. A wife doubles his capa[-] bilities, and a second or third wife boosts hi[s] potential further.

Of course, like anywhere else, there ar[e] sometimes confidence artists. Chiefs serve a[s] the "banks" in Moni culture, so individual[s] with shells or pigs that they don't have a[n] immediate use for will "invest" them with [a] chief they trust. Because of his position, h[e] will have many more opportunities to trade and will be able to do so more successfull[y.] The end result should benefit both him an[d] his "investors."

Wealth and politics

However, a fast-talking con artist can hood[-] wink investors into believing he has enoug[h] personal wealth to repay their investmen[ts] when in reality he has borrowed from hu[n-] dreds of people and only shuffled their pig[s] and shells around (much like a U.S. bank, i[n] fact). If too many debts come due at the sam[e] time, the whole pyramid collapses.

A famous chief, Wanda Wome, died wit[h] thirty borrowed high-grade *indo* shells le[nt] out to clans scattered around his village. [A] war nearly broke out when it was discovere[d] he had no wealth of his own to cover thes[e] debts. A genuine chief with real assets i[s] called a *mbusu-maga nanga-baga;* a ligh[t] weight chief is said to be a *mbogo.*

Hoarding is not the answer, however. [A] fine line needs to be walked. The more gene[r-] ous a chief is with lending, the larger th[e] group of loyal followers he has, and thus th[e] more political clout he can wield. This ver[y] importance form of social cohesion has bee[n] threatened with the arrival of outside source[s] of money.

The importance of lending and not hoar[d-] ing money was brought home to me recentl[y.] A group of prominent Moni leaders gathere[d] in the yard, and spoke to me.

"You're a chief today because we raise[d] you with Moni insight and wisdom. You ar[e] young, and still learning how to tell goo[d] shells from bad, evaluate people as honest [or] not, and talk chief's talk and ideas convincin[g-] ly. You're a chief, but you don't divide yo[ur] wealth properly. You have much to learn stil[l."]

My attempts at community developme[nt] by advancing their cause by helping the[m] help themselves was only seen by these vi[l-] lagers as selfishness and a desire to hoar[d] wealth I obviously had.

The industrial capabilities of the Mo[ni] have never been developed. Always durin[g]

ny time with them they wanted explanations: How do planes fly? Where do steel axes come from? How are clothes found? Never having een these items made, of course, they are ery susceptible to a kind of cargo cult thinking.

Development and discontent

Jnus, a close friend for 15 years, turned to ne one day and asked: "Where did you find hat shirt?" I replied that I bought it in a store. t this point he lowered his voice. "Listen. lave we not been friends for years? Please ell me where is the hole in the ground that ields all these treasures. I promise I won't ell another soul."

Recently, a group of Moni men pproached me and said they believed I eturned to the Monis and the place of my hildhood because I knew there was a mounain of hidden treasure here. A breathless eam of men had arrived to report that 50 eople had died in the past several months in n area just a day's walk away. They had also ound a rusty machete along a river bank. 'ould it be that the fumes from an underround factory, pushing to the surface, had illed these people?

The real question coming from the Moni s: How can we improve the condition we are ? Which leads to: Why do you have all you eed and we don't? And finally, the question at hurts the most: Are you somehow keep-

ing this cargo from us, its rightful owners?

These questions are difficult and persistent, and I struggle with them to this day. My involvement in a full-scale community development project with P.T. Freeport which is addressing their basic needs encourages me to believe they will find answers to these questions. Helping them discover their capabilities and then providing avenues through which they can express these skills in a changing world can replace vain hopes with tangible results that can be understood.

Recently, on the way to a "killing of a white pig" ceremony I asked my Moni companions: "Do you feel the coming of the missionaries and other outside influences have hurt you as a tribe?" The question was answered very explicitly.

"If the missionaries had not come, today we would be killing one of our own warriors to even the score of battle and bring peace. Instead, we will give 63 pigs in exchange for his life. We are glad your parents came and taught us about God and loving others. It is good not to live in constant fear."

I must add that I too am glad. It was a privilege to be raised in the midst of such beautiful people. And with that privilege comes an awesome responsibility.

—*John Cutts*

Above: *John Cutts today, chatting with some of his friends in the Moni lands east of Enarotali.*

AROUND WAMENA

Exploring the Grand Valley of the Baliem

Wamena, the administrative and communications hub of the Baliem Valley, boasts decent accommodations, the lively Pasar Nayak market, a variety of souvenir shops and good restaurants. But to really get the experience of the Grand Valley and Dani life, you must leave Wamena.

Roads lead across the river and north, all the way to Pass Valley, northwest to Pyramid and beyond, and south to Sugokmo. Minibuses can take you to see Dani villages, the mummies at Akima and Jiwika, brine ponds, or to the jumping off points for more ambitious hikes—west to Lake Habbema, south to the spectacular Baliem Gorge, or east, over the mountain wall to Yali lands.

Wamena town

The town of Wamena is growing dramatically. More than 1,000 tourists a month are now arriving in the valley, and several flights a day from Jayapura bring in tons of subsidized merchandise and gasoline. The Air Force's Hercules cargo planes bring up Japanese minibuses for just $300 each. From a few thousand people in the early 1980s, estimates of Wamena's population now top 8,000 people.

Much of this increase is due to Indonesians arriving from elsewhere in the archipelago (mainly from East and Central Java, Manado, Ambon and South Sulawesi) to take advantage of job and business opportunities. The district's only high school and a number of specialized colleges—for example, for teacher training—have added hundreds of students to Wamena's population.

There's a post office, a bank to change travelers' checks and cash (at a slightly lower rate than in Jayapura), a movie house, and a sprawling covered market. Recently a satellite telecommunications office was built, and one can now make calls to anywhere in the world.

The daily Merpati flight arrives early in Wamena and there's plenty of time to settle into one of the small hotels and still take advantage of most of the day. The market, a short walk from the airstrip (everything in Wamena is a short walk from the airstrip) should be your first stop.

The **Pasar Nayak** market is crowded with the colorful produce of Dani gardens and equally colorful crowds. Souvenirs include bows with a bunch of multipurpose arrow

hunting, killing humans), stone axes, penis ourds and belts of cowrie shell money. You an buy color print film here (no slides) and ottled water, as well as rice, sardines and ther rations for a trekking expedition.

Pugima Village

Perhaps the first thing to do upon arriving in Wamena, after finding a hotel and a guide, nd having lunch—is to make the two hour ound-trip to the nearby village of Pugima for taste of traditional Dani life. (See map page 38–139.) Like all Dani "villages," Pugima is ctually a loose grouping of house com- ounds, each of which is home to from two to ix related families. A strong wooden fence ncircles several thatch-covered huts: the ound men's house, the similarly shaped omen's houses and a long, rectangular itchen adjoining the covered pig sty.

The walk itself travels along level ground well, there's a tiny hill). A taxi can even drop ou off on the far side of the airfield, cutting a alf-hour off the walking time. At Wesaput, on he way, an Ambonese couple who work in he local department of culture manages a mall museum of Dani artifacts. The sign by he road reads "**Pusat Alat Seni**" (Art Center). Vith a day's notice, this couple can arrange o have schoolchildren perform a traditional ance. Wesaput was the site of the first Dutch overnment post in the valley.

From Wesaput, you cross the Baliem

River on a steady suspension bridge, hike over a small hill and you're in Pugima. There are several traditional hut compounds as well as a few "modern" houses scattered around the valley. Have your guide show you around a compound. Some local men have started irrigated rice cultivation here and a market has been built in preparation for the harvest. There's plenty of time to return to Wamena before dark for dinner (try the crayfish) and sleep before the next day's explorations.

To Jiwika: mummies and brine pools

The most popular and easy jaunt from Wamena is to Jiwika (pronounced either Djiwika or Yiwika), some 20 kilometers to the northwest along one of the few roads in the Baliem. A crowded public minibus will take you there for about 75¢, or you can charter one for $5.50 an hour. It's about an hour each way, and there is a comfortable *losmen* in Jiwika for overnight stays.

Shortly after crossing the bridge, a short side road leads to **Akima Village** and its famous mummy. Men of importance—war *kains*—were not given the usual cremation after death. Their bodies were desiccated and

Overleaf: *Dani men at Wunin, ready for mock battle.* **Opposite:** *The Pasar Nayak market at Wamena attracts men and women from all over the valley.* **Below:** *Soaking banana stems in the brine pool above Jiwika to extract salt.*

kept in the men's house as a conduit to the supernatural to obtain good health, abundant harvests, wives, pigs and victory in war. No one knows the age of the Akima mummy. (Most Dani don't know their own ages, and consider this unimportant.)

The Akima mummy is the earthly remains of Werapak Elosarek, a powerful warrior and "Big Man." The people of Akima are a good-humored bunch, and are really the highlight of the visit. The keeper, Akima Ulolik, is current chief of the Akima area. After a bit of bargaining, the usual price is $3 per person to have the mummy brought out. The body, blackened by the smoke, sits in a compact, knees-to-chin pose and is set out on a chair.

Approaching Jiwika, modern rectangular houses replace the native compounds. These were built by the government in an attempt to give the Dani healthier living quarters, apart from their beloved pigs. Some Dani obligingly moved in while building traditional huts in the back. Eventually they moved into the huts and the "modern" houses were only used for storage and as pig sties.

Jiwika, a *kecamatan* or administrative center, lies a couple of hundred meters off the main road. The market (Sundays only) is a quiet, if crowded affair. Early arrivals grab the shaded spots on long tables inside two open-sided, tin-roofed sheds. Others set their produce on the ground in an open area next to the sheds and gossip with friends. Sweet potatoes, bananas, red chillies, cucumbers, peanuts, cabbage, fried bananas and an occasional chicken are offered for sale.

The **La-uk losmen** (meaning hello/welcome in Dani women's speech) in Jiwika, run by a long-term resident Christian Javanese couple, with its thatched roof and dirt floors, has been a hiker's haven for years. The guestbook is full of recent hiking info, and stories and humor from past travelers.

About a hundred yards past the losmen in Jiwika on the main road is a footpath that leads to a **Kampung Sampaima**, with another mummy. This is the earthly remains of the war *kain* Mabel Mimintok, who is said to be 360 years old. The price here is about $2 per person for viewing and photography.

The mummy is a major tourist stop now, and on your approach you will be swarmed by bare-chested women in grass skirts, soliciting you to take their picture. For this, they will ask for Rp100 and probably some cigarettes. It's all rather stagey and aggressive, so be prepared to feel a bit uncomfortable.

Another path starts out from the back of

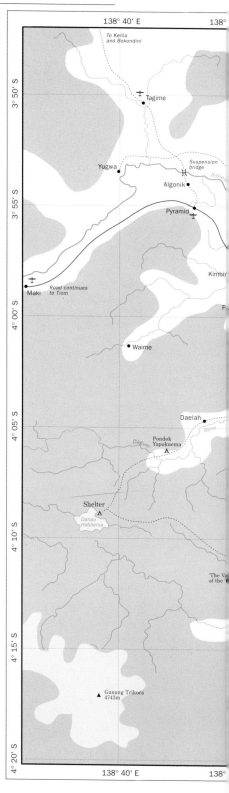

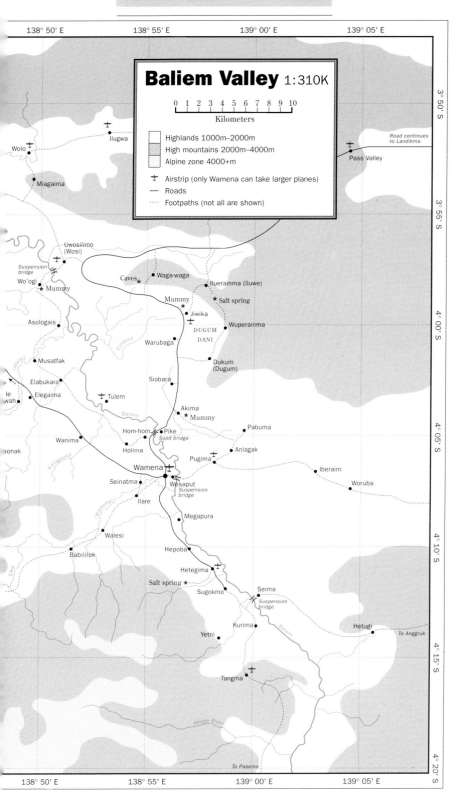

Baliem Valley 1:310K

0 1 2 3 4 5 6 7 8 9 10
Kilometers

Highlands 1000m–2000m
High mountains 2000m–4000m
Alpine zone 4000+m

✦ Airstrip (only Wamena can take larger planes)
— Roads
···· Footpaths (not all are shown)

138° 50' E   138° 55' E   139° 00' E   139° 05' E

3° 50' S
3° 55' S
4° 00' S
4° 05' S
4° 10' S
4° 15' S
4° 20' S

Ilugwa
Wolo
Miagaima
Road continues
to Landikma
Pass Valley

Uwosilimo
(Wosi)
Suspension
bridge
Wo'ogi
★ Mummy
Caves ★
Waga-waga
Iluerainma (Iluwe)
Mummy ★
Jiwika
✦
DUGUM
DANI
Salt spring ★
Wuperainma
Asologais
Eilokera
Warubaga
Musatfak
Elabukara
Elegaima
✦ Tulem
Siobara
Dukum
(Dugum)
le
wah
sonak
Wanima
Holima
Hom-hom ● Pike
Solid bridge
Akima
★ Mummy
Pabuma
Baliem
Pugima ✦
Anlagak
Iberaim
Wamena ✦
Seinatma
Wesaput
Suspension
bridge
Ilare
Woruba
Megapura
Walesi
Babililok
Hepoba
Hetegima ✦
Salt spring ★
Sugokmo
Seima
Suspension
bridge
Yetni
Kurima
Hetugi
To Anggruk
Baliem
Tangma ✦
Hedge River
To Pasema
Kulagaima
Uwe
(Wamena)

the Jiwika market, up a steep mountain side to a saltwater spring called **Iluerainma** (or just Iluwe). The salt pool is about 300 meters above the valley and the steep climb takes about an hour. Beware of the slippery footing.

The brine pool is frequented by Dani from the valley as well as Yali living to the east—for whom the trip is a two to three day walk. The same procedure is used by everyone to gather the salt. Banana trunks, peeled and cut into segments, are soaked in the brine for about half an hour, then carried home. The saltwater permeates the fibrous trunks which are dried and then burned, yielding salty ash. The ash, wrapped in blocks, was formerly an essential trade item, and is still preferred for its taste.

At **Waga-Waga**, further north from Jiwika, is a limestone cave called Kontilola. Minibuses let you out within a hundred meters of the cave entrance. A dark passageway (bring a flashlight) leads from a large chamber to a pool of water and a section of the cave filled with bats. The cave-keeper will charge 75¢ to $1.

South to Kurima: the Baliem Gorge

Some of the Grand Valley's most spectacular scenery lies southeast of Wamena, where the mountain wall parts in the Baliem Gorge. Public transportation (about $1.10) leads as far as Sugokmo village, 20 kilometers from Wamena, where the road peters out. From here, it's an hour's walk to Kurima at the head of the gorge, and the scenery all along the way is well worth the effort.

The easy, level walk from **Sugokmo** takes you across a long and narrow (but solid) steel suspension bridge over a steep-sided gorge. A bit further ahead, you will have to ford a stream, the Yetni, which is easy when the water level is low, but tough when the river is high. Willing porters will carry you across piggy back. A porter weighing 60 kilos can carry a bulky 85-kilo westerner. It may look and feel a bit ridiculous, but it's a lot better than slipping into the rushing current.

Kurima is a tiny, spread-out town with schools, military and police posts and the administrative center of the *kecamatan*. An airstrip and a mission perch on a flat ledge above town. Tuesday is the weekly market day here. If you stay overnight, report on arrival to the police, where your *surat jalan* will be checked and the information laboriously copied down. Possible places to sleep in Kurima include the military post, the police station, or one of the schoolteachers' homes.

Hikes out of Kurima lead to incredible mountain scenery. Good boots, drinking water, and a porter/guide with knowledge of the local trails are all absolutely essential. The hike described below can be covered in eight hours by experienced mountain hikers, but to photograph and enjoy the scenery you should plan on two or three days.

From Kurima, the trail leads straight up a short but steep mountainside on the western bank of the Baliem River. The trail then levels off, following stone fences and leading past traditional compounds for some two or three hours. Most of the way, the sheer mountain wall on the other side of the gorge looms in the near distance. The steep slopes are blanketed by neat gardens, some on an unbelievable 60 degree slope. The terraces are supported by stone retaining walls or stout Y-shaped branches (sometimes both) to keep the fertile soil from eroding.

About one and a half hours out of Kurima, you can clamber down to **Wamarek Village** where a suspension bridge spans the river. Continuing along the Kurima mountainside, a wide panorama opens where the Moki River tumbles down a steep valley to join the Baliem. You feel like you are on top of the world. Then comes the tough part—the path down to the village of Tangma must have been laid out by mountain goats. In about 40 minutes, you drop an almost vertical 250 meters to the airstrip at **Tangma** (market day here is Wednesday), an evangelical center with irregular weekly flights.

From Tangma, it's about one and a half hours to the highlight of this walk, the Wet–Pasema suspension bridge. Here the Baliem River twists and turns through frightening rapids. During the rainy season, the tumbling waters lick the bridge with an occasional wave, giving those brave enough to cross a soaking.

You might be lucky enough to catch a flight out of Tangma, but don't count on it. It's also possible to spend the night here (bring a sleeping bag) with a schoolteacher. Otherwise, it's a tough three hour walk back to Kurima.

If you walked from Kurima on the west bank of the Baliem River, switch to the east bank for your return. At Kurima, a suspension bridge crosses the river, then it's an easy two hours' walk upstream to the next bridge, near Sugokmo, where you can catch public transportation back to Wamena. About one and a half hours' walk up into the hills to the west of Hetegima, there are salt springs similar to those above Jiwika.

North to Pyramid

A mostly paved road now runs the entire way from Wamena to Pyramid (and beyond, to Tiom) in the northwest corner of the Baliem Valley. You can also find public transportation leading there.

On the way to Pyramid, a side-trip leads to **Lake Habbema** (where Archbold landed in 1938) and Mt. Trikora, which, at 4,743 meters, is one of Irian's highest peaks. This excursion requires organization: tents, a warm sleeping bag, food, and porters. (See "Lake Habbema," page 142.)

One can stay on the road all the way to **Pyramid**, the site of the main highland base and conference center of the fundamentalist Protestant Christian and Missionary Alliance (CAMA). Here there are clapboard houses, lawns and American creature comforts.

If you decide to stay overnight here, ask a schoolteacher and don't pester the missionaries. A better idea would be to spend the night at **Kimbim**, the district center, just 5 kilometers south of Pyramid. You have to report to the police there anyway. The *camat* has spare beds and so does the school. Figure on $5 for accommodations and meals.

From Kimbim, there is a good trail—about one and a half hours—to the village of Wo'ogi, where your hosts will show you the village and its mummy. Very few tourists ever stop here.

Opposite: *Flimsy suspension bridges like this one near Karubaga span the many rivers and gorges in the highlands.* **Above, left:** *The mummified remains of Werapak Elosarek at Akima.* **Above, right:** *Pulling a truck back onto the main road, just past Elegaima.*

LAKE HABBEMA

Trekking to the Shadow of Trikora

Bare, spectacular mountains stretch across the horizon, a long rocky backdrop culminating in Gunung Trikora, at 4,743 meters, Irian's second-highest mountain. In the foreground is Lake Habbema, wide and cold, reflecting the mountains and sky. Habbema sits in a broad alpine marsh, a sponge of mosses, tea-brown streams and strange vegetation. The air is thin and cold, and at night every star is visible. The nearest village is a hard day's hike below.

The trek to Lake Habbema requires no mountaineering skills, but it helps to be in good physical condition. At a good pace, from Wamena to the lake and back takes five days, but we suggest planning on 7 or 8 days to enjoy the scenery and keep the trip from degenerating into a test of endurance.

You will need a guide and several porters to lug your gear. The guide ($14 a day) and porters ($3 a day) will make life as easy as possible for you, cooking hot meals two or three times a day, making fires, arranging your bedding and lending a helping hand over tricky spots–such as the long, slippery logs which constitute the path through sections of the thick upland rainforest. For two people, we suggest four to six porters. June, July and August, the driest months, are best for this journey.

Boots with good grip are essential. You will also need a tent (there are no permanent settlements in the area of the lake, and the shelters are sometimes in very bad shape), sleeping bag, food and cooking utensils. You should also bring a rain-proof jacket, and some plastic to waterproof your gear, and a sweater and even long underwear will not go unused at night.

Daelah Village

To save time (2–4 hours), start your trip by chartered minibus for you and your team, $18 and 13 kilometers to the end of the bridge just past the village of Elegaima, near the eastern edge of the Baliem Valley.

From here, it's an easy two hours along the Bene River, to the village of Ibele Atas where you could overnight with the school teachers if you started your hike at Wamena. But we suggest pushing on to spend the night at Daelah village, the last one before the long hike to Lake Habbema. It's 3–4 hours from Ibele Atas to Daelah, following ridge and hillside contours above the Bene River. Lots of little creeks cross the path, offering pure drinking water.

The views improve considerably as the gorge narrows. A short, but steep uphill stretch opens into the valley, with Daelah's compound scattered at the bottom. You can overnight at any of several compounds on your side of the river or cross it on a suspension bridge of rattan and planks to pick an inviting place on the far side of the Bene.

Our second day started with a steep half hour through yam gardens to the uppermost compounds of Daelah, which offered a great panorama of steep forested slopes and gardens. Then an unpleasant hour of mud brought us to the Dagum River, one of two joining to form the Bene. On the far side of the Dagum, the path became much drier as we entered the dense forest which reached up to the high swampy plateau on which Lake Habbema sits.

Pandanus madness

No one lives permanently in this forest, as the altitude and thick vegetation preclude sweet potato cultivation. But the men of Daelah who own most of this forest, know it well, for it provides them with cuscus for meat and decorative fur, birds for flesh and feathers and timber for their houses and to sell in Wamena. And, most of all, here grows the highland pandanus.

The fruit of these distinctive trees (*Pandanus juilianetti* and *P. brosimos*) produces great quantities of tasty, oily nuts. The trees are immediately identifiable by their thin trunks, crowns of strap-like leaves, and downward-pointing prop roots.

As grown men elsewhere go crazy over the durian, so do the Dani over the pandanus. When the fruit ripens, between March and August, men are known to neglect their potato fields and families to gorge themselves on pandanus. Our porters were not in the least immune to pandanus-mania.

Shortly after we entered the forest, our lead porter stopped dead in his tracks: he had spotted a couple of men from Daelah, cutting

o a pandanus fruit trailside. The spiky, oval-shaped fruit, 40 centimeters long and 25 centimeters across, is made up of hundreds of tapered nuts. These taste something like Brazil nuts when eaten raw, and more like almonds when roasted. Our porters got busy chatting up the owners, who were chopping away the outer husk.

After their bargaining had bottomed out (1/3 the price it would have cost at the market in Wamena, I was informed) I was asked for some money to buy several already roasted chunks and a whole fruit, the latter weighing 12 kilos. The fruits were split into halves for ease of portage. The curved shape balanced perfectly on a man's head, and this was how they were always carried by our men.

This scene repeated itself several times on the way to Lake Habbema, and from this point on our expedition had a soundtrack: the constant cracking of nuts.

After only about three hours out of Daelah, it started drizzling and our guide suggested spending the night in a *pondok* we had come across. These shelters, used by hunters and pandanus gatherers, vary from quite comfortable huts to mere lean-tos of bark and wood. Pondok Yapokuema, a couple of hundred meters off the path, was of excellent quality, with a tight, overlapping bark roof and well joined sides. There was another *pondok* some 2–3 hours further and we were not tired yet. But we gave in and decided to

spend the night there. (This proved wise: when we passed the pondok the next day, we noticed it was a very skimpy affair, and the higher altitude here and last night's rain would have made us most uncomfortable.)

But to reach the first *pondok,* we had to climb up a huge, long trunk, with only slight notches for footholds. Our porters walked up as if it were a flight of stairs, but we inched up the slippery wood, grateful for constant stabilizing hands.

Our team

As we relaxed that afternoon, we got to know the men on our team. Markus was our cook and my partner's personal porter. He was always solicitous for our comfort on the trail and in camp, laughing and hugging us at the slightest pretext. Markus was tireless and always high-spirited, and his command of Lani (he is from a village west of the valley) often came in handy.

Jery was my personal porter, and even though he was stuck with a heavy camera bag which had to be always within my reach, was the liveliest of the bunch, constantly cracking jokes in Dani and Indonesian. He is also more than a little vain, decorating his hair, armbands and beard with flowers, bits of moss, leaves and whatever catches his fancy. When

Above: *Just past dawn, wood smoke filters through the thatched roofs of Daelah.*

he spotted an attractive tuft on top of a tall pandanus tree, he bound his ankles with a hoop of rope, and scampered up in record time to bring down the coveted ornament. Needless to say, he loved to pose for photos.

Izack was the most reserved and intellectual of the group. As a former school teacher, he was always called "Pak Guru" (Father Teacher) in spite of his youth—24 years. He always thought things through before speaking, and expressed himself articulately in either Indonesian or English. Isack was born near the coast, in the Yapen–Waropen district. He put himself through school in Jayapura, then taught in the Baliem Valley, learning Dani and taking great pride in his students' academic success. He has adopted the Grand Valley as his home (although his coastal blood shows: he packed on as much clothing as we did against the highland chill.)

And there was Beni, my old friend and guide of many a trek. Although never overbearing, it was always obvious that he was in charge. I was his first client years ago, and we have been friends since. At the time he spoke only Dani and Indonesian, but he now has a good working knowledge of English. He knows the trails, the weather, the plant and animal life, how to build a *pondok,* how to fry up rice, noodles, salt-fish and vegetables into a crowd-pleasing dinner, and just about any other skill one might need on such a trip.

That night, as we all huddled around the fire in the *pondok,* our normally talkative cre' was silent. They had roasted the pandanu fruit and settled to one of the great pleasure of life. We drifted off to steady tapping sound of nut-shells being hammered between tw smooth stones and cracked by strong teeth.

Up to the swampland

The next morning we hit the trail early und clear skies. The forest was unusual her made up of huge trees, their trunks draped i moss of several colors. As always in rai forests, the undergrowth was sparse, as littl sunlight reaches the jungle floor.

The track was fairly level for the first hou then began a steep climb. We followed as w followed the course of a creek, crossing an recrossing it many times. A couple of hou of this, including one brutal, near vertic climb, and the trail crested. Here the veget tion thinned, and we entered a field of mos and lichen, with only a few tree ferns an scraggy conifers. Lake Habbema gleamed the distance.

The trail quickly deteriorated, however, a we discovered this strange field was a swam Eyes glued downward, we sought to place ou feet so as to keep our boots from sinking ov of sight in the muck. It was all very frustrat ing. A bit of moss (green, silvery, copper even red) might yield solid ground, or might be floating on a foot of water. It wa almost impossible to tell. Bits of fine whit sand usually offered surprisingly firm footin, but occasionally would part like quicksan Since visual cues were unreliable, so w stabbed the ground with our walking stick like blind men.

The landscape here is truly eerie, lik something out of a dinosaur movie. Most the vegetation hugged the ground, includir strange mosses and tiny ground orchid Clumps of tree ferns, stout trunks supportir a crown of fringed leaves, sprang up here ar there. Weathered conifers sprouted tumo like growths: anthouse plants (*Myrmecod* sp.). These epiphytes have a swollen base th size of a watermelon, honeycombed with pa sageways which serve as home to a colony ants. A rosette of stiff green leaves pokes o from one side, and the whole swollen base covered with spines.

But we had little time to concentrate

Above: Beni Wenda, the best guide in the Baliem Valley. *Opposite:* Jerry, mistaking himself for a movie star, adjusts his decorations in his ever present pocket mirror.

e swamp's fascinating ecology—our bodies ad to move to campsite. This took a couple f hours which we finished with boots thoroughly soaked. To cross some sections, near r to the lake, we had to wade through knee-eep water. It was of little consolation to us to e told that during the rainiest months—ctober through December—this entire wampy meadow is knee-deep in water.

Camp Habbema

he *pondok* at Lake Habbema sits atop a nall hill on the north side of the lake, over-oking it and the mountain backdrop. It was most welcome sight. We got there exhaust-d, and in strangely bad humor.

Only after a bit of rest did we determine hy we were angry with the world. It was the titude (3,300 meters). Once we realized hat was affecting our mood, we cheered up.

Our crew was busy preparing for the cold ight: patching the the low shelter and xtending the roof with plastic tarps and ranches, gathering firewood and setting up ur tent. We took a barefoot stroll down to e lake which, we were told, is locally called gu. (We were also told that it used to harbor ocodiles, but decided to take this informa-n with a grain of salt.)

The shore is partially fringed with reeds. he water, stained brown with tannins, was o cold for extensive wading or swimming. ucks swam in the lake, diving periodically for what we assumed were juicy tidbits, but they kept a respectful distance. We had read in Archbold's journal that the lake was full of large crayfish and had looked forward to a tasty meal of the crustaceans. But our crew was evasive when we tried to encourage them to catch a batch of crayfish for supper, saying that they had never seen any in the lake.

In the late afternoon, a chilling rain began and we took refuge in the *pondok,* where two fires were keeping the cold at bay. But we were soon driven outside by the thick smoke from the wet wood, coughing and eyes running. When we recovered and got cold again we ducked back in for a dose of warmth—and more smoke.

The Dani are oblivious to a level of smoke that would suffocate a western mortal. In most *honai,* it isn't a problem as the design pulls the smoke upward, and guests usually sleep on the straw floor. But the low roof of the *pondok* greatly compounded the ventilation problem, and we sucked at the walls for air, eyes tearing profusely.

Matters cleared up for supper, but it was still too smoky for comfort so we exiled ourselves to the tent. We could barely sleep for the brutal cold, despite several layers of clothing and a sleeping bag for one and a heavy blanket for the other.

But the awful night was followed by a warm, sunny morning, revealing Trikora and the rest of the mountains in back of the lake.

While Trikora forms a distinctive anchor to the mountains at the far eastern end, it does not really stand apart from the rest in size. The mountain, formerly Mt. Wilhelmina (after the Dutch Queen), takes its current name from an acronym for the three-branched Indonesian military: Tri Komando Rakyat.

We took advantage of the photo op offered by nature. And then our porters put on their penis gourds, decorated themselves with materials at hand and insisted on group photos with Habbema and the chain of mountains in the background.

By noon we broke camp and started back, deciding to take a different, slightly longer route back to Wamena. According to Beni, this way offered more spectacular scenery. As usual, he was right, although it did not seem so at first as we sloshed our way across the swamp for a couple of hours.

Getting up from a quick rest stop, we spotted a group of men armed with bows and arrows heading toward us. A magnificent set of lean bodies, carrying nothing but their weapons. A quick chat with our porters and they were on their way, heading for some distant village, keeping an eye out for cuscus along the way. They were the only people we saw during three days in the high plateau around Habbema.

The Valley of the Tree Ferns

Coming up on a ridge, we looked down on a green valley, far below, which sloped upward to low hills and the base of Trikora. Most of our porters scrambled ahead, and we carefully picked our way down a narrow, steep walled canyon that opened into the valley we saw from above. The men were already setting up camp, just across a small river winding its way along the near side of the valley. These were the headwaters of the Uwe River which, swollen by many tributaries, reached the Baliem River at Wamena. (It is sometimes called the Wamena river).

Here it was little more than a wide creek flowing through a bed of smooth stones. As we relaxed on a bit of dry ground we took in the sight of the valley, covered with extensive stands of fern trees. From our position below, Trikora barely peeked above the hills on the far side of our depression. We dubbed the site the Valley of the Tree Ferns. As the sun lowered itself, it crossed clouds of dark shade interspersed with tufts of white. It was a magical moment.

The moment was not so magical for our men. We had our tent, but there was no *pondok* here, and they had to build a shelter for the night. While a two stayed behind to fix supper, the others disappeared up a steep forested hill. Soon we heard trees toppling over. Logs were hurled down the almost vertical face of the hill, picked up and hauled across the river.

Sharpened at one end these became post

which were stuck into the spongy soil to form he *pondok*'s frame, with thick branches ashed to them to support roof and sides. 'wo men came back from the forest under arge, rectangular strips of bark—these became the roof. The sides were created rom tree fern fronds, loosely woven and tied 1 place. Presto, a *pondok*.

Gathering the materials took almost three hours; the *pondok* went up in about 15 mintes. Profiting from out previous night's experience, we placed our tent in front of the open *pondok*, close to the fire. That night, the clear sky was filled with stars as bright as we had ever seen, so much that it seemed we were within touching distance of the Milky Way.

Next morning, everyone was up bright and early, but we insisted on staying around until the sun filled the valley for a series of photos. This mistake we were to pay for later in the day. Most of the porters took off before us to set things up at Babililok village, the first one on the way to Wamena. We took off after them, slogging through some four hours of swamp before entering the forest again. On the way, we crossed the path to Trikora, whose base-camp was about a half day away.

Our joy at leaving the swamp was fleeting, as the dry path soon became a series of large, slippery logs joined end to end. Steadying hands were always ready, but that did not prevent a well-bruised coccyx, not to mention ego. Even the porters fell several times.

Darkness dropped and still no village in sight. Now we realized the importance of an earlier start. As the darkness grew, the forest, which had been quiet all day, came alive with the sounds of insects. The porter carrying our flashlights was one of those who had gone on ahead, but fortunately we had a small penlight with us. Not much for four people, but better than nothing. Our already slow progress became a snail's pace, and it took another hour to reach Babililok.

Having learned our lesson, we got a very early start the next day, content to breakfast on a cup of coffee and a handful of pandanus nuts. We crossed the Uwe River on a shaky rattan suspension bridge to face a path of more slippery logs—infinitely easier to negotiate in daylight. A couple of hours of relatively level trekking brought us out high on a ridge top with the Uwe, now a considerable river, rushing through rapids far below. About three hours of steep downhill followed, hard on aging, operated-on knees.

Great expanses of yam gardens and small

Dani compounds marked our downwards progress. Shortly after we reached the Uwe River, we crossed a big government school. A bit further, a hanging bridge over the Uwe—stopping at an island in the middle—provided the perfect place for lunch. We washed our clothes and lounged around, watching the butterflies.

Downhill to Wamena

From here on, the path is in good shape, mostly downhill. Even so, we were quite happy to get our first glimpse of Wamena. We crossed Walesi village, where there are clusters of "modern" houses put up by the government. These were to replace those burned during a conflict with a Dani group from Wamena. The houses were almost all unused however, and new traditional huts had been built behind them.

We were nearing the end of our second 10-hour day, and growing anxious for the comforts of civilization. Within an hour we were rewarded at our hotel with a delicious hot bath. No cold beer or Glenfiddich to celebrate, however. Wamena is "dry" for Dani, tourist and trekker alike.

Opposite: *Lake Habbema, with the rocky peaks around Trikora (at far left) in the background.* **Above, left:** *A tannin stained stream in the alpine marsh near Habbema.* **Above, right:** *Gunung Trikora, Irian's second-tallest peak.*

TREK FROM KARUBAGA

North to Western Dani Country

One of the best ways to see the highlands north of the Grand Valley is to fly to Karubaga, in the home of the Western Dani, and trek back to Wamena along relatively easy trails, staying along the way at friendly villages. The trip takes several days, and the scenery is magnificent.

Weather permitting, Merpati offers a weekly flight from Wamena to Karubaga on Saturdays, for $14 one-way. The window of the De Havilland Twin Otter displays the highlands in all their panoramic splendor.

Tin-roofed Wamena quickly gives way to the valley's neatly arranged sweet potato gardens, here and there dotted by the thatched roofs of Dani compounds. The creamy brown Baliem River snakes its way along the valley floor. Flying north, the valley floor rises and becomes covered in forest, yielding only occasionally to painstakingly cut agricultural fields. The small plane barely clears the 2,000 meter peaks, and the land below opens again into a huge valley with long missionary airstrips.

Twenty minutes out of Wamena, the plane makes a short, bumpy landing on Karubaga's grass-and-dirt airstrip, steeply inclined and a an elevation of 1,400 meters. An expectant crowd rushes forward to unload the plane embrace relatives or stare at the white strangers with their strange gear and heavy hiking boots.

Karubaga Town

The tiny town of Karubaga, like the other 1 sub-district centers of the Jayawijaya *kabupaten,* is the administrative center of a wide are and, in this case, a scattered population o some 20,000 Western Dani. Karubaga snuggles just below the mountains at the head of wide green valley, ending in the distance i steep mountains, shrouded in blue haze.

Three rivers—the Kano, the Konda an the Kurege—spring from the mountains i back of Karubaga, flow through the valley and eventually empty into the Mamberam River which then winds its way down t Irian's north coast. The town started as a mis sionary outpost in the 1950s, shortly after th arrival of American fundamentalists. Th whites are gone now, replaced by Dani pas tors of the Indonesian KINGMI Protestan denomination, overseeing some 50 churche

near town and more than 100 district wide.

The legacy of the missionaries in Karubaga and among the Western Dani generally includes an end to tribal warfare, the eradication of diseases such as yaws (a debilitating skin condition), the introduction of a variety of fruits and vegetables, and the end of witch-killings. While in the old days missionaries frowned on penis sheaths and bare breasts, the current and more rational policy permits the native attire, taking into account that many of the Dani are too poor to afford clothes and soap to keep them clean.

Some local pastors allow a bit of the old-style ancestor and spirit worship by some of the few remaining pagans—but only if a fine is paid to the church. Weddings, funerals and even ceremonies connected with the Christian calendar, such as Christmas, are celebrated in the traditional ways. And groups of villages periodically hold huge feasts in the old style, which result in the slaughter of 500 or more pigs.

Although missionaries have successfully stopped witch-burning, they have not ended a widespread belief in witchcraft. Many of the Western Dani continue to believe in heredi-ary occult powers. Black witches can become bats in order to eat people, or can become the wind that blows away a whole village. One recently acquired power allows black witches to burn airplanes, but fortunately this technique has not yet been tested.

The American missionaries also left a legacy in Karubaga of a more material nature: many neat wooden houses surrounded by lawns and flowers. One of these buildings serves as the best little guesthouse in the highlands. The mission-built complex on the highest part of town gives way to the police and administrative buildings, an army out-post, two primary schools and two junior high schools. The church and government main-tain separate school facilities, which include board for children living too far away to make the trek to Karubaga each day.

Arriving in town

The first thing to do is check into the *rumah tamu,* or guesthouse. With five bedrooms, a sit-down toilet and a bucket shower, this is a bargain at $5 a night. Mattresses, pillows, sheets, blankets, mosquito netting (not need-ed most of the year) and towels are provided. In the daytime, the well-lit living room offers comfortable chairs and a couch, a rug and lots of uplifting missionary literature as well as old *Readers Digest*s and Peanuts cartoons. At night, you can read by candlelight and if it gets chilly, start a fire in the Franklin stove.

Opposite: *Crossing the Jekni River near Kurima. While some visitors prefer doing things the hard way, sure-footed porters are always willing to carry their clients across.* **Below:** *A Western Dani couple pause on the trail above Wunin.*

The guest house kitchen is equipped with a wood stove (the $5 includes wood) and a full set of pots, pans and crockery. You can cook your own meals or delegate the chore to either your guide or the guest house caretaker, who is available to do all kinds of domestic work for a very reasonable rate.

After settling in, you should report to the police station, a short walk on the other side of town. They might want to look at your passport but the critical item is your *surat jalan* or travel permit. On the back of this essential document, they will stamp the Karubaga permit, then fill out various forms with an antique typewriter. The clean-cut young policemen are friendly chaps with little to do in life except play ping-pong and check out the occasional tourist. Give them a chance to practice their nonexistent English.

Police business over, see to the logistics for your upcoming trek. If you have not brought a guide from Wamena, a local one—as well as porters—can be found, but none can speak English. Even for tough walkers carrying their own backpacks, we suggest at least one guide because trails around villages and gardens can be confusing, requiring frustrating backtracking.

If you did not fly into Karubaga with all the essentials, there are a half-dozen small stores around town to buy basics such as batteries, candles, tinned food, biscuits and instant noodles. You do not have to buy food here for the whole trek as vegetables and fruit—including, of course, sweet potatoes—are available along the way. To make the walk enjoyable, hire a porter (about $3 a day). Taking only essentials, one porter should be enough for each person's load, with another for food and cooking gear.

Karubaga hosts a market on Mondays, Wednesdays, and Fridays, which brings to the town the produce of the subdistrict. The first transactions take place in the uncovered market area around 8 a.m. and by 2 p.m. most of the action is over. Peanuts are the biggest local cash crop, selling here for 25¢ a kilo, half the Wamena price. Other marketables include pineapples, 10¢-20¢ per fruit; oranges, red onions, chickens and the occasional pig. Local government employees stock up here, and some of the produce is flown to Wamena at subsidized rates.

The Karubaga market makes a great place for photographs, with lots of Western Dani men and women gossiping, buying and selling. Outside of the Baliem Valley, you don't have to pay to photograph the locals. They love to have their picture taken. The problem is obtaining natural poses, although this can usually be accomplished with patience and a telephoto lens.

The trail

The trail between Karubaga and Wamena lies along a planned, but not yet built road. The

right of way leads from Nabire (near the coast at the base of Cenderawasih Bay) to Wamena, through the western highlands.

Many sections of this trail have been widened enough to allow sunshine through, drying up the mud below, but elsewhere the trail is just a narrow footpath—especially on the steepest inclines. Even in the driest season, June and July, there is always the chance of a shower, lasting a couple of hours or more. And after a good rain, there will be mud (not very deep). But, unless you have absolutely awful luck, day-long rainfall is most unlikely. On the contrary, chances are better for sunburn. Bring a wide-brimmed hat, long sleeves and pants, and sunscreen.

The level distance between Karubaga and Wamena—through Wunin, Bokondini, Kelila, Tagime and Pyramid—is just 70 kilometers. But this does not account for laboring up the mountainsides or easing one's way down the incline on the other side. A strong hiker can make it in three days (the Danis do it in a day or two), but it is much better to allow yourself four or five days. Then you can enjoy the changing scenery, take lots of breaks and photos, and arrive at your sleeping destination early enough to bathe, relax and dine during daylight.

While tennis shoes will probably do, hiking boots offer ankle support, keep mud out of your toes and grip better on slippery surfaces. Some rivers are spanned by bridges, but small creeks and mudflats are traversed on a round log or two, which are more likely than not to be slippery. If you don't think you can manage, let your porters give you a hand or carry you across. They are tough chaps, well able to carry even an overweight body across a waist-high raging river with only loose, slippery stones as footholds for their bare feet. (Make sure someone gets a photo!) Even if you can make it across on your own, the lift prevents wet boots or wasted time taking your boots off and putting them on again.

Along the trail there are many places to drink clear mountain water but take a canteen for those stretches of two hours or more under the hot sun. And have your guide bring along some pineapples, delicious at breaktime. Keep your camera handy, because you will often meet locals along the way. Only one word of Western Dani language suffices for close encounters: Wah!

Wunin

Get an early start, 8 a.m. at the latest, and in six easy hours you will reach Wunin. The early start is important—each day begins with an uphill climb (towns are generally in

Opposite: *The spectacular Baliem Gorge, south of Kurima.* **Above:** *A group of Dani girls at Wunin. Dani women do not wear the distinctive low-slung skirts until they marry. Until then, they wear grass skirts such as these.*

valleys) and you don't want to be making this during the heat of the day.

From the edge of the Karubaga plateau the trail drops to a river, with a well-maintained, rattan and cable bridge. Most of the floor planks are in place. After the crossing, be ready for a two-hour climb. The slopes, near and far, are covered with gardens and highlands forests. Once the climb is over, you pass through a village of thatched huts. This signals the beginning of two hours of flat trekking. Towards the end of this part of the stroll, Wunin will appear, but it's further than it looks. First a long drop, then a river crossing on a solid bridge, and finally a short level stretch before Wunin comes back into view. Another short drop and you are crossing the Warom River, the last before Wunin. The river makes an excellent place for a swim before the short climb to Wunin village.

The altitude here, 1,460 meters, is just slightly higher than Karubaga. Wunin is dominated by a huge airstrip, flatter than Karubaga's, which receives sporadic MAF flights when building materials or supplies are urgently needed. The village hugs one side of the airstrip. All the buildings are "modern"—clean, tin-roofed and without character. The inevitable church, school and teachers' houses hold together this tiny mission-built village. During clear weather, the upper end of the landing field affords a fine view of the brooding mountains.

At Wunin you can sleep at a school-teacher's house, but first take a look at the bed offered and agree to a price. Expect to pay about $3 per person, but you might have to bargain. Forget about sit-down toilets—a little outhouse over a hole in the ground is standard. You can relieve yourself anywhere away from the houses, preferrably at night.

Commissioning a Dani festival

There are also several Dani compounds just off the main trail, which starts at the upper end of the landing field, where you can overnight in a *honai* or men's house. The huts have no beds, but soft grass on the floor makes a decent mattress. (Foreign women are also allowed to sleep in the huts.) A central fire, double wood walls, and a number of bodies ward off night time chills. The disadvantages of a Dani hut include the possibility of fleas or ticks. And it can get quite smoky, but it is usually not too bad if you keep your head close to the floor, and stay away from the door. Pay $1–$2 per person for the *honai* stay. Dani guests (your guides and porters)

are usually put up on a complementary basis.

If you are too sore to continue the next day, rest up for 24 hours. Get your legs rubbed with oil and crushed red onions. Have your guide organize a festival. If there are several members in your group, it's not very expensive—say $200. The price depends on the size and number of pigs killed as well as the number of participants.

In the "show" my guide organized, three pigs were killed ($75) and about 140 men and women took part, all in traditional dress. The guide got things going by visiting four Dani compounds at daybreak, and by 8:30 a.m. things were underway.

First the tribesmen dug a pit about one meter-deep and 1.5 meters long and then nearby, arranged huge armfuls of firewood into a rectangular pile and covered the pyre with stones. The traditional method, rubbing a tough liana against a piece of softwood started the fire. When the firewood under the stones was blazing, each pig was held by two men while a third shot an arrow into its heart from close range. Bamboo knives quickly cut up the meat. After the pigs were dispatched the Dani lined the pit with leaves, and then with stones that had been heated in the fire. More leaves were laid over the stones, and then sweet potatoes and chunks of pork.

While the food steam-baked for two to three hours, the men and women danced and whooped, yelling and singing with abandon. The men organized themselves into two teams and staged an enthusiastic mock battle with plant stems as spears. A few of the men were superbly decorated with soot and pig grease, white lime paint, flowers, cuscus fur and feathers. Everyone had a good time, and I took plenty of photos before the food was cooked and divided among the participants.

On to Bokondini

From Wunin, it's a flat stretch for a half hour before coming to the mountain at the head of the valley. Another half hour and you reach the topside forest and begin a nice, shaded stretch. The trail touches the edge of an artificial lake, a fairyland opening in the high misty forest. The water is stocked with carp and tilapia. An hour of hiking brings you to the top of the long drop to the Bokondini Valley. If the weather is clear, the looming mountains appear through openings in the

Opposite: *A arrow shot at close range is the traditional way to dispatch a pig. This one became roast pork for a feast at Wunin.*

orest. At the bottom of the mountain is a stream that makes a perfect resting place for weary knees. Then it's flat again for a while before dropping down to the Bogo River below Bokondini. There is no bridge here, but your porters will either built a temporary one or carry you across. A short, steep climb ends at the little town and subdistrict center of Bokondini—six easy hours from Wunin.

The urban "center" of Bokondini resembles Karubaga, but with an important difference. A Cessna plane owned by MAF has its home base here, along with its pilot and missionaries. They live in neat wooden alpine houses surrounded by fences, lawns and flowers—in the American style. Don't expect missionary hospitality—they are not in the business of putting up hikers. Try a schoolteacher or the infirmary staff house, just across from the clinic (*rumah sakit*). Again, look over the facilities and agree on a price before settling in and reporting to the police with passport and *surat jalan*.

Back to Wamena

Try to get the earliest possible start out of Bokondini because there is a long day ahead. The first part is easy: a stroll of some two and a half hours with little climbing and one solid ridge crossing lands you in Kelila, another subdistrict center where you report again to the police. Kelila has a regular Merpati flight once a week (on Friday) to Wamena, and

occasional missionary flights. From Kelila you face the trip's toughest climb, 2 to 3 hours uphill on a wide road to the top of the pass.

Here you are on the island's divide. The watershed to the north drains into the Memberamo and the Pacific; to the south all the rivers head to the Baliem and the Arafura Sea. The wonderful view of the southern valley is your reward as your knees take a pounding during the 1.5 to 2 hours downhill to Tagime, a 6-hour day. The pastor in Tagime runs a guesthouse.

From Tagime, it is an easy 3 hours to Pyramid, the missionary center at the head of the Baliem Valley. From Pyramid, you can catch a flight (10 minutes) to Wamena. Or continue to Kimbim, one hour further. The *camat* (subdistrict head) has guest rooms where, for $5 a day, you can room and board. Kimbim requires a police stop.

From Kimbim, Landcruisers and trucks take passengers to Wamena once or twice a week for $2 a head ($60 for a chartered ride). You can also walk, flat but hot, another 4–6 hours to Sinatma, where there is regular bemo service to Wamena. Or walk across the valley to the Baliem River, cross on a small raft or a canoe, and from Uwosilimo, just on the other side, take a public minibus to Wamena. Minibuses from Uwosilimo make the run several times a day, and the fare is less than $1 ($15–$20 charter).

Highlands Practicalities

All prices in U.S. $

Leaving Sentani, you soar up over the lake, across the wide swamps of the Mamberamo Basin, through Pass Valley and on into the Grand Valley of the Baliem. Your airplane touches down at Wamena, 45 minutes from Sentani. You pick up your bags, and as soon as you reach the main part of the terminal, a small army of eager hands (each expecting a tip, of course) grabs your bags to carry to one of the local losmen, all of which are easily within walking distance.

(Note: The Baliem Valley is officially "dry," meaning no alcohol is allowed. Bag searches have loosened up, and there is some tolerance of small amounts for a tourist's personal use, but we still suggest you respect this rule.)

SURAT JALAN

Upon arrival in the Baliem, the police have to check your passport and *surat jalan*. The desk clerk at the hotel/*losmen* will ask for these, and will usually be able to send someone to the police station (which is just behind the Pasar Nayak) to take care of this for you. If you are planning on leaving the valley itself, you will have to show your *surat jalan* and passport (or a photocopy thereof) to the police at *kecamatan* (subdistrict) centers. The *kecamatan* centers for the Jayawijaya *kabupaten* are marked on the highlands map on pages 116–117. For more on the *surat jalan,* see "Travel Advisory," page 188.

ACCOMMODATIONS

Other than the Hotel Jayawijaya, 3 km out of town, all the hotels/losmen are within walking distance. The best rooms are at the Nayak Hotel, just across the road from the airport.

Baliem Palace Hotel. Jl. Trikora ℂ 19. 17 rooms, all with indoor facilities. A new, clean hotel. Good restaurant serving shrimp or steak ($4), rice or noodle dishes ($1.50–$2) or soup and vegetable dishes ($1–$2). $22 S, $24 D.

Hotel Nayak. Jl. Gatot Subroto 1, P.O. Box 1. Directly across from the airport. ℂ 26. 12 rooms with bath. The best rooms in town. $16 S, $21 D.

Baliem Cottages. Jl. Thamrin, P.O. Box 32. Some 600 meters from the airport. 15 thatch covered cottages, a bit run down but spacious. The restaurant on the premises is not always open. $13 S, $21 D.

Wamena City Hotel. Jl. Trikora, next to the Sinta Prima Restaurant and Sam Chandra's travel agency. 20 rooms. Good rooms, all facili-

ties and breakfast included. $13 S, $21 D.

Marannu Jaya Hotel. Jl. Trikora, across from the Baliem Palace. 20 rooms. $8–$11 S, $16–$21 D.

Losmen Anggrek. Jl. Ambon, P.O. Box 12. 8 rooms. Includes breakfast and tea or coffee. $10.50 S, $15–$20 D

Losmen Sri Lestari. Great location, In front of the Pasar Nayak market. 10 rooms. A bucket of hot water upon request. The higher priced rooms have attached facilities. $8–$11 S, $13–$15 D.

Losmen Sjahrial Jaya. Jl. Gatot Subroto 51 ℂ 151. 23 double rooms with bath attached. Highly recommended guide Beni Wenda works out of here. $7 S, $13 D.

Outside of town

Hotel Jayawijaya. 3 km out of town off the road to Pyramid. 18 rooms, none with attached bath. 5 bathrooms upstairs, 5 downstairs. There are rice paddies and Dani huts in back. This hotel is only for tour groups.

Losmen La-uk Inn. On the west side of the main road, in Jiwika. $6 for bed and full board.

DINING

Most hotels/*losmen* serve meals, and there are foodstalls around the market serving inexpensive Indonesian food. **The Sinta Prima**, on Jl. Trikora, is the best restaurant in town, serving Chinese food and freshwater crayfish. Meals range from $2 to $5.

There are also three restaurants in back of the market: The **Vemalia,** specializing in Chinese and Indonesian dishes ($1–$2.50); the **Gembira,** rice dishes (75¢–$1); and the **Minang Jaya,** rice and meat (75¢–$1).

Banks and money-changing

Bank Rakyat Indonesia. Will change $US, $A, ¥, D.M. and French francs. They accept American Express, Bank of America, Thomas Cook's, Bank of Tokyo, and Visa Australia traveler's checks. Hours: Mon–Thurs, 8 am to 12:30 pm; Fri to 11:30 am and Sat to 11 am.

Communications

The post office, on Jl. Timor, is open Mon–Thurs from 8 am to 2 pm; Fri to 11 am and Sat to 12:30 pm.

The satellite telephone office, on Jl. Panjaitan, is open 24 hours. One minute to the U.S. costs $3; to Europe, $3.50.

Shave and a haircut

Pemangkas Rambut Bangkalan. Jl. Trikora, next to the market. Haircut $1, shave 30¢. A massage is included.

Souvenirs

You can find these at the Pasar Nayak market, in the "Souvenir Shop" across the road from the market. You will probably also be offered

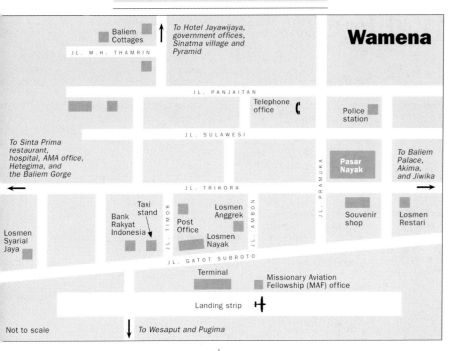

ems while you are sitting in your hotel lobby or a restaurant.

The most popular souvenir is a *horim,* or yellow penis gourd, available in various sizes and shapes. Prices range from 25¢ to as high as 1 if "decorated" by a local (non-Dani) merchant. A bow with a set of arrows, $2–$3; *oken* (net bags) $2.50–$5, depending on size. trands of shell money, sewn on belts, cost $2 n up, depending on the quality of the cowries. ong, narrow breast-plates of tiny shells sewn together (*wali noken*) run $10–$18. Various namental necklaces, with pig's tusks and eathers, $3–$5. Determining a fair price for a tone adze is difficult. They range from $4 to a hopping $150, depending on the type of tone used: greenish is the most expensive, llowed by the bluish hues. Check the binding make sure the stone won't fall out even efore you get it home.

Note: Some of these items may be made ith protected species, so look at them carefully. Feathers of any kind will alert a baggage spector back home, as will lizard skin. Stick the net bags and gourds if you are not sure.

TRAVEL AGENCIES

s interest in Irian Jaya has grown, so have the umber of operators bringing in tourists. A umber of groups, based in Jakarta or Bali or ung Pandang have begun bringing clients to e Baliem Valley and the highlands. We suggest sticking with the three pioneering agencies at have been operating out of the Baliem for ears. For any tour that requires an inland flight ut of Wamena, at least two weeks notice are required to reserve a plane. All the operators will meet their clients at Sentani airport and provide accommodations there for the first night. We suggest you figure out where you would like to go, and write or fax one of these operators well ahead of time.

Chandra Nusantara Tours and Travel. Jl. Trikora 17 (next to the Sinta Prima Restaurant), T.Pos 41, Wamena. ✆ 143. Telex: 76102 CNTWMX IA. Or fax, in Jayapura: (967) 22318. This outfit is run by Sam Chandra, who is very experienced in taking people to the highlands. Chandra offers 11 different tours, covering the Baliem Valley, Yali country, Lake Habbema and Trikora, the Asmat, and some very traditional lowlands groups. His operation is very well run. A sample of Chandra's tours (all minimum of two people):

5-day Baliem Valley tour. Exploring the valley around Wamena, a pig feast, and two nights in traditional Dani huts slightly modified for westerners. $345/person.

7–14 day tour of Yali country. Fly to Kosarek, and after 5 days of trekking, reach Anggruk. Either fly back to Wamena, or continue trekking for 6 more days back to Wamena through the Baliem Gorge. $480–$655/person (depending on length) plus plane charter: $160 per flight (for the whole group).

Highlands and lowlands. Fly to Korupun, and trek to the lowlands around the Brazza River, in the area of the Momina people. By dugout down the Brazza to the area of the Cain, who live in tall tree houses. Continue downriver, through Citak land, to Senggo, whence to fly back to Wamena. This route passes through some of the least-known territory in Irian Jaya,

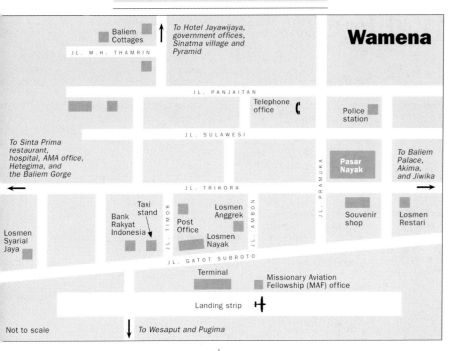

Wamena

JL. M.H. THAMRIN
Baliem Cottages
To Hotel Jayawijaya, government offices, Sinatma village and Pyramid

JL. PANJAITAN
Telephone office
Police station

JL. SULAWESI

To Sinta Prima restaurant, hospital, AMA office, Hetegima, and the Baliem Gorge

Pasar Nayak
JL. PRAMUKA

To Baliem Palace, Akima, and Jiwika

JL. TRIKORA

Taxi stand
Bank Rakyat Indonesia
JL. TIMOR
Post Office
Losmen Anggrek
JL. AMBON
Losmen Nayak
Souvenir shop
Losmen Restari

Losmen Syarial Jaya

JL. GATOT SUBROTO

Terminal
Missionary Aviation Fellowship (MAF) office

Landing strip

Not to scale
To Wesaput and Pugima

and where the missionaries have had zero success. A real adventure. $770/person plus plane charter: $320.

10–14 day Asmat tour. By boat to various Asmat villages. $990–$1,250/person, plus $135/day for boat rental. If your schedule is loose, you can take the weekly Merpati flight to Ewer. If not, add $650 each way for charter.

12-day climbing Mt. Trikora. Tent and cold weather clothes are essential. Your guide will only go halfway up the mountain with you. In good weather, you can climb up to the peak and back again from base camp in a day. Bring very heavy leather gloves, as the rock is extremely sharp on Trikora. This is a mountaineer's trip, not for tourists. $610/person.

Insos Moon. Run by John Wolff, P.O. Box 57, Wamena, IRJA. He can be contacted through Airfast in Jayapura: Jl. Sam Ratulangi 3, P.O. Box 1234, Jayapura, IRJA. ✆ (967) 31730, Fax: 99012, Telex 76122 AIRFAST.

We recommend John Wolff for his pioneering work in opening up many areas to trekkers, his connections with the military in getting permits and the fact that he has himself walked to many places with his groups. He owns the Nayak and Jayawijaya hotels in Wamena, and lives there most of the year. Some samples:

7-day Yali trip. To the Yali lands around Anggruk and Ninia, for $300/person.

8-day Senggo expedition. Visiting the traditional people around the Brazza River. $450–$525.

Wolff also offers plenty of long hikes for those in good physical condition.

Insatra Exclusive Tours. Jl. Kemiri #1H1, P.O. Box 211, Sentani, IRJA. ✆(967)21224. A reputable firm run by Rudi Willem. Write or call for any special requests.

AREA AIR TRANSPORT

Merpati now regularly connects Wamena to the many small grass strips in the highlands, and their schedule is supplemented by the mission airlines, which offer charters. Be sure your *surat jalan* specifies any area you wish to visit outside the Baliem Valley proper.

Merpati. In the air terminal or Jl. Trikora 41. Book early, check and re-check. Flights can be cancelled for lack of passengers, breakdowns, and bad weather. Scheduled flights from Wamena at press time:

Apalapsili	Tu	$13
Bokondini	F	$12
Ewer	M,F	$36
Jayapura	2–4 times daily	$34
Karubaga	Sa	$14
Kelila	Tu	$10
Mulia	Tu, Th	$14
Nabire	Tu	$24
Oksibil	Sa	$14
Tiom	Th	$15

Note: Other flights could be listed by the time you read this, so check when you arrive.

MAF. The Missionary Aviation Fellowship maintains light aircraft and a helicopter and flies from Wamena to numerous landing strips in the Irian highlands. Their weekly schedule (Mon–Sat) is confirmed and posted each Thursday. Check it at their office, next to the Wamena air terminal.

Their first priority, of course, is logistical support to the Protestant missions. But they also take paying passengers on a space-available basis.

Bokondini	(3 times weekly)	$13
Tiom	(4 times weekly)	$13
Karubaga	(3 times weekly)	$17
Anggruk	(once weekly)	$17
Maki	(2 times weekly)	$11
Boma	(once weekly)	$44
Mamit	(once weekly)	$17
Kelila	(once weekly)	$13
Kangime	(once weekly)	$18

You can also charter the MAF's planes and helicopter. You have to pay for return time, unless they can do some business on the way back. They will, however charter for less than 1 hour flights. They normally need two weeks notice for charters.

Cessna 185 or 206 (5 people)	$160/hr
Cessna 208 (9 people)	$420/hr
Hughes 500 helicopter (4 people)	
	$600/hr + $100/day

To estimate your cost, figure the Cessnas fly at 200 km/hr (the 206 is a turbocharged version of the 185 and thus has a higher ceiling). For 185/206 this works out to 80¢/km or, split four ways, 20¢/km.

Note: arriving on a MAF flight doesn't entitle you to missionary hospitality. Missionaries lead busy lives and are not in the field to entertain travelers. Try not to bother them. They will, of course, help you in an emergency.

AMA. The Associated Mission Aviation, the Roman Catholic equivalent of MAF, also sometimes offers charters out of Wamena airport. Check with the AMA office on Jl. Trikora, towards Hetegima. The planes are Cessna 185s. From Wamena:

Enarotali	$480 + 10%
Ok Sibyl	$370 + 10%
Ewer	$650 + 10%
(also to Kokonau and Timika)	
Sentani–Ewer	$1,050

TRAVEL IN THE HIGHLANDS

Several tourist attractions around the Baliem Valley can now be reached by minibus on a dirt road network from Wamena: Dani villages, mummies, markets and caves. Of course, all the crowds go to these places, and the experience may not be what you had in mind. In and around the Baliem (as in life in general), the further you walk, the more rewarding the view, and the more personal, and more unsullied by commercialism, the experience.

One of the best strategies for a long trek

fly out and walk back. This is particularly important if you are under any time constraints, as it lets you get much further out. These walks are real adventures, through beautiful country and not very difficult if you have time and are in relatively good physical shape.

Make sure your *surat jalan* covers your destination before you leave, and bring along any supplies you need that you don't think you will be able to get in your destination. Remember, in most Dani villages you cannot so much as buy a pack of cigarettes (although if there is a school teacher there, he might have a few items) although sweet potatoes and other essentials are available.

If you have a good guide in Wamena you have worked with before, you may want to fly him out as well, but remember that although guides from Wamena might speak English, they probably know their way well only around the valley itself. You can find guide/porters at the other end, perhaps enlisting the aid of school-teachers or policemen to arrange this. (If you have the budget, you could bring one guide from Wamena who speaks English, and hire another at your destination who knows the trails.)

Guides. If you arrange your trip through a travel agency, a guide and porters will come with the package. On your own, you can pick up a guide when you arrive in Wamena—either at the airport or at your hotel/*losmen*. Local guides who speak a bit of English charge $10 per day, plus their food and cigarettes. Porters run $3 plus food and smokes.

If you know some Indonesian, you can hike by yourself, frequently asking for directions (if there's anyone around to ask). But trails often run off into the gardens and you might have to backtrack—often. We recommend always using a guide. For a longer trip, your guide can help you estimate how many porters you will need.

Minibuses. Public minibuses run everywhere in the valley the road does. Some sample fares from Wamena: Ibele (55¢); Uwosilimo (80¢); Sugokmo ($1.10). To charter, multiply the usual fare by 12, or figure about $5.50/hour. You can negotiate a separate price for waiting time. Taking a minibus to the furthest point it can reach on your planned route is a good way to get out of the valley quicker.

Hiking. As long as you stay in the valley, walking is level and easy. If the side valleys require uphill trudges, the scenery makes the effort worthwhile, especially in the Wolo and Welesi valleys. Agency tours cover several areas of the Baliem, but with a little Indonesian and some initiative, you can easily plan your own itinerary.

The rainy season in the Baliem is from October to December with the driest months (theoretically) being June and July. But it's not worth it to plan your trip for the drier season, because it still rains plenty. When it does rain, it's usually in the late afternoon, at night or early morning. It's much more pleasant to walk under a cool, cloudy sky than the blazing sun, although parts of the trail can get very muddy and slippery. In many places you have to clamber over stone or wooden fences but there's always a system of stones, logs and branches where the trail comes up to a fence.

For short hikes (2 hours or less) and returning to Wamena or Jiwika to overnight, only a few essentials are required: hat, sunscreen, drinking water, sunglasses, tennis shoes and a waterproof jacket. For longer hikes, bring all all of the above plus sturdy, comfortable boots. For overnighting, bring a sleeping bag or blanket, and insect repellent.

You can almost always stay with government officials or in a Dani *honai*. (If you will be traveling to places where there are no villages, bring a tent.) Figure on paying $3/night for accommodations. Although you can often purchase food (but not meals) in villages, it's best to bring some of the essentials such as rice, tinned fish, coffee, sugar, spoons, plates and cooking gear. Toilets, if any, are of the squat-over-hole variety. Bring toilet paper unless you can adapt your sensibilities to the prevailing water and left hand method.

Walking Times. For the estimates below, figure a day equals 8 hours of walking:

Wamena–Pyramid	1 day
Pyramid–Bokondini	1 day
Bokondini–Karubaga	1 day
Karubaga–Mulia	3 days
Mulia–Sinak	3–6 days
Sinak–Beoga	4–5 days
Beoga–Ilaga	7–10 days
Wamena–Lake Habbema	3 days
Wamena–Daelah	1 day
Daelah–Tiom	1 day
Tiom–Karubaga	1 day

Photography. Men in penis gourds and grass-skirted women make exciting photo subjects. They will also ask to be paid for participating in your exotic photo opportunities—usually with a red one hundred rupiah note. Don't grumble, as this is only direct benefit most Dani receive from foreigners, who spent a lot of money getting to the Baliem to see them. Aside from a few menial jobs in hotel restaurants, tourist dollars flow into non-Dani pockets. Sometimes, if you take a series of photos, your subjects might ask for more money. We suggest going along with any reasonable demand, up to, say, Rp 1,000. Outside of the valley, most people will not ask for payment to be photographed.

Ceremonies and dances. As soon as you arrive in Wamena, and wherever else you go, ask if there are any ceremonies. Births, marriages, first menstruation, first wearing of the penis gourd and funerals are occasions for Dani rituals throughout the year. If you happen on any of these ceremonies, find the *kepala suku* (clan chief) or whoever is in charge to obtain permission to photograph. Expect to pay $6–$30 for the privilege.

PART V

The Asmat Region

The tidal swamplands of Irian's south coast are one of the best-known, but also least accessible parts of the island. This is the land of the Asmat, now world-famous for their spectacular wood carvings, and previously notorious as head-hunters and cannibals.

The Asmat found themselves on the front pages of newspapers worldwide in 1961, when Michael C. Rockefeller, son of the then governor of New York, disappeared here. Rockefeller was collecting art for the New York Museum of Primitive art when his boat, an underpowered contraption consisting of two lashed-together dugouts, encountered the swift tidal bore at the mouth of the Betsj River and overturned.

Some people (and *all* of the yellow press) assumed Rockefeller had been captured and killed by the Asmat. Cooler heads suggested that the strong, unpredictable tides and crocodiles were likelier villains. A small, but committed minority thought that the governor's son "went native" and still lived, and more than one adventurer went off toward this great island to find Michael Rockefeller.

Until very recently, the Asmat area was closed to visitors, and the infrastructure for tourism is still very limited. Fuel, bottled water and other staples are shockingly expensive here, and many other items (insect repellant, suntan lotion) are simply unavailable. There are no telephones anywhere in the region, and news filters in through radios.

At the time of this writing, air service was very unreliable. If you are on a tight schedule, do not go to the Asmat region unless you are on a group tour with a chartered airplane.

The capital of the Asmat region is Agats, a small town on Flamingo bay. Because of the tides, the entire town is built on stilts, and the "streets" are plank walkways. Despite that it might sound so, it is not a very charming place. Visitors should come with a serious interest in Asmat culture and a willingness to tolerate mud and heat and insects.

Fewer than 1500 people live in Agats. Small-time merchants and traders, shark's fin fishermen, and dealers in ironwood form the economic base. The businessmen are all from western Indonesia, mostly Bugis from South Sulawesi. The Catholic mission has its headquarters here, as well as schools, the Asmat museum and a sawmill.

The Asmat Museum of Culture and Progress should be the first stop for any visitor. The mission has accumulated a very good collection of Asmat art, and everything is accompanied by clear and informative explanations.

Visiting the Asmat region around Agats requires hiring a dugout canoe and guide, and sleeping at night on the bark floor of a *jeu,* the long, raised men's huts that serve as the architectural and cultural centers of Asmat villages.

In the villages, you can watch woodcarvers at work, see how canoes are hollowed out and decorated, and generally look around the place and chat with your hosts. Everywhere, small carvings, bone knives, bags and other crafted items will be offered. You may be able to organize a visit to the sago fields (often quite far from the village) where you can watch the operation of felling the trees and washing out the starch.

If you get lucky, you might even stumble onto a festival, accompanied by night-long drumming and dancing, feasts of sago grubs, special carvings and general high spirits. There are many occasions for celebrations—a new *jeu,* carving of *bisj* poles, rites of passage—but they are rather infrequent and the timing is sporadic. But you could always organize your own festival, and for a reasonable fee commission a canoe demonstration, or drumming and dancing.

Overleaf: *Heading back to Agats at sunset on Flamingo Bay.* **Opposite:** *Drummers at a festival to dedicate a new* jeu *house in Biwar Laut.*

THE ASMAT

Artists and Former Head-Hunters

Powerful wood sculptures coveted by collectors the world over, a reputation for head-hunting and cannibalism, and the well-publicized disappearance of Michael Rockefeller here in 1961 combine to make the Asmat Irian's most notorious group.

The south coast of Irian Jaya is inhospitable. Tangles of mangrove line the shore, and inland from the rivers the vegetation is so thick as to be almost impenetrable. Only the riverbanks are habitable, and the muddy ground and up to 5-meter tides force all houses to be built on posts. The air is hot and humid, the water is brackish, and malaria is a constant problem. It is not a salubrious place.

The tides determine the rhythm of life here. The land is so flat that tides are felt up to 100 kilometers inland. Near the coast, the salient current in the wide, brown rivers is generated by the tides, and reverses twice a day. Trying to paddle against this force is folly, and even trips by motorboat are timed with the tide: upstream on an incoming tide, downstream on an outgoing tide.

In this environment, the Asmat developed a rich and volatile culture, revolving around a cycle of spirit appeasement that required huge, expressive woodcarvings, lavish feasting, and deadly warfare. The banning of head-hunting has affected this cycle deeply. Today, after decades of mission and government influence, the identity and culture of the Asmat is still in transition.

The Rockefeller incident

Michael C. Rockefeller, 23-year-old son of New York Governor Nelson Rockefeller, arrived in West New Guinea in 1961 as part of the Harvard Peabody Expedition, to study and film the Baliem Valley Dani. (See "The Dani," page 122.) He shot stills for the group, and rolled sound for the documentary film *Dead Birds*. Rockefeller had a chance to briefly visit the area near Agats, and was amazed by the Asmat sculpture he saw. After a short trip back home, he returned to obtain as many pieces as he could for an exhibit in New York at the Museum of Primitive Art.

His partner on this collection trip was René Wassing, a Dutch expert familiar with Asmat art who was to help Rockefeller choose the best pieces. The two hired a couple of Asmat guides, Simon and Leo, and obtained an outboard-powered catamaran. Rockefeller, who was also shown around by Adrian A. Gerbrands, bought a number of fine carvings. (They are now at the Metropolitan Museum of Art in New York.)

But on Saturday, November 18, disaster struck. Crossing the mouth of Betsj River at the change of tide, their boat capsized. Simon and Leo swam ashore to get help, and the collectors spent the night on their upended craft. (The river Betsj—pronounced "betch"—takes its name from mournful, ritual wailing.)

The next morning, Rockefeller became impatient. Although Wassing urged him not to go, the young man was determined, and seeing the shore several miles away he emptied the gas tank, strapped it and an empty jerry can together with his belt, and headed for shore. It was the last anyone saw of him.

Wassing was soon rescued, because Simon and Leo had made it to shore and gone for help, but Michael was nowhere to be found. Governor Rockefeller and Michael's twin sister, Mary Strawbridge, flew to Agats to direct the search effort, attracting some 70 reporters in their wake. The press had a field day, reporting that Michael had been eaten by cannibals. No trace of him was found, and Governor Rockefeller and Strawbridge returned to the United States, grief-stricken.

"I don't know what happened to him," Wassing later told a reporter. "But I am almost certain that he didn't get to shore. Even if you are only 30 feet from the shore, you don't stand a chance against that abnormally heavy tide."

Although the rough seas in particular (the crocodile and shark hazards are overstated) mitigate against Michael having ever reached shore, it is not impossible that the press headlines were correct. After all, the guides made it, and Rockefeller was an excellent swimmer.

Proponents of the theory that Rockefeller was killed by the Asmat offer some intriguing circumstantial evidence. Several years earlier Dutch police sent to investigate a head-hunting incident killed the chief, two warriors and

Opposite: *The men of Biwar Laut, dressed for the occasion, racing down the Jiwe River.*

wo women in the village of Otsjanep, on the Ewta River south of the Betsj. It would have been conventional for the village to avenge hese deaths. Any member of the white "tribe" who came along would have made a suitable victim.

Given the strong tide, it is impossible to letermine exactly where he may have come ashore. But it is possible that he landed in Otsjanep's sago fields, which were in the area.

Ajam, then chief of Otsjanep, was the son of a man killed by the Dutch police in 1958. Moreover Rockefeller, who had visited Otsjanep earlier to commission some carvings, had then brought along men from Omadesep as guides, unaware that the two ribes were the bitterest of enemies.

A lone white man, tired from a long swim, naked and unarmed, would have made the ideal victim. Rumors persisted among area ribesmen long after the search parties had eft, of a pair of spectacles, shorts, and the skull of a white man. The mention of glasses in particular is significant, because other than one local missionary, no one in the area except Michael wore glasses.

Life on the rivers

The 64,000 Asmat live in scattered riverbank villages of from 35 to more than 2,000 people. The largest village is Atsj (pronounced "atch"). Perhaps the most important division is not village, however, but the *jeu* (one sylla-ble, pronounced "jayu") or men's house. Each village may represent from one to a half-dozen or more *jeu* communities. Tensions between *jeu*s sometimes cause them to break off and resettle. In the past, Asmat villages moved around frequently, although because of schools and other services, and the standard governmental distrust of nomadism, this is now actively discouraged.

The word "Asmat-ow" is equivalent to "people" or "real people." The etymology of the word comes from that for a division between two things, and the particular meaning of "Asmat-ow" is: people as distinct from ancestral or animal spirits. "Asmat" is commonly used to refer to the people (who speak several dialects) and also to their land.

The staple of the south coast is sago, a gummy starch that comes from the pith of a tall palm tree (*Metroxylon rumphii*). New Guinea harbors the most extensive sago forests in the world. In western literature, sago is often disparaged as "tasteless," but the Asmatter would no sooner give up his *amos* (sago) than the French his baguette, or the Javanese his rice.

One advantage sago has over all other crops is time. It is an easy way to get calories. Cutting down the tree, pounding the pithy trunk and washing out the flour is hard work, but a man and his wife working together can obtain 50 kilos of sago flour in half a day from just one tree. And, of course, the palms are

gathered and need not be tended at all.

Almost nothing of the tree is wasted. The bark, split into strips, is used as flooring, the leaf ribs serve as walls, and the leaves themselves are woven into thatch. And, for ritual occasions, a fresh tree is cut, poked full of holes, and left as an incubator for beetle larvae. A month or so later, the fattened grubs are collected and eaten with gusto.

Traditionally, the Asmat kept no domestic animals except dogs. Missionaries have tried to introduce chickens and ducks with limited success. Protein and other nutrition is provided by the shrimp and small mudfish that women seine from the creeks, as well as clams, crabs, snakes, lizards, small mammals and birds, including the large cassowaries.

Until metal pots were introduced by outsiders, the only method of cooking was roasting over the fire, and this is still preferred.

Strangely, there is not a single stone in the Asmat land. In the past, the Asmat obtained fully-formed stone tools from upriver groups, trading sago, shells, jewelry, lime (for coloring), cassowary bone tools and bird of paradise feathers for the precious items.

Head-hunting and spirits

The world of the Asmat is alive with spirits. Animals, trees, even whirlpools and eddies in rivers are possessed of a power beyond man's direct reckoning. The success of an Asmat community—good sago harvests and hunting, healthy children, smooth social relations—requires a proper relationship to the spirits. Asmat life and art is directed at balancing and appeasing these spirits.

In such a hostile environment, death never came about from old age. Life, in this system, comes only from the death of another human. A human head is a powerful source of spiritual energy, and at times of crisis or spiritual depletion, many were needed to rebuild the community.

Before head-hunting ended, the skull of a deceased relative, particularly one who was a successful warrior in life, provided the best protection against malevolent spirits. At night, this provided the most "secure" pillow—as it was during sleep that one was most vulnerable to the supernatural world.

According to Father Gerardus A. Zegwaard, a missionary who arrived in Agats in 1953 and wrote the seminal study of Asmat head hunting practices, "The human head captured at war is believed to possess a germinative power comparable to the fallen seeds of trees." The heads, he writes, were hung in the sago grounds to promote good harvests.

Head-hunting is of course today considered an intolerable practice, and has been banned for decades. But this ban caused great instability in Asmat culture. Many people died in head-hunting raids, and it created a constant atmosphere of fear.

But head-hunting was never as frequent or destructive a practice as one might assume. At its height, anthropologists have estimated that 1–2 percent of the Asmat population yearly died in raids. Even today, malaria is responsible for almost 20 percent of the total mortality in the province. Infant mortality in parts of the Asmat region is more than 65 *per hundred*. Outbreaks of cholera and other diseases are distressingly common.

The jeu houses

Asmat villages were typically built at the bend of a river to keep a lookout for canoes carrying incoming raiders. (Most still are.) To increase their safety, villages were large, housing several clans with a population in the hundreds. Each clan owned and maintained a large *jeu,* sometimes reaching 90 meters in length. These long, rectangular houses faced the river and had many doors, each leading to a fire pit located against the back wall.

These men's houses were the focus of all social life, and fulfilled essential religious and social functions. The organization of the fireplaces denoted status, and the *jeu* was the political and religious center of the village. Here is where important decisions (such as whether to carry out a raid) were made, where the carvings were crafted, and where festival drumming and dancing took place. Women do not enter the huts (although today this rule is said to have loosened up in some areas). They live in small, individual family huts, built on piles between the *jeu*s.

In 1964, the Indonesian government banned traditional celebrations and carvings throughout the Asmat region, and ordered the destruction of the *jeu*s, burning many of them down. The men's houses were considered unsanitary, politically suspect (headhunting raids, for example, were plotted in the *jeu*) and just plain backward. The Catholic missionaries counseled against these measures, but the program went ahead.

The destruction of the *jeu*s removed one of the most secure sociological and psychological anchors for the Asmat, who, with outside involvement in their affairs and land, were already facing a crisis. Villages split up, and many families went further upriver and deeper into the forest, living in shelters far from the eyes of the government.

The eradication program peaked in the late 1960s. From 1968 to 1974, the Asmat Art Project, a collaboration between the United Nations and the Indonesian department of small industries, helped rebuild the cultural roots of the Asmat. But it was the Catholic mission in particular that can be credited with reestablishing Asmat culture. Today, carving is commonplace, almost all villages have *jeu*s, and grand festivals (like the *bisj* pole ceremony) are once again being celebrated.

Ceremonial life

In the past, head-hunting provided a kind of energy and climax to the Asmat ritual cycle, and with its ending—and the government ban on ceremonies—many villages withdrew from ritual life. In the past decade, however, Asmat ritual life has experienced a noticeable renaissance. (See also "Asmat Art," page 168.)

The Asmat celebrate five general categories of festivals: *jeu pokmbu,* the feast for a new *jeu*; *bisj mbu,* the feast for which *bisj* ("beesh") poles are carved; *tsji mbu,* the feast for which numerous canoes are carved; *jipae or mbi pokmbu,* the costume feast, for which full-length mask costumes are made; and the *imasj pokmbu,* the shield feast.

Some of these are regional, for example the *bisj* feast, which takes place only among the Bisjmam (literally "*bisj*-makers") villages

of the central coast. Some are now very rare, such as the shield feast. The one a visitor is most likely to encounter is the *jeu pokmbu,* the dedication ceremony for a new *jeu*.

Asmat feasts are days-long affairs accompanied by drumming, dancing, and eating. Some, such as the mask feast, are associated with rites of passage, and include, for example, specific instructions and rites designed to bring a group of boys to manhood.

In the days of head-hunting, the most important food was the brains of the victims, cooked and mixed with sago grubs. Today, the sago grubs alone serve this function. The rich larvae are solely a ceremonial food, and while the artists are preparing the woodcarvings for the festival, the grubs are being incu-

bated in sago trunks felled for this purpose.

Within Asmat culture, the phallus or *tjemen* ("chemen") represents life, power and regeneration. The *tjemen* of various carvings—particularly the *bisj* poles—is central and often exaggerated in size.

During times of great crisis, such as the arrival of a steam ship, an epidemic of disease, a large and devastating raid, or any other event of imponderable dimensions, an Asmat community would engage in an orgy of

Opposite and **above:** *Clamshell nosepieces, hats of cuscus and cockatoo feathers and other ornaments are de rigueur at Asmat festivals. These men are from Biwar Laut.*

sexual activity. During this mass *papisj* ("papeesh"), men and women would have sex with their own spouses and many others. These orgies occur, writes one missionary scholar, because an "enormous flow of seminal fluid was necessary to obtain an end beyond the reach of normal behavior."

Papisj does not always—or in fact often— take the form of mass orgies. The more usual form of *papisj* involves an occasional, temporary wife exchange. Two men who are very good friends will become *papisj* partners, a relationship that lasts for life. At each instance of having sex with their friend's spouse, the wives (who must have already borne children) must agree, and both husbands must be in the village. The exchange lasts for one night, and is preceded and followed by a somewhat ritualized preparation of food.

Europeans in the Asmat region

The first European to meet the Asmat was Captain James Cook, who stopped for water at present day Cook's Bay on the Casuarina Coast near Primapun. According to his journal entry on September 3, 1770, he and two of his officers went ashore in a small boat, but had not gone more than 200 yards before 3–4 hostile-looking men emerged from the woods. Cook fired, and the men disappeared, but the English explorer decided to head back to the ship. As he did, 60–100 men in canoes appeared to chase his pinnace back.

After Cook's experience, the Asmat were left alone for a half century, until 1827, when Lieutenant D.H. Kolff sailed by in the *Dourga* He blamed exploitation by Seramese traders for the disposition of the Asmat. The following year, a Dutch explorer named de Rochemont landed briefly at Flamingo Bay.

In 1902, the establishment of the Dutch colonial government post and military detachment at Merauke gave a secure base for inland explorations. The first foray into the Central Asmat region took place in 1904, and between 1903 and 1917 several expeditions sponsored by the Royal Netherlands Geographical Society set out to chart Irian's rivers and mountains, sometimes passing through Asmat territory on the way inland.

After 1925, when the colonial government inaugurated its post in Kokonau, in Mimikan land, contact with the Asmat became more frequent. These were still far from friendly. The Mimikans were terrified of the Asmat and frequent raids made this a far from irrational fear. In 1928, an Asmat raiding party hit the village of Atuka, taking a number of heads and stealing everything in sight, including the merchandize in a Chinese-owned store and the nails from the school benches.

With the Dutch around, however, this raid was to be avenged. Two years later, a war party of 400 Asmat was caught in an ambush. With the Mimikans, bent on revenge, at one end, and the Dutch colonial police—armed

with guns—at the other, the Asmat were slaughtered. Only 16 remained to be escorted to the jail in Fakfak.

During the war years, the Japanese occupied the Mimika area around Kokonau with ,000 troops. This was their furthest outpost on New Guinea's south coast. The Australians hung on at Merauke. Japanese patrols reached into Asmat territory as far as Sjuru (next to present day Agats) and Ayam.

The immediate post-war years were marked by greatly increased raiding. In 1946 the Sawa-Erma alliance initiated a long series of bloody battles which eventually led 6,000 Asmat to flee to Mimika for safety. By 1948, the number of Asmat refugees in Mimika approached one-third of the total Asmat population, and threatened Mimika's food supplies.

The Asmat community in Mimika gave Father Zegwaard the opportunity to establish a school for the Asmat, and learn their language and some of their culture. Soon thereafter, he started exploring Asmat country and in 1953 established the mission headquarters in Agats. (See "Agats" page 174.)

The missionaries arrive

The first Asmat was baptized a Roman Catholic in 1954. By 1956, the mission claimed 2,000 converts. The missionaries set about proselytizing in earnest, learning the various Asmat dialects and finding out about Asmat custom and ritual life.

The Protestants have never had as strong a presence among the Asmat, although the first protestant missionaries have been in the region almost as long as the Catholics. The Evangelical Mission Alliance (TEAM) opened its first post at Ayam in 1956, a few months after the Catholic Church set up a permanent presence there. Calvin and Ruth Roessler, who brought the evangelical faith to Ayam more than four decades ago, were still ministering their flock in 1991.

While the missions and the Dutch govern-

ment were beginning to re-shape the Asmat culture, chiefly by prohibiting head-hunting and encouraging fixed and centralized villages, the world of commerce took note of the Asmat land.

The Dutch import-export company IMEX, based first in the police post of Agats in 1953, and later locating its headquarters in Jamasj, started a large coconut plantation and set up a sawmill for lumber exports. In 1958 a Dutch oil company based in Sorong began explorations of the Asmat area from Jaosakor, but

the findings were disappointing. Later, the U.S. company Conoco came to the same conclusions, fortunately for the Asmat.

Lumber, particularly two local varieties of hardwood called redwood and ironwood, became the only commercially important export from the Asmat region. Chopping down these trees and floating them out to the coast was hard work (for example, the ironwood didn't even float, and had to be lashed to canoes) and the Asmat were forced to do it for little or not pay.

Woodcutting is in principle not a bad occupation for the Asmat. It gives the men some time in the forest, and by local standards is fairly lucrative. But particularly when Indonesia took over administration of the land in 1963, exploitation by merchants, administrators and police became common. The men were threatened, beaten, and regularly cheated on their pay.

Persistent efforts by the diocese and a series of muckraking articles in Jakarta papers finally brought an end to the practices in the early 1980s. Now, most of the ironwood cut is used for local consumption.

Opposite: The famed bisj ancestor poles line the rear wall of an Asmat jeu. **Above, left:** When the tide has reduced the Jiwe River to a trickle, women work the brown water for small fish and shrimp. **Above, right:** A carver at work on a canoe prowhead in Warse.

ASMAT ART

World-Class Traditional Woodcarving

Collectors and scholars consider Asmat woodcarving to be among the world's finest. The powerful lines and coarse, expressive motifs appeal strongly to the contemporary western eye. Collectors today pay thousands of dollars for good Asmat carvings, and sometimes even hundreds for bad ones. One of the great admirers of Asmat art was the young Michael Rockefeller.

"The key to my fascination with the Asmats is the woodcarving," he said. "The sculpture which the people here produce is the most extraordinary in the primitive world."

Although wood is plentiful in the Asmat lands, pigments were scarce, limiting the artists to three basic colors: red, from ocherous clay; white, from calcined clam shells; and black, from soot. Until the introduction of metal tools, the stone, shell and bone implements used forced the artists to work in rather soft, fibrous woods.

Woodcarving and the spirits

To the Asmat, woodcarving was inextricably connected with the spirit world. Important carvings were always produced in a ritual context, and served as powerful materializations of ancestral and other spirits. Carvings were often named for those who recently died, serving to remind their owners that vengeance was still not served. (Only babies and the very old died a "natural" death. Everyone else was killed, either physically in battle, or by magic.) Also, the first humans were carved out of wood, and then brought to life by the creator Fumeripitsj.

In this context, the carvings cannot be principally considered aesthetic objects. They are far from identical expressions of mythic forms, however. Motifs are highly schematic, and vary dramatically in their style of execution from carver to carver. While all Asmat did some carving, the best pieces were sculpted by specialists, and their work was immedi-ately recognized as superior. These master carvers, or *wow-ipitsj,* acquired status almost equal to the greatest warriors.

New Guinea's other famous artists are the people of the Sepik River in northern Papua New Guinea. Dr. Carleton Gajdusek, Nobel prize winner in medicine, has concluded based on blood typing that the Asmat and the Sepik are related. He postulates that the Asmat left the Sepik river area at least several hundred years ago, crossed the central cordillera and settled in their present location on the coast. The work of traditional art expert Douglas Newton shows a marked similarity in motifs between the work of Asmat and Sepik carvers, lending even more credence to Gajdusek's hypothesis.

Style regions and objects

The Asmat area is divided into four major zones based on art styles: Northwest Asmat Central Asmat; the Citak region to the east around Senggo and the Dairam Rivers; and the foothill region around the Brazza River to the northeast, around Bras. In terms of designs and motifs, the Northwest and Central Asmat regions are the richest. In the Citak and Brazza River areas, shields are the only elaborate carvings one encounters.

War shields (*jamasj*), sometimes more than two meters high, are the Asmat's most famous art pieces. In the coastal areas they are carved from the thin, wide buttress roots of a type of mangrove tree; in the foothills and inland, they are made from cut planks.

The shield, emblazoned with strange and magical motifs, was a warrior's most important weapon. It gave him strength and courage, and was an offensive weapon as well. A man would rather go into battle with only a shield than with only his bow and spear. Some mysterious designs were so powerful they could paralyze the enemy with fear.

Shields show most distinctly the differences among style regions: Northeast shields tend to have a complex pattern of many small motifs, and are topped by a flat stingray motif. Central shields have larger, somewhat simpler designs (very often a human) and are topped by a small, three-dimensional figure and usually decorated with rattan tassels. Citak shields have large, geometric designs often seeming floral (almost Matisse-like) and the top displays divided fields of color but is uncarved; Brazza shields are similar to Citak shields, with perhaps more rectilinear

Opposite: *Raising the* bisj *poles.*

designs, and curious, tiny "eyes" at the top.

Monumental carvings

The most dramatic sculptures created by Asmat artists are the tall totem poles called *bisj*. These stand 3–5 meters, and are carved into a lattice of small clambering figures. At the top, a wing—the *tjemen* or phallus of the carving—sticks out like a flag. The *bisj* were one of the most powerful carvings, and were historically associated with head-hunting. The figures represented were real people, clansmen crying out for revenge. The carvings were part of a ceremonial cycle that culminated in a retaliatory raid.

Bisj are carved only in certain villages (called Bisjmam, for this reason), in the coastal region south of Agats, from the Unir to the Ewta rivers, and inland as far as Atsj. The ceremony, which requires months of preparation, is infrequently held. The carving begins with the selection of an appropriate tree (a species of mangrove) which has a buttress root large enough to serve as the pole's *tjemen*. The tree is harvested, and brought into the *jeu* to be carved.

After the ceremony, the *bisj*—like all the monumental carvings—were taken to the sago fields, broken up, and allowed to rot. In this way the spirit in the carving would pass to the sago trees, promoting a good harvest. (Today, of course, such carvings would be snapped up by a collector.)

Long soulships, called *wuramon*, are another expression of fine monumental art. They were (and very occasionally, are) made only in the northwest Asmat area, in the villages of Jamasj-Jeni, Ao, Kapi and As-Atat. These bottomless canoes contained human-like figures crouched face downward and several symbolic animals. The soulships were used in conjunction with initiation rituals.

Not all the products of Asmat artists were carvings. Full body costumes, great shaggy cloaks of rattan called *jipae*, serve in another initiation ritual. The costumes, which have strange, otherworldly shapes, are made in secrecy, and unveiled only during the celebration. These costumes serve to drive spirits from the village. The *jipae* festival is still a rather poorly understood event, and it is probably a very rare occurrence.

In the coastal and central areas, skulls of ancestors and head-hunting victims were decorated by filling the eye sockets with beeswax, and then pressing in blue-gray Job's tears seeds and the crinkled red seeds of the crab's eye vine. The tops of the skulls were also decorated with seeds and cockatoo feathers. Ancestor and trophy skulls are easy to distinguish: the latter have no jawbone (these were given to women to wear as neck laces), and have a large hole in the temple where the brain was removed.

Useful objects

The work of artists also decorates more mundane, workaday objects such as canoes, paddles, drums, spears, and a variety of small bowls and utensils. Light, dugout canoes, the main form of transportation in the Asmat region, are still decorated with fine prow heads and carvings along the gunwales. The long paddles (the Asmat always stand up in their canoes) used to have knobs at the top that bore the face of a relative killed in a raid, thus serving as a daily reminder of a death that required payback.

Asmat drums (*em*) all have the same basic hourglass shape, and all bear a drumhead of lizard skin. But each shows unique decorations on the side, carved into the wood after the body has been hollowed out by fire. The handles may be plain, carved with intricate

Above: *Shields from the Asmat Museum in Agats, representing four style regions. From left: Central Asmat (Pirien); Northwest Asmat (Esmapano); Citak (Bras); and Brazza River (Asa-Ijip-Enam).* **Opposite:** *Carvers in Atsj, the largest Asmat village and one famous for carving*

bstract lace-work or shaped like humans. As
is being played—around a fire in the
u—the skin is periodically held over the
re to tighten it up. Lumps of beeswax on the
urface are used to tune it.

Art in transition

/hen Irian Jaya was first integrated into
idonesia, over-zealous officials, anxious to
civilize" the Asmat, burned down the *jeu*s,
irbade festivals and destroyed most existing
culptures. At this time, Protestant missionar-
s backed the officials, as they thought their
achings could find better reception if there
ere no men's houses, traditional feasts and
rts. The Catholic mission was a notable, and
utspoken opponent of this cultural genocide.

Fueled by the then new, liberal and far-
aching tenets of Vatican II, the young
rosier order priests believed that, as much
s possible, the Asmat should retain their cul-
ire. Although teaching Christian doctrine,
iey encouraged the use of Asmat ritual
bjects in the Catholic liturgy, and encour-
ged traditional feasts and art. Churches
ere decorated with Asmat designs, and inau-
urated just like a new *jeu*.

The Catholic missionaries, together with
nited Nations officials and others, worked
) convince the Indonesian government to
escind the ban on traditional art and festi-
als. Already, some local officials had discov-
red just how valuable Asmat art was on the

international market, and had been making
good money shipping out this contraband. In
the early 1970s, the order was rescinded.

During the period when art was being
destroyed by officials, the Catholic Church
stepped in to buy carved items for safekeep-
ing. The church's plan was to preserve the
Asmat cultural heritage so a later revival of
the carving tradition would still be possible.

This policy eventually led to the Asmat
Museum of Culture and Progress, officially
opened on August 17, 1973. Here was a museum, with a fine collection of Asmat art, set up
where the Asmat themselves can visit. In the
history of western collection of so-called
primitive art, this is a rare thing indeed. (In
fact, the very best and earliest Asmat sculptures were taken out during the time of
Dutch colonialism, and these now exist in
European museums.)

In addition to continuing to buy fine traditional carvings, the museum also sponsors a
yearly contest to look for new styles. We must
admit that the prizewinners from these are of
very low quality compared to the other pieces
in the museum.

But in at least looking for quality, the contest bucks a strong, and unfortunate tide:
profit-minded merchants, paying pennies a
carving, who are exporting thousands of
units of very low-quality, churned-out Asmat
woodcarvings for sale in Wamena, Jayapura
and especially Bali and Java.

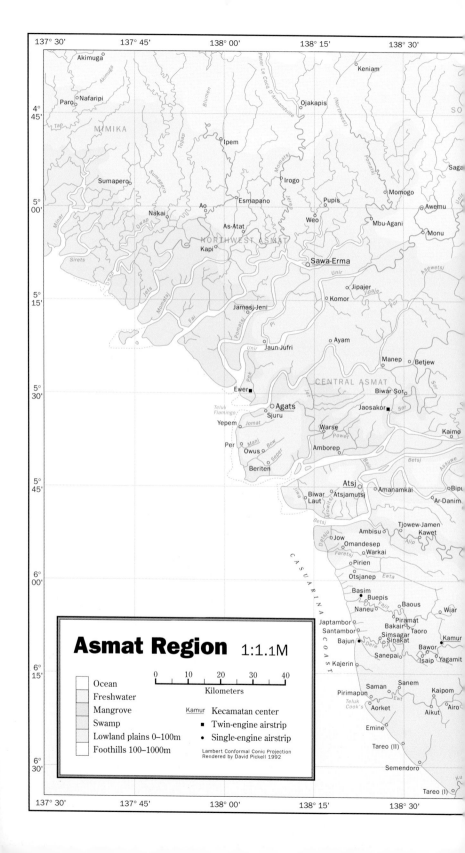

Asmat Region 1:1.1M

0	10	20	30	40

Kilometers

☐ Ocean
☐ Freshwater
☐ Mangrove
☐ Swamp
☐ Lowland plains 0–100m
☐ Foothills 100–1000m

Kamur Kecamatan center

■ Twin-engine airstrip

● Single-engine airstrip

Lambert Conformal Conic Projection
Rendered by David Pickell 1992

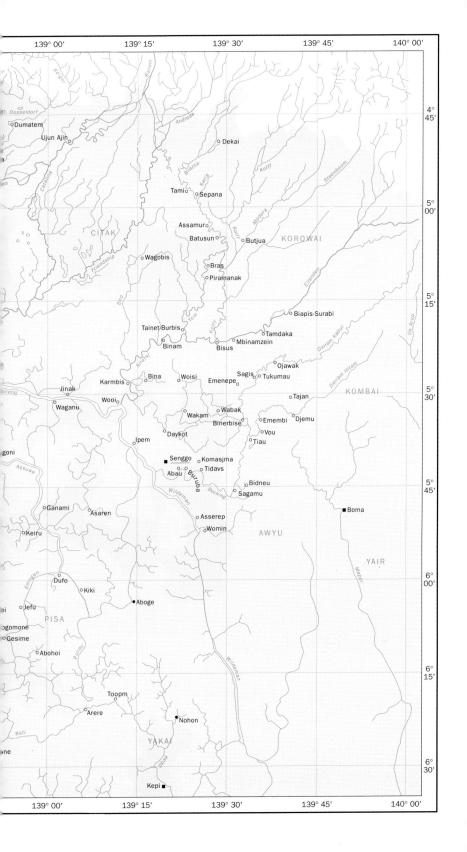

AGATS

Rickety Capital of the Asmat Region

The small town of Agats sits barely propped above the mud on the south bank of the mouth of the Aswetsj River, where it empties into Flamingo Bay. Wooden walkways, raised on posts, serve as streets. The planks are not everywhere in good repair, and even in broad daylight walking about requires a keen sense of balance. Walking about at night without a flashlight is courting disaster. For the first few days you get a bit of a neck ache from looking down, but after a while the boards become familiar. Overconfidence, however, can quickly land you in the mud.

When the tide is in, the water reaches to within a meter of the boards, and little boys jump in with glee, using either the boardwalks or half-submerged trees as diving boards. When the tide goes out, the town garbage is mercifully washed out to sea. Twice a year, just after Christmas and in June,

the tides can exceed five meters. When this happens, great stretches of boardwalk can be submerged. This is not really the best season to visit.

When the tide is out, mud remains. At this time the little mudskipper fish quarrel over their territories, and small orange and blue crabs scuttle about. The boys are out in force then, armed with homemade slingshots, powered by dozens of little rubber bands tied into fat ropes. Mudball projectiles are aimed at the crabs with a triumphant cry of "Mati!" (Dead!) when a target is hit.

Some five meters of rain falls each year in Agats, but it is spotty. Since the town's drinking water all comes from cisterns fed by the tin roofs, a two or three week dry spell can mean a lack of good water.

A humble capital

Agats is the capital of the Asmat region, the communications center, the commercial center, the educational center and the center of the Catholic mission. Of the four sub-district capitals in the region, Agats, with 1500 residents, ranks only third in population. Both Atsj and Sawa-Erma have more than 2,000 people; Kamur is less populous than Agats. Senggo is another *kecamatan* center, further inland and to the east. This is the center of a region occupied by a number of ethnic groups, including the Citak, who are usually considered a subgroup of the Asmat.

Although one might think so, the town did not take its name from the bothersome little gnat-like biting bugs called *agas,* but from the Asmat word for "good"—*akat*—which degenerated into the current Agats. The first post was set up here in 1939 by Kei Islander Felix Maturbongs, a university graduate appointed District Officer by the Dutch. Maturbongs tried to start the post at the far more important village of Ayam, then the largest in all the Asmat region, but repeated flooding forced him to look for another site.

This first post was, however, short-lived. Maturbongs himself destroyed it to prevent the site from being used by the Japanese, who occupied the Mimika area in 1942. After the war, many Asmat fled to Mimika, and from the refugees Father Gerardus Zegwaard learned the Asmat language.

Zegwaard then decided to set up the center of the Catholic mission in the region at Agats, on February 3, 1953. A month later, the Dutch set up a police post there, and following a visit by the governor in 1955, Agats grew into a small town. After the Indonesians took over Irian, they retained Agats as the principal administrative center of the region.

Trade outpost

Just in and to one side of the old dock is "downtown" Agats, a stretch of a couple dozen small stores and shops selling clothing, canned or packaged food, tobacco, cheap household items and basic hardware. The proprietors of these businesses are almost all Bugis from South Sulawesi, with a few Torajans and one ethnic Chinese family.

The stores line both sides of the boardwalk near the dock, and a few spill over into the town's main walkway. The wares are all very expensive, as they are freighted in from Surabaya, sometimes via Merauke. No other place in Asmat holds nearly so many stores.

Agats also has a daily green market, **Pasar Bhakti,** held in a small building in

front of the Asmat Inn. Its activities start at 5 a.m., and an hour later, it's deserted. Not much appears here—some green bananas, a few papayas, taro, manioc and manioc leaves, used as a vegetable, called *singkong.*

The Bugis also own a fleet of some 15 seagoing fishing boats which specialize in catching sharks, for their fins. The dried fins are exported to Singapore, Hong Kong and Taiwan to end up in shark's-fin soup. These boats, which stay out at sea for up to a month at a time, motor out of Agats most of the year.

During the local season of high waves, November / December through March / April, the vessels shift their operation to the seas around Merauke. Walking around the dock area where the Bugis live, you will see large nylon nets piled up, some being repaired by the fishermen enjoying a few days ashore.

Agats also serves as the area communications center. Merpati flights to Merauke, Wamena and Jayapura land in Ewer, a small village just a few minutes by motor launch from Agats. Important visitors come by chartered helicopter, landing on the wooden helipad in front of the *camat's* office in Agats. Mixed freighters stop in Agats to pick up passengers on their Merauke–Sorong runs, and other smaller craft plying the coast of the Merauke district do the same. In 1991, the Pelni passenger ship *Tatamailau* began regular—but only monthly—service between Agats and western Indonesia.

The Roman Catholic church, which pioneered the proselytization of the Asmat, continues to maintain its headquarters in Agats, largely run by American Crosiers today, under Bishop Alphonse A. Sowada. The

Opposite: *At high tide in Agats, the mudflats between the boardwalks become waterways.*
Above, left: *Decorated skulls in the Asmat museum. Those with mandibles intact are ancestor skulls.* **Above, right:** *Black-capped lories at the teachers' quarters at Pusat Asmat.*

church looks after the worldly needs of the Asmat as well as the spiritual ones. Thanks to its efforts, while there are many schools now in the Asmat region, but the area's best education is still to be found in Agats.

The Asmat Museum

It is perhaps in the field of cultural preservation that the Crosier Fathers and Brothers deserve the most credit. It would be difficult to find a more liberal and intelligent group of clerics anywhere. The missionaries have actively encouraged the retention of most of the essential elements of Asmat culture (with the notable exception of head-hunting and cannibalism), even in the face of governmental pressure.

While this is not immediately evident on the surface of things—the Asmat now wear clothes and rituals are not a daily occurrence—it is obvious in the preservation of fine woodcarving. Literally tons of junk art is produced, bought up for pennies a piece by Bugis and Chinese middlemen, and shipped off to western Indonesia for sale to tourists. This is not simple exploitation. The price most visitors will pay, and the unwieldy scale of traditional Asmat carvings, conspire against fine craftsmanship and art.

But beneath this torrent of mass-produced junk, Asmat woodcarving survives, in a large degree thanks to the church. The Crosiers occasionally commission pieces, made in the context of feasting and ritual. The finest of these art pieces are on permanent display across the boardwalk from the mission headquarters in Agats.

The Asmat Museum of Culture and Progress is a "must" for all visitors. The museum was inaugurated in 1973 by Bishop Sowada, partly with money from the Michael Rockefeller Fund. On display is an excellent selection of different objects from various regions. Shields and large monumental carvings, mask costumes, small items like bowls and bamboo horns, and even decorated ancestor and trophy heads are represented. The catalog, which explains the provenance and context of each piece, is excellent, having been written and illustrated by Tobias Schneebaum.

The Asmat Center

The Pusat Asmat, still under construction in 1991, is a large educational and cultural center just north of town. Follow the boards out and you will encounter a large open hall with two long wings housing the region's only high school. Financed by the Asmat Foundation out of Jakarta, there are teachers quarters, classrooms, dormitories, and main hall for carving and cultural training and demonstrations.

Plans for the rest of the complex look like something meant for Bali or Waikiki Beach. There is a bar, a sports center and even a swimming pool. This part of the center is being funded by the deep pockets of Freeport Indonesia, and so far some U.S. $700,000—a veritable fortune in these parts—has been slated for the construction.

The appropriateness of all this has been questioned by locals. The lavish use of red wood (which has become very scarce here) in building has been questioned, as has the durability of the swamp cedar posts supporting the building. These materials have never been used to construct such a large edifice, and under the best of circumstances, the insect and rot resistant cedar posts last only 10 years. The style and scale of the building makes replacing these an almost impossible job. Anyway, only time will tell. If the center comes about as planned, Agats will quickly become a very different town from today's small and easygoing village.

A trip down the coast

Other than to see the museum and to stock up on supplies, there is really no reason to spend much time in Agats. If you have time to spare, take the boardwalk to Sjuruh (Seeyoo-roo) village, less than 15 minutes walk, past the Cathedral of the Sacred Heart. The raised plank walkway, which along several stretches here is always in need of repair, spans a creek and crosses part of Sjuru village, ending at the water.

There's a *jeu* set back towards the Aswet River, next to the church, but getting there requires a long balancing act over logs and planks. Canoes lie in the tidal creek close to the walkway, as well as in the river. Sjuru is a good place to organize a trip up the coast, to the nearby Bisjmam villages of Jepem, Per Owus and Beriten.

If you go there early enough, you might be able to arrange a trip for the same day. But it is more likely that you can set things up for the following day. Ask for Demianus, if he's around. But if not, you could certainly find other willing paddlers.

Demianus and a crew of four more pad

Opposite: *A shark fishing boat at Agats. The fins are dried and sold to the Chinese market.*

lers picked us up at the old Agats dock early
ne afternoon. We would have left earlier, but
e had to make our ritual pilgrimage to Ewer,
here Merpati pulled its fourth consecutive
o-show in a row.

The canoe was a long one, with its side
rved inward high above the water line. A
ng plank had been laid down for the three
f us—long enough to stretch out if we
ished. The prow was carved, as well as
rts of the inner gunwales: on each side, for-
ard, a man was strangling a snake; aft, two
en were trying to chin-up over the canoe's
dge. These little men watched over us.

The men worked standing, Asmat-fash-
ned, with four-meter oars. Two men for-
ard, three aft, dipping their paddles in uni-
n with barely a splash, scraping lightly
gainst the hull, then lifting them out togeth-
r for a second's rest. A steady, powerful
rhythm sped us along the Aswetsj River, then
ong the coast to the south. After our earlier
ip spent listening to the constant buzz of the
0HP outboard, this silence, interrupted only
y the paddling, was like magic.

Occasionally one of the men broke out in
ong, a few chanted phrases followed by a
rong, sustained note with just a hint of
emolo. These songs, Demianus said, told of
omen mourning men who had died in bat-
e, of slain fathers and brothers, and of the
ve of a handsome warrior for a beautiful
aiden. Flights of birds crossed overhead

and small waves rocked us gently as we skirt-
ed the coast, meeting an occasional canoe out
for an afternoon's fishing or heading to the
"big city" of Agats. In a couple of hours we
turned into a creek and landed at the village
of Jepem.

Jepem village

Just as we balanced our way out of the canoe
and over a long log, one of our party recognized a handsome elderly man, an excellent
carver whom she had met the previous year.
Unfortunately, he had not received the photos
she had sent to him six months ago, but he
was still obviously happy to see her—and
held her hand for all of the hour or so we
spent at Jepem.

After a stroll through the village, escorted
by every child between the ages of three and
ten, we returned to the creek-side *jeu* where
our canoe was tied up. The long men's house
was raised on a series of low piles, these
carved with some very nice figures.
Unfortunately, the small carvings we had
been offered here were not very good.

The people of Jepem were all pleasant and
smiling, willing to answer questions. The men
did a lot of carving here, and at the time we
visited were planning a *bisj* festival. Many
men would work on this carving and it would
require three months' preparation, culminating in feasting (including lots of sago grubs),
drumming, singing and dancing.

VISITING THE ASMAT

Through the Asmat Lands by Canoe

The atmosphere in the new *jeu* or bachelor's house was charged. Scraps of late afternoon light filtering in revealed a tight circle of seated men beating away on old drums, polished smooth by years of use. Plaintive songs filled the air, starting slowly, building in tempo, and then ending in a frenzy of drumming. When the pace picked up, men stood, and danced the knee-fluttering Asmat Charleston.

Only men were present, some with feather head-dresses, large, curved shells through pierced septum, woven armbands some of which held bone daggers. Except for the tattered shorts, the scene could have come out of the time when the Asmat were dreaded head-hunters. Our luck at stumbling onto this festival had been extraordinary.

Into the swamps

We organized our trip through the Central Asmat region in Agats. We hired Amhier Oedhien, who owns a bright blue, 10-meter dugout with a 40HP outboard, to take us around. The pilot of the craft was Herman Jisik. We couldn't have asked for a better team. Both Amhier, a Bugis migrant to Agats, and Herman, an Asmat from Biwar-Laut, were good humored and very capable.

Time and budget constraints put a limit on our trip—two days. Amhier charges $135 a day, very steep for Indonesia. His fee is justified, however, by the shockingly high price of fuel and equipment. Kerosene here costs three times what it does in Jayapura, and a simple outboard costs almost three times what it would in the United States.

We were three passengers: myself, my friend and editor David, and Linda, a Boston-based art collector and dealer. There was also another, unwelcome, guest. Deddy Junedy, a young, Uzi-wielding policeman from Agats. "Some of the Asmat do not yet understand government regulations," was his tersely delivered argument for accompanying us. To our relief, he turned out to be more or less well-behaved. (See "South Coast Practicalities" page 182, for more on this practice.)

As we buzzed upriver at about 12 kilometers an hour, the shoreline vegetation underwent several changes. The species of tree changed, as the water became less brackish. Small birds performed acrobatic acts for us and occasional flocks of noisy lories crossed overhead. Except for a very few huts on stilts, a timber-loading dock, and an odd canoe there were no signs of human life in the vast expanse of river and swamp.

Warse: craftsmen

In less than an hour, we reached the Jet River and turned south. We passed crocodile traps attached to floats (there are few of the animals left in the area) and several canoes. A hour and a half from Agats, where the Jet reaches the Powet River, we reached Warse (pop. 788). Clusters of stilt-perched huts followed the riverbank and extended a short distance inland. These were flanked by two *jeu* one upriver and one downriver. Children and adults waved as we bumped into the mud bank and scrambled ashore.

We set out to have a look at the village balancing over logs which, above the mud connected the houses to a drier inland path. Linda disappeared in a crowd of eager sellers as soon as word was out that she was buying. David and I climbed into one of the long *jeu* which was nearly deserted. We watched a man making bird hunting arrows, straightening the long thin shafts by warming them in fire. He then set the barbed tip to the shaft by smearing one end with a ball of resin.

While we watched our man working, others came to the house with bone knives for sale. These were made of cassowary femur a large bone almost the size of a human femur. The knob was covered with a knitted cap, and decorated by strands of grey Job tears seeds, and the grey, hair-like feathers the cassowary. The bone on some of these had a fine patina, and some were etched. One of the knives, brown and coarse, was made from the jawbone of a crocodile.

When we emerged from the hut, Linda was still surrounded by eager sellers, so we took our boat a short way downstream to the other bachelors' hut. Here the men showed us some really awful carvings, which we rejected politely, and one quite nice stylized ancestor figure, which we bought immediately

Opposite: *Late afternoon high tide at Biwar Laut. At low tide this river disappears.*

ly. There were also some spears for sale. Using a wooden mallet and chisel, a man was sculpting the projecting prowhead of a new canoe. Several almost complete canoes were lying around, awaiting finishing touches.

Out of nowhere, an Asmat man in a safari suit demanded peremptorily to see our travel permits. Until this unpleasant chap came around (nobody else seemed to like him much, either) everyone had been friendly, all smiles and cooperation for our photos, and happy to smoke a cigarette and tell us about their village. Not interested in being pushed around by this petty officer, I told him in Indonesian to go take his grievance up with our Uzi-packing policeman. He disappeared as quickly as he had made his entrance.

Amborep: modern town

When Linda finished her purchases we continued on the Powet River to where it met the Siretsj, at Amborep (pop. 738). This place had a much more "modern" look than Warse, with better walkways, several outhouses and not a *jeu* in sight.

The people of this village, involved for two decades in lumbering activities, moved their village to its present site in 1973. A year after settling in, Amborep held a *bisj* festival, the first one allowed by the government after it rescinded its ban on large feasts and ceremonies. But we saw little evidence of traditional life at Amborep and the crafted items

the men showed us were not appealing. We pushed off, crossed the Siretsj and took a small river south, to the wide Betsj River. A large village stood around the first bend.

Atsj: woodcarving center

The village of Atsj ("atch") is the largest in the Asmat region, with more than 2,000 people. (Note: Indonesianization of the spelling has led to "Atsy," which has in turn prompted an Indonesian pronunciation, "at-see.")

Atsj is a lumber center with a small sawmill and numerous tin-roofed houses. The boardwalks here are in better repair than those in Agats. The many Bugis and Javanese living here give it a non-Asmat look. We had coffee, cookies and an instant-noodle lunch at the home of the local policeman, an affable man who keeps crocodiles in his back yard. We then walked over to watch the woodcarvers, as Atsj is a well-known carving center.

The items produced here are of a new style, that began with the introduction of pit-saws and hardwood planks. Called *ajour,* these are openwork sculptures taken from a single board of *Intsia* wood. This style has evolved, and several men were working on small ancestor poles, miniature *bisj* of hard-wood. All the hardwood figures are for the tourist market. These figures are occasionally sold to passing tourists for $25 or more, but the bulk of the production goes to Bugis merchants, who pay some $10–$12 per piece.

Each takes about 18–20 hours to carve, but it is not hard work. Although we have seen nice modern hardwood carvings in the museum, none of those we saw here was very good.

We were rather disappointed with the place. Then a distinguished looking man came up and introduced himself as Ari Markus, the chief of Biwar Laut village. He needed a ride back home, and thought we might like to witness a *jeu pokmbu*, the festival to dedicate a new *jeu*. Of course, we accepted his offer immediately. In less than an hour we were pulling up to Biwar Laut. As soon as the engine shut down, we know we had made the right move.

Biwar Laut: the new jeu

We could hear drumming and singing coming out of the *jeu*, perched on a forest of stilts, 10 meters back from the bank of the small Jiwe river. The new *jeu* was decorated with a fringe of leaf strips from the top of the front porch area running the length of the building. Canoe paddles, each covered with a sheath of white cockatoo feathers, projected from the roof, giving it a festive appearance. We walked up a plank to the narrow front porch.

We could hear the drumming and singing from the river, but entering one of the doorways, we were immediately struck by the scene. A couple of the men glanced up at us, but everyone went about the ritual without paying attention to the three white persons who had just entered. I asked Ari Markus, who had followed us into the *jeu*, if photography was allowed, and he said I was welcome to take as many as I liked.

I went about my work with glee. David's flash self-destructed after one pop, so I even had a willing assistant. No one minded as I stepped around seated men and wormed my way to good shooting angles. Some shifted to let me through, others turned slightly so I could have a better shot. After I worked my way through a couple of rolls, I could no longer contain my joy. As a song ended with its fast drum rhythm, I too danced the wiggly-kneed Asmat Charleston, to roars of approving laughter. At dusk, the singing ended, and the men went home for supper.

Markus invited us to spend the night in the *jeu* and disappeared into the night. We settled on the front porch and ate some noodles and sardines with Amhier, washed down with coffee. As we commented on the day's events, men came out of the darkness, entered the *jeu*, then shyly approached us from nearby doorways to offer seed neck-

laces, knives and a few drums for sale. As Linda was doing the buying, she became the focus of attention, leaving us to chat with our hosts. One man was particularly talkative. This was Mohammed, an Asmat from Biwar Laut who had converted to Islam during a long stay in Ternate. Feeling like a bit of an outsider himself, perhaps he needed to talk to the outsiders.

The drumming and singing resumed after dinner, this time around a fire in front of the *jeu*. Just a few diehards kept up the tradition of all night drumming (and this was the second day of the festival). Eventually we retired to the *jeu*, listened to BBC and drifted off to sleep on the springy bark and branch floor. When we awoke around 5 a.m., the drumming was much louder, and a quick glance outside revealed a full complement of men and boys in the faint pre-dawn light. Soon after, the playing stopped. The inauguration of the *jeu* had been completed.

A muddy morning

When we walked over to the river, we were shocked. The wide stream we had come in on, was reduced to a trough of mud, with barely a trickle down the middle. As we drank our morning coffee, Ari Markus came by, and I asked him if we could hire ten of his men to paddle one of the large canoes for photographs. We bargained a bit and settled on $3 per man for a quick run.

In an hour or two, as a thin stream was forming between the mudbanks, women set out for a morning's fishing in Siretsj River. A little later, as the water rose a bit more, two elderly women worked their way upstream, a large net between them, hung from an oval wooden frame. An occasional small fish, coming inland to forage with the tide, ended up in their woven bag.

Soon the men appeared and began preparations for the paddling session. For the sake of re-creating the atmosphere of a head-hunting war party, I had them cover their shorts with grass skirts. (Some of these, ironically, were of the type worn by women.)

In the good old days, men set forth for battle stark naked, but resplendent in personal adornments—clam-shell nose ornaments, dogs' teeth necklaces, cuscus hats, mother-of-pearl forehead pieces. With all their accoutrements in place, the men began to paint each other with lime (from burned clamshells) and orange powder (from ocherous mud). The men were ready to set forth into battle.

The river had risen, and each man grabbed his long oar and stepped into the canoe. They paddled downstream, and after briefly terrorizing a few boys who were swimming there, turned around and swept back, dashing by the village, presenting a magnificent spectacle of color and power.

Otsjanep, Owus and home

We left Biwar Laut amidst shouting and farewell waves for our second and last day of village-hopping. Everything that second day was anti-climatic. And damn uncomfortable. As soon as we emerged from the Jiwe River and started crossing the wide mouth of the Siretsj, salt spray started pouring aboard, wetting everything, including our clothes and bodies. An hour and a half later, cold and miserable, we turned into the small Ewta River. A few minutes later we reached Otsjanep.

Trees were cut down, and grassy fields planted here. The neat houses have tin roofs. There is a new church under construction. Overall, the town has a clean, modern appearance. But the open fields, in the mid afternoon, make it blazingly hot. Otsjanep is a regular stop on the tourist circuit, and song-and-dance performances here run $160 a pop. We were rather disappointed, as we had thought that there must be a reason that so many visitors come here. There doesn't seem to be.

(Note: Just about everyone who comes to Otsjanep makes some half-witted comment

about Michael Rockefeller, and nobody here finds this particularly clever. Please refrain.)

As we pulled out to sea from the Ewta River, we wished for Ostjanep's burning sun as we shivered under a constant stream of spray. Ours was not a sea-going craft, and after two hours crossing the wide mouth of the Betsj, and then the Siretsj, we were cranky and soaked with the sticky seawater.

The short ride up the narrow river to Owus was a dry, pleasant god-send. The setting here is pleasant enough, with stilt-perched huts along the banks of the Bow River. But the town is very tourist-oriented, and seems to be almost owned by one travel agency. We were not even allowed to pull up to the company's dock, and had to scramble ashore over the mud. We were shown a guesthouse, erected especially for tour groups, boasting of twin-attached toilets over the waters. Exclusive or not, we inaugurated the toilets and sped away.

At this time, the seas had calmed, and we had a pleasant ride home in the late afternoon sun, catching one of Flamingo Bay's famous sunsets just as we pulled into Agats.

Opposite: *A man braids armbands on the porch of the brand new jeu at Biwar Laut.* **Above, left:** *The Ewta River, near Otsjanep, is almost completely overgrown.* **Above, right:** *Ten men, paddling in unison, can make a light Asmat dugout fairly leap across the water. Biwar Laut.*

Agats
Practicalities

(includes Merauke)

The Merpati flight lands in Ewer, 15–20 minutes from Agats by motorized dugout. Boats wait on the river to whisk you to Agats. There is no official price, so find out the fare before you get in. (Should be $3–$6.) If there is more than one boat, bargain. The losmen may have a boat there to meet incoming planes. If you are going to stay there, try to get a free ride. Be prepared: depending on the tide, your luggage and yourself could get soaked with salt spray.

AIR TRANSPORT

Merpati. Merpati has a radio and a desk in Ewer, next to the grass strip (reinforced with interlocked steel strips). Scheduled flights:

Wamena	M,F	$36
Jayapura	M,F (via Wamena)	$70
Merauke	Tu,Th	$48

The Merauke flights are crowded, but mostly on schedule. The flights to Wamena and Jayapura are not particularly crowded, but the scheduled Friday flight seems to be strictly mythological. During our visit, so was, in fact, the Monday flight. You can (we were) easily be stuck in Agats for two weeks. Due to lack of radio contact, you have to motor to Ewer each morning to find out if the plane is coming in or not. You hang around there for 3–4 hours, and find out that the plane still needs repairs, the weather over the highlands is bad, or the pilots are on vacation. Then you return to Agats to try the next day. It does not help to strangle the Merpati agent in Ewer.

SEA TRANSPORT

Pelni. Pelayaran Nasional Indonesia's new, big ship *Tatamailau* calls at Agats once a month on the following run: Surabaya–Ujung Pandang–Maumere–Dili–Merauke–Agats–Tual–Fakfak–Bandaneira–Ambon–Ternate–Bitung, and returns by the same route. It's about a week to Bitung or Surabaya from Agats. Check at the Pelni office in Jayapura [Jl. Halmahera 1, ✆ (967) 21270, Fax: 21370] for dates the *Tatamailau* calls at Agats.

Coasters. Two local mixed freighters out of Merauke call at various places along the coast and rivers on the following routes:
1) Merauke–Kimam–Bade–Agats–Sawa Erma and back the same way.
2) Merauke–Kiam–Bayun–Atsj–Asgon–Senggo and back.

Each of these ships makes the run, on the average, once a month. Two other ships, making coastal stops between Merauke and Sorong, also call at Agats every few weeks. While conditions are excellent on the *Tatamilau*, on these ships they are what most people would call deplorable.

ACCOMMODATIONS

There are two *losmen* in Agats.
Losmen Asmat Inn. 11 rooms. Fairly clean, but the rooms are seldom made up and no towels are provided. Bathrooms are attached. Lots of junky Asmat "art" for sale. Price includes breakfast, and meals can be ordered. $12/person for the better rooms; $8.50/person for the more basic rooms.
Pada' Elo. 8 rooms. Pool table, excellent breakfast (including noodles, vegetables, egg, tea or coffee), but pretty crude out-of-room toilet/bath facilities. $8.50/person.

DINING

Buetkawer. Next to the dock. Simple meals rice or noodles, vegetables, and if available fish. Can get beer cold for you at night with sufficient notice at $1.60 per can. (They need an hour to get the beer chilled at a nearby fish cooler.)
Dahlia. Just off the main walkway opposite the helipad. Good chicken soup $1.10. Fried chicken (about half of a tough bird), vegetables and rice $4. Fried manioc and fried bananas sometimes available.

Note: Neither restaurant has a sign outside so follow map and ask.

SURAT JALAN

Like most parts of Irian, you have to show your *surat jalan* and passport to the police here. By itself, this is fine, except the police here have the irritating habit of accompanying you in your boat when you leave Agats. They will insist that this is strictly for your own safety, which, of course, is nonsense.

Southern Irian Jaya is probably the least desireable station in all of Indonesia, so the military and police here are either very young, very poorly connected, or incompetent. Sometimes all three. And they seem to have an overwhelming fear of the Asmat.

When a 20-year-old Javanese kid with a string around his head, sitting in his office surrounded by Rambo posters and holding a sub machine gun tells you he is going to accompany you on your trip to visit the Asmat, you can be forgiven for your rising anger. But keep it in check, as it will only make things worse. You cannot avoid the escort.

These trips are really the only way for the police to get out of Agats; it is a little junket for them. Best to try to work out a modus operandi, as diplomatically as possible. If you set on of these bundles of machismo off, you really are going to ruin your trip. Firstly, do not pay for his "services." You may be asked for some money for this man. Tell the guide you have

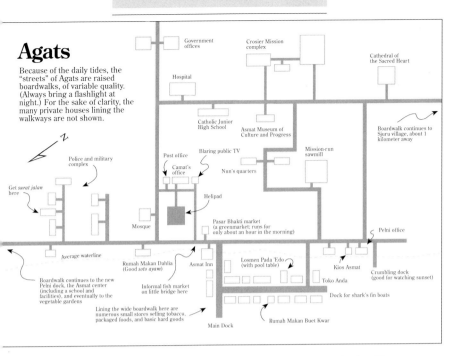

Agats

Because of the daily tides, the "streets" of Agats are raised boardwalks, of variable quality. (Always bring a flashlight at night.) For the sake of clarity, the many private houses lining the walkways are not shown.

Government offices

Crosier Mission complex

Cathedral of the Sacred Heart

Hospital

Catholic Junior High School

Asmat Museum of Culture and Progress

Boardwalk continues to Sjuru village, about 1 kilometre away

Post office

Blaring public TV

Mission-run sawmill

Police and military complex

Camat's office

Nun's quarters

Get *surat jalan* here

Helipad

Mosque

Pasar Bhakti market (a greenmarket; runs for only about an hour in the morning)

Pelni office

Average waterline

Rumah Makan Dahlia (Good *soto ayam*)

Asmat Inn

Losmen Pada 'Edo (with pool table)

Kios Asmat

Crumbling dock (good for watching sunset)

Toko Anda

Boardwalk continues to the new Pelni dock, the Asmat center (including a school and facilities), and eventually to the vegetable gardens

Informal fish market on little bridge here

Dock for shark's fin boats

Lining the wide boardwalk here are numerous small stores selling tobacco, packaged foods, and basic hard goods

Main Dock

Rumah Makan Buet Kwar

---

red that the police officer can eat from your provisions, but he gets no money.

It really helps to speak Indonesian in these circumstances. When you get to a village, the police officer will sometimes try to "take charge," jumping off the boat with his gun handy and barking orders at the people who, out of curiosity, have come up to meet you. Do not let him do this. It is your trip, you have paid for the boat, and you do not want him bullying people and spoiling it. Be very firm about this.

The police escort is just a fact, and not worth ruining your trip over. There may even be some circumstances where it comes in handy. Local officials in some villages have been running little woodcarving rackets, and the presence of tourists threatens to push up prices or reveal to the carvers just how much they are being exploited. These folks will often say things like "tourists aren't allowed here." The presence of your own private police officer will shut this kind of thing right down.

CARVINGS AND SOUVENIRS

Toko Anda. Near the old disused dock. Run by Pak Mansur, who bargains, wheels and deals, but still keeps his prices low. A very mixed bag of carvings, some quite nice, expecially his shields. Ask to also see the items in the back of his house.

Kios Asmat. Next to the Pelni office. A much more orderly place, with a large room full of average quality commercial art.

The Asmat Inn. The lobby here has lots of art, ranging in quality from truly awful to barely acceptable.

Buying carvings in the villages

You will probably see some carving being done at most villages you visit. Forget about finding fine old Asmat pieces—too many dealers have been through, offering top dollar. Stick to souvenir class carvings, and remember you have to lug things home, so length and weight matter. Small sculptures are cheap, $3–$20 for most items, and there is usually no reason to bargain.

By buying in the village, you cut out the middlemen and more money goes into the carver's own pockets. Certain regions produce distinct items and styles. The Sawa–Erma area specializes in stylized, scaled-down shields with geometric patterns, in hardwood. Astj produces *ajour*, flat openwork carvings in hardwood, and small and medium-sized figures in hardwood. Per and Beriten make fairly well-finished figure sculptures in softwood.

Some fairly decent full-scale shields are still being made in the Brazza area, but obtaining these at the source requires an extensive trip. Boatloads occasionally arrive in Agats, and you might be fortunate enough to be there when this takes place. With no middleman involved, you can pick one of these up for $20.

Some of the more interesting small items sold in the villages are cassowary bone knives, small feathered bags, woven armbands, and necklaces of seeds. The only thing to be cautious of with these is that customs officials in the United States and Europe tend to be very suspicious of animal products in general, and it might not be legal to bring them in. Especially if the item prominently displays feathers, you may have problems. Find out the relevant customs restrictions.

Money Exchange

There is no bank in Agats. Change plenty of money into Rupiah before you come. It is also handy to have smaller denomination bills in the villages, when buying craft items.

Electricity

From 5:30 pm to 11:30 pm. You will know because the public TV will be blaring.

BOAT RENTAL

Motorized dugouts. This is the key to travel in the region. If you have relatively little time and want to get around, the only way to do this is hire a long dugout powered by a 40HP outboard. This is expensive—about $125–$150 a day, but since at least 10 people can fit in it, if your group is large it is not too much on a per person basis.

The high daily costs are justified by the freight costs to Agats which brings the cost of a 40HP outboard in at around $3,000 (the boat itself costs some $1,200), and actual cost of fuel runs $14 per hour. Add to that the wage of the boat driver, maintenance of the engine and boat, and the price seems far from outrageous. Worse still, sometimes there is no fuel available so you can't motor anywhere.

There are two or three boats available for charter out of Agats, all costing about the same amount. We were quite satisfied with the services of Amhier Oedhien, who often meets incoming planes at Ewer and can be contacted through the Asmat Inn. He took good care of us, and cooked up our meals at no extra charge. You can also try at the Pada 'Elo, whose owner, Pak Nurdin, seemed quite willing to bargain.

Some travel times from Agats: Beriten, 1.5 hrs, Jamas-Jeni, 2 hrs; Ayam, 2.5 hrs; Sawa-Erma, 3 hrs; Atsj, 3.5 hrs; Omadesep, 5 hrs; Otsjanep, 6 hrs.

A motorized boat is the only realistic way to go to the Brazza River area from Agats. Count on a week or so. One day to Jinak, second day to Senggo, third day to Tami. From here, you walk. Outside of the main towns, the people living in this area are shy of outsiders, and you may spend your whole trip without meeting anyone. Pick up an interpreter in Jinak or Senggo.

From the end of November to sometime in March, the season of the waves (*musim ombak*), sea-going canoe trips can be very dangerous. Sometimes you can reroute inland, but this can add time, depending on where it is that you plan to go.

Paddled canoes. An alternative to motorized travel is to hire a smaller boat and five or so paddlers at Sjuru village, a short gangplank walk from Agats. This is much cheaper: $3 a day per paddler, $3 for the boat, which can fit 2 to 4 passengers. It is also more pleasant, with the sounds of the jungle broken only by the songs of the paddlers.

But you cannot travel as far as quickly this way—it takes a full day to cover the distance spanned by outboard canoe in a couple of hours. To Ayam, it's a day, same for the Jamas-Jeni area. About two days to Atsj or to Sawa Erma. Depending on seas and tides, it could be four days to Otsjanep.

For a good boatman who can get a team of paddlers together, try to locate Demianus in Sjuruh village. On overnight trips, he will cook for you as well.

Tides. Whether by motor or paddle power you have to go with the tides. Many villages are accessible only at high tide. At low tide, you have to make your way up deep mud banks to reach the villages on the larger rivers, although felled logs are often strategically placed to save muddy feet. Tides of over 5 meters are usual in June and late December, and even the normal twice daily tides often exceed 4 meters. You have to go far upriver before the tide no longer affects the river height.

Provisions. On any journey, you can obtain sago to eat in the villages, but we suggest buying all your provisions in Agats before setting out. Bottled water is very expensive in Agats (Rp1000 for a small bottle, the only size available) and you can either drop a lot of money for a case of the stuff, or buy fresh coconuts (very inexpensive) along the way. We did the latter and were never thirsy. Take some Minyak Gosok, a locally sold insect repellant of citronella and eucalyptus extracts. Aside from its bug-repellant properties, the oily liquid (55¢ for a small bottle, 80¢ for a larger one) serves as a perfume, and at least according to the label treats fungus, intestinal problems, hemorrhoids, burns, and even knife wounds.

Some essential items are simply unavailable in Agats. Buy all the film you will need before you arrive or in Jayapura, as well as sun tan lotion and insect repellant. Batteries and any other items of a similar nature should also be bought beforehand.

TOURIST EVENTS

Many villages will put on "traditional" events for tourists, such as racing by in canoes, and drumming, singing and dancing. These performances cost $30–$200 depending the number of participants and the length of the event. These are not too difficult to organize. Some tour groups even go through adoption "rituals."

WEATHER

It rains a lot, for a total of some five meters a year. Sources conflict as to which is the driest season—some say May–June, others January–March, still others August—so be prepared for rain no matter when you come.

Also be prepared for occasional weeks without rain, which puts great stress on the water supplies in Agats. This means no laundry, and a steadily shrinking *mandi* bath reservoir.

Travel in canoes is impossible along the coast during the season of the waves, which could start as early as October and continue as late as March. Late December, January and February bring the worst waves, and forget about visiting any of the coastal villages at this time. Temperatures year-round range from 21°C to 31°C.

Merauke

The airport at Merauke is about 3 km from town, and the trip costs $3 by chartered minibus (or 15¢ by public transportation.)

ACCOMMODATIONS

There are 5 hotels/losmen in this town of 43,000 people, with a total of 54 rooms.
Nirmala. Jl. Raya Mandala. Generally considered the best in town. $16/person.
Megaria. Jl. Raya Mandala. $15/person.
Flora. Jl. Bambu Pemak. $11–$14/person.
Asmat. Jl. Trikora. Dutch built, with some character, but not much service. $8–$14/person.
Merauke. Jl. Bambu Pemali. $6/person.

DINING

Mostly Indonesian food, a bit on the expensive side. Venison is usually available. (Rusa deer were stocked in the savannahs just outside of Merauke in the early 20th century.) Figure on about $3–$5 a person at the following places.
Nusantara. Jl. Raya Mandala.
Cafeteria Mandala. Jl. Raya Mandala. Chinese dishes.
Toba. Jl. Taman Makan Pahlawan.
Kawanua. Jl. Biak.

There are also two Padang style restaurants in town, both on Jl. Raya Mandala.

DISCO

Open daily 10pm to 2am, Saturday night until dawn. Cover charge $3 for men, $3 for a small can of beer, $11 for a woman to sit at your table.

AREA TRANSPORTATION

Merpati. Jl. Raya Mandala, Merauke 163. © (971) 21242. Scheduled flights:

Bade	Tu,Th	$33
Ewer	Tu,Th	$48
Jayapura	Tu,Th,Su	$85
Kepi	Tu	$33
Kimaam	W	$34
Mindiptanah	W	$45
Okaba	Th	$16
Senggo	W	$50
Tanahmerah	F	$43

Also: Aboge ($59), Kamur ($59)

An Asmat vocabulary

Hello	Dormum
Goodbye	Dormum
Yes	Awangbis
No	Opak
What is your name?	Or uncum jeusam?
My name is…	Dorjous…
Where are you from?	Ocayo yipicam?
I am from…	Dorsuru pisipit…
Which way to…?	Dorsuru bayofa…?
I am going to…	Dorsuru bandi…
To Ewer	Do Ewer
To Agats	Do Agasta
How much?	Ucumaram?
Men's hous	Jeu
Ancestor pole	Bisj
Soulship	Wuramon
War shield	Jamasj
Figure carving	Kawe
Drum	Em
Bowl	Jifai
Bamboo pipe	bus
Men's bag	Ese
Ancestor skull	Ndambirkus
Trophy skull	Ndaokus
Bone dagger	Pisuwe
Canoe	Tsji ("tchee")
Prowhead	Tsji tsjemen
Paddle	Po
Spear	Otsjen
Stone club	Onok pak si
Stone axe	Si
Shell nosepiece	Bipane
Sago	Ambas
Sago grubs	Tou
Sago pounder	Amosus
Cassowary	Pi
Cassowary bone	Pi emak
Crocodile	Eu
Snake	Amer
Lizard	Utsj
Turtle	Mbu
Frog	Woro
Cuscus	Fatsj
Hornbill bird	Fofojir
King cockatoo	Ufir

Travel Advisory

The good old days of facing spears and deadly diseases as you hack your way through the New Guinea jungle are over. You will not see a cannibal feast. There are a few small groups of people living in the Mamberamo basin and between the highlands and the south coast swamps that have not been contacted by outsiders, but you will not be the first to meet them.

None of this, however, means Irian is now Bali. It is a huge, beautiful, out-of-the way place unlike no other in the world. One-fifth of the world's languages are spoken here. The cultural differences between, say, the Dani in the highlands and the Asmat of the south coast are vast. The island's wildlife is among the most interesting on the planet, and perhaps the least well-described.

Much of Irian Jaya still remains impassable. The government's road-building program is ambitious, but so far the whole province—half of the second-largest island in the world—has about as many miles of road as a medium-sized Los Angeles sub-division. Travel here means flying in on relatively small airplanes, and walking from there.

Some of the regions are inaccessible for political reasons, and a lack of tourist infrastructure: the area around the Paniai Lakes and Enarotali, for example, or parts of the Bird's Head.

In this book, we have concentrated on the most interesting, and most accessible places. It is impossible to describe in detail (within a budget a publisher would accept) an area as large as Irian.

Everyone traveling to Irian Jaya should fly to Wamena and spend at least a few days in the Baliem Valley. The temperate climate, the stunning scenery, and the hospitality of the Dani are not to be missed. Right in Wamena, the administrative center of the valley, there are more traditional (non-Christian) villages than in the more outlying parts of the valley.

A more adventurous trip would be to visit the Asmat lands of the south coast, although flights in and out are unreliable, and it is nowhere near as inviting a place as the Baliem. If you think mud, salt, humidity and the lack of anything except basic services will dampen your enthusiasm, then they probably will. On the other hand, this may just whet your appetite to be one of the mere handful of people who visit this fascinating place each year.

TRAVEL IN IRIAN JAYA

International flights and most flights from within Indonesia land in Biak, which is the hub for flights around Irian. From Jayapura, Merpati flights spread out around the province. In the practicalities sections for each area of Irian, we have listed all the Merpati flights scheduled at press time. Check when you arrive, however, as these things change rapidly. (Note: See "Indonesia Travel Primer" following this section for more basics on flying and traveling in Indonesia.)

Garuda. Jl. Sudirman 3, Biak. ✆(961)21416 (ticket office); ✆21331 (District Manager); ✆21199 (Station Manager). Jl. Percetakan 2, Jayapura. ✆(967)21220.

Merpati. Jl. M. Yamin 1, opposite the airport. ✆(961)21213, 21386, 21416. Telex: 76186 MNA IA. Jl. A. Yani 15 Lantai I/21, next to the Hotel Matoa, Jayapura. ✆(967)21327, 21913, 21810, 21111.

Flying in the highlands. The fastest way to reach Wamena in the Baliem Valley is to fly into Biak, catch the next flight to Sentani, either get your *surat jalan* there or catch a ride into Jayapura to do so, overnight at one of the *losmen* in Sentani, and take the next morning's flight to Wamena.

Once in the highlands, you can catch a flight to any number of small highland's airstrips. At last count, there were a total of 246 airstrips in Irian Jaya. Merpati regularly schedules a number of flights, and the Missionary Aviation Fellowship (MAF) and the Associated Mission Aviation (AMA) have flights to the others. It is also possible—and even practical, if you are in a group—to charter one of the mission planes. See "Highlands Practicalities," page 154 for more details.

Travel by sea

Pelni, Indonesia's national shipping line, has several mixed passenger/cargo ships that run occasionally along Irian's north coast, and the new *Tatamailau* stops in Agats and Merauke in the south. Prices are very cheap, and this can be an interesting way to see the coastal villages and towns. Yotefa shipping, a cargo outfit, offers deck passage on its tramp coasters. For more information, see "Jayapura Practicalities," page 88. Ferries run in some areas (e.g. Sorong) and small boats can be chartered to explore the coastal areas. See the relevant sections for more information.

Pelni (P.T. Pelayaran Nasional Indonesia). Jl. Halmahera 1, Jayapura. ✆(967)21270, Fax 21370.

Yotefa shipping lines. Jl. Percetakan 90A Jayapura. ✆(967)31687, Telex: 76148 YAKJ.

Land transport

In the relatively few places in Irian with developed road systems—major cities, some of the smaller villages and parts of the Baliem Valley—the standard Indonesian form of mass transport, the "Colt" or minivan, plies the road. Along the regular route, these vehicles are quite cheap, but since their drivers usually wait for at least a half a load before departing, and often swing through populated areas to round up passengers, the eager tourist might find them a bit slow for his schedule.

These vehicles can almost always be chartered, however, and the best way to do this is have your hotelier round one up for you. There's no harm in bargaining a bit for rates, but expect to pay $5–$10 per hour. Irian is off the beaten path, and things like truck parts and fuel are expensive.

THE SURAT JALAN

To travel outside of Biak, Jayapura and Sorong, you need a document called a *surat jalan* (literally "travel letter"). This permit is a letter with information like your passport number, a pasted in photograph, and at the bottom, all the places to which your travel has been approved. The *surat jalan* is necessary, but easily obtained.

Technically, one can get the document at the main police office at Biak, Jayapura or Sorong. In fact, you are best off getting it in Jayapura. The Biak office seems to have little authority, and in 1991 were nervous even about giving permission to Wamena(!) Don't waste your time there. If Sorong is your point of entry to Irian, you of course need to get your document there. If you are going directly to Jayapura from Sorong, you may as well wait. The Jayapura city map on page 89 shows the location of the police station.)

It takes one to four passport-sized photos and half an hour to get the *surat jalan*. You hand over your photographs and passport, and sit for a little interview in which you tell them where you want to go. Don't be conservative about your travel plans. Remember, flights are unreliable in Irian, and you may be stuck somewhere and decide to set out in another direction. Try to get as many cities on the list as possible.

Be polite and use your head. Offer a coherent itinerary and talk about the scenery and the wildlife and other noncontroversial aspects of the region to which you want permission to go.

There are some areas for which you will not be able to get permission to visit. At the time of this writing, these were: the corridor along the border with Papua New Guinea, the Mamberamo River basin, and the Paniai Lakes and adjacent highlands, including Puncak Jaya. The reasons for this are various, having to do with politics, lack of infrastructure, and—in the case of Puncak Jaya—proximity to the Freeport Indonesia copper mine.

[Note: One possible way around this is to sign on with a travel agency. Some of these are well-connected enough to get permits for, say, Puncak Jaya or the Paniai Lakes area. Write to some of the agents listed in "Highlands Practicalities" page 154 and see what they say.]

When you arrive at each stop on your trip, you need to show your passport and *surat jalan* to officers at the local police station. In most areas, your hotel/*losmen* will send someone to take care of this chore for you. If you meet with the police in person, just tell them where you will be going, and some idea of a schedule. If you disappear in their jurisdiction, it is their heads that are going to roll, so don't be impatient and rude. In most cases they just want to meet you and practice their English.

In most cases, the police will just check your papers and send you on your way. The Asmat area—which we visited fairly soon after it was opened to tourists—is a different case. Here an officer will want to accompany you on your trip. Although it is very disappointing to have a gun-toting policeman mediate your interaction with everyone you meet, there seems to be no simple way around this rule. We suggest you make it clear that (1) it is *your* trip, and you will define the schedule; (2) this is not a paid vacation for the police officer, and he can share your food but you will not be paying him any bribes disguised as a per diem fee.

Accommodations

Hotels in Irian range from one star-rated hotel in Jayapura (and at least one other planned for Biak) to very basic. Most are mid-range *losmen*. At this level, one can expect reasonably comfortable rooms, good service, and tea and coffee service.

Check the place before you settle in. Many of the cheaper digs have only squat toilets (no toilet paper) and ladle-type, "mandi" baths. This is usually adequate, but try to get a room with an attached bath, if possible. Whether or not AC is a priority depends on where you are. In the highlands, it is not usually necessary. On Biak, and the muggy coasts, it can be almost essential.

We suggest you bring your own towel and soap (although many places provide these for their guests) and a packet of mosquito coils. Mosquito nets are the best protection, but they're a hassle to put up in most hotel rooms. If you request, your room will usually be sprayed for insects. Be sure that this is done long before you are ready to sleep if you want to avoid the smell.

Where there are no commercial lodgings, you have to rely on local hospitality. In the *kecamatan* centers, either the police or the *camat* could help you find a place to sleep. In the villages, you should find the *kepala desa* (village chief), who will help. Sleeping in thatched Dani huts is actually quite comfortable in the chilly night of the highlands, and we slept like logs on the springy bark of the Asmat *jeu* floor.

When staying outside of *losmen*, keep in mind that you are a bother, because you will certainly not be treated like one. Insist on paying about $5–$6 a day for the privilege of sleeping and for the meals, to which you will no doubt be invited. Gifts such as sugar, salt, cigarets, instant noodles, batteries and clothing are always appreciated.

FOOD

The only place in Irian Jaya you will find western-style meals is in the better hotels and up-market restaurants in the larger cities. The cost is usually high, and ingredients like beef are imported frozen.

Indonesian food sits far better in the hot climate of the tropics. A typical meal consists of heaps of rice, perhaps garnished with vegetables, small fish, or shreds of chicken. Fish, at least the way westerners are used to it being served, is not that common, despite that the sea is never far away. (Jayapura, however, has some very fine and inexpensive grilled seafood stalls.)

The main cities in Irian offer a few basic types of restaurants: Padang style (named after the region in Sumatra where it originated) which consists of a plate of rice and numerous small dishes of spicy goodies, of which you pay for only those you eat; Chinese style food, soups, fried vegetables, steamed seafood; and basic stalls, with spicy fried rice or noodles, chicken soup, or some other staple. Indonesian food is often quite spicy; Chinese food is, on the other hand, usually quite mild.

Because the restauranteurs in Irian are from western Indonesia, the island's staples—sago, sweet potatoes, manioc—will not be found in restaurants. When traveling through the interior or along the coast, try to eat at least some of the local food, which—compared to western Indonesian cuisines—tends to be monotonous and bland. But you may find yourself really liking these after weeks of rice. (For example, thin pancakes of sago spread with peanut butter and jelly make a delicious breakfast.)

The beers available in Indonesia are Bintang and Anker, both brewed under Dutch supervision and rather hoppy and light (perhaps appropriate for the tropics). With electricity such a precious commodity, however, in many places the only way to quaff it cold is to pour the beer over ice.

WHAT TO BRING

Bring wash-and-wear, light cotton clothes. (Synthetic fabrics are really uncomfortable in the tropics.) A light rain jacket with a hood and a good sweater (it can get very cold at night in the highlands) are also essential. For cold nights in the highlands, you may even want to bring long underwear. Tennis shoes are fine for basic footwear, but for hiking you will need sturdy shoes. Bring a pair that is already broken in. Also, bring a cap to keep the sun off during long boat rides or walks.

You should also bring any film you need,

although stores in Jayapura offer a good selection, including Fuji B&W emulsions, and Fujichrome (but not Kodachrome). Also, personal care items like contact lens solutions, tampons, prescription drugs, even dental floss can be impossible to find in a place like Irian Jaya. Bring what you will need.

HEALTH

Indonesia is a tropical country, and with that comes certain health risks, particularly for temperate-accustomed visitors. Ideally, you should get a a thorough medical (and dental) checkup before leaving. Ask which inoculations your doctor recommends—tetanus, definitely, and the cholera vaccine, although it is painful and doesn't eliminate the risk, can help. A gamma globulin shot, effective for about six months against some strains of hepatitis, may also be worth getting. Get another medical checkup when you get back home, including blood and stool tests, to see if you picked up any microscopic tropical creatures.

Malaria

Malaria is a problem in parts of Irian Jaya. It is worse along the coasts, particularly where it is swampy. It is much less of a problem in the highlands (although, the oft-heard rule of thumb that malarial mosquitos do not live at altitudes higher than 500 meters is simply not correct. People have gotten malaria in Wamena, a 1500 meters). The disease accounts for some 18 percent of the province's total mortality, and is nothing to be irresponsible about.

Malaria is caused by a protozoan *Plasmodium*, which affects the blood and liver. The vector for this parasite is the *Anopheles* mosquito. After you contract malaria, it takes a minimum of six days—and up to several weeks—before symptoms appear.

If you are visiting Irian, you *must* take malaria pills. Do not think that pills offer complete protection, however, as they don't. If you are pregnant, have had a splenectomy or have a weak immune system, or suffer from chronic disease, you should weigh carefully whether the trip is worth the risk.

Chloroquine phosphate is the traditional malaria prophylactic, but in the past 10–15 years, the effectiveness of the drug has deteriorated. Deciding on an appropriate anti-malarial is now more complicated. There are actually two forms of malaria: *Plasmodium vivax*, which is unpleasant, but rarely fatal to healthy adults, and *P. falciparum,* which can be quickly fatal. *P. falciparum* is dominant in parts of Indonesia.

Malaria pills. As a prophylactic for travel, take two tablets of Chloroquine (both on the same day) once a week, and one tablet of Maloprim (pyrimethamine) once a week. Maloprim is a strong drug, and not everybody can tolerate it. If you are planning on taking Maloprim for more than two months, it is recommended that you ake a folic acid supplement, 6 mg a day, to guard against anemia. Note: The anti-malarial drugs only work once the protozoan has emerged from the liver, which can be weeks after your return. You should continue on the above regimen for one month after returning.

Another recent drug that has been shown effective against both forms of the parasite is Mefloquine (Larium), although unpleasant side effects have been demonstrated for it as well. Mefloquine is also very expensive, about $3 a tablet. However, it can be a lifesaver in cases of resistant *falciparum* infection.

These drugs are not available over-the-counter in most western countries (or, indeed, even behind the counter at most pharmacies), and if you visit a doctor, you may have trouble convincing him of what you need. Doctors in the temperate zones are not usually familiar with tropical diseases, and may even downplay the need to guard against them. Do not be persuaded. Try to find a doctor who has had experience in these matters.

You can also buy Chloroquine and Maloprim over-the-counter in Indonesia, for very little (a few dollars for a month's supply). Maloprim, however, may still be difficult to find. [Note: there is a non–chloroquine based drug sold in Indonesia called Fansidar. This drug is NOT effective against the resistant strains of *P. falciparum*.]

Treatment. Malaria in the early stages is very hard to distinguish from a common cold or flu.

A person infected may just suffer from headache and nausea, perhaps accompanied by a slight fever and achiness, for as long as a week until the disease takes hold. When it does, the classic symptoms begin:

1) Feeling of intense cold, sometimes accompanied by shaking. This stage lasts from 30 minutes to two hours.

2) High fever begins, and victim feels hot and dry, and may vomit or even become delirious. This lasts 4–5 hours.

3) Sweating stage begins, during which the victim perspires very heavily, and his body temperature begins to drop.

If you think you have malaria, you should call on professional medical help IMMEDIATELY. A good medical professional is your best first aid. Only if you cannot get help, initiate the following treatment:

• Take 4 Chloroquine tablets immediately.

• Six hours later, take 2 more Chloroquine tablets.

• The next day, take 2 more.

• The following day, take 2 more.

Note: If the Chloroquine treatment does not cause the fever to break within 24 hours, assume the infection is the very dangerous *P. falciparum* and begin the following treatment immediately:

• Take 3 tablets (750 mg) of Mefloquine (Larium)

2) Six hours later, take 2 more tablets (500 mg) of Mefloquine.

3) After 12 hours—and only if you weigh 60 kg (130 lbs) or more—take one more tablet (250 mg) of Mefloquine.

Prevention. Malaria is carried by the *Anopheles* mosquito, and if you don't get bit, you don't get the disease.

1) While walking around, use a good quality mosquito repellent, and be very generous with it, particularly around your ankles. Wear light-colored, long-sleeved shirts or blouses and long pants. (Effective insect repellent is very hard to find in Indonesia, so bring some from home.)

2) While eating or relaxing in one spot, burn mosquito coils. These are those green, slightly brittle coils of incense doped with pyrethrin that were banned in the United States some years ago. They are quite effective and you will get used to the smell. (If you are worried about inhaling some of the poison they contain, re-read the classic symptoms of malaria above.) In Indonesia, the ubiquitous coils are called *obat nyamuk bakar*. In some places where there is electricity, there is a repellent with a similar ingredient that is inserted into a unit plugged into the wall.

3) While sleeping, burn *obat nyamuk* and use a mosquito net. Some hotels in Nusa Tenggara have nets, but not many, and you should bring your own. The *obat nyamuk* coils last 6–8 hours and if you set a couple going when you go to sleep you will be protected. Remember that mosquitos like damp bathrooms—where few people bother to light a mosquito coil.

Stomach Problems

While traveling in Indonesia, drink only boiled or bottled liquids. Bottled water is widely available, if a bit expensive. Try not even to brush your teeth with tap water. Hotels usually provide boiled water, but ask to be sure.

Diarrhea is a frequent problem, and it does not necessarily come from bad food. Most cases can be traced to a combination of climate, fatigue, change of food and culture shock. Your system has to get used to a new set of bacteria in Indonesia.

While affected, drink plenty of water with a bit of salt and some sugar, or better yet, bring oral rehydration salts. And keep your diet simple. No meat, spicy foods or milk products. Start with plain boiled rice or dry biscuits, then papayas and bananas.

Remember that you have diarrhea, not dysentery. If you contract the latter, which is much more serious, you must seek medical help. Do this if your stools are mixed with blood and pus, are black, or you are experiencing severe stomach cramps and fever.

For starters, if no medical help is available, try tetracycline and Diatab, effective for bacillary dysentery. If you feel no relief in a day or two, you have the more serious amoebic dysentery which requires additional medication.

To prevent stomach problems, try to eat only thoroughly cooked foods, don't buy already peeled fruit, and stay away from unpasteurized dairy products. If you encounter constipation, eat a lot of fruit.

Cuts and Scrapes

Not every mosquito bite leads to malaria, but in the tropics a scratched bite or small abrasion can quickly turn into a festering ulcer. You must pay special attention to these things. Apply Tiger Balm—a widely available camphorated salve—or some imitation thereof to relieve the itching. Treat any broken skin with strong disinfectant—Dettol, Betadine—and/or antibiotic powder (try Trofodermin), and change bandages at least once a day. For light burns, use Aristamide or Bioplacenteron.

Exposure

Visitors insist on instant sun tans, and overexposure to the heat and sun are frequent health problems. Be especially careful on long boat rides where the roof gives a good view. The cooling wind created by the boat's motion disguises the fact that you are frying like an egg. Wear a hat, long-sleeved shirt, pants, and use a good-quality sunscreen (bring a supply with you). Tan slowly—don't spoil your trip.

To avoid exposure, drink plenty of fluids and take salt. Wear loose-fitting, light-colored cotton clothes. Do not wear synthetic fibers that do not allow air to circulate.

First Aid Kit

A basic health kit should consist of aspirin and multivitamins, a decongestant, an antihistamine, disinfectant (such as Betadine), antibiotic powder, fungicide, an antibiotic eyewash, Kaopectate or Lomotil, and sunblock. Also good strong soap, perhaps Betadine or other antiseptic soap. Avoid oral antibiotics unless you know how to use them. For injuries, make up a little kit containing Band-aids and ectoplast strips, a roll of sterile gauze and treated gauze for burns, surgical tape, and an elastic bandage for sprains. Also very important are Q-tips, tweezers, scissors, needles and safety pins. Keep your pills and liquid medicines in small, unbreakable plastic bottles, clearly labeled with indelible pen.

Pharmacies—*apotik*—in Jayapura carry just about everything you might need. You can readily get malaria pills here, and an excellent anti-bacterial ointment called Bacitran. Tiger Balm is available everywhere in Asia, and it is excellent for itching bites and lots of other things. Mycolog is a brand of fungicide sold in Indonesia. Oral rehydration salts are usually sold in packets to be mixed with 200 ml of (clean) water, a glassful. Outside Jayapura and the other larger cities, it's nearly impossible to purchase medicines or first aid supplies.

Doctors and Hospitals

In the larger towns, especially Jayapura, there are decent government hospitals and medicines are widely available. Your hotel or *losmen* will probably be able to find you doctor who speaks English. The highlands aren't this deveoped. Like anywhere in the world, medical facilties decline in direct proportion to the distance from urban centers. Missionaries are usuall equipped for medical emergencies—but at least pay for whatever medication/help you receive from them.

Doctors and health care are quite inexpensive by western standards, but the qualit leaves much to be desired. (At least they're familiar with the symptoms and treatment otropical diseases, however, which is somethin your family doctor might have a real tough tim recognizing back home.)

Consultations with doctors are very cheap i Indonesia, usually about $2–$5 for genera practitioners, $4–$10 for specialists. If yo check into a hospital in Jayapura, get a VI room ($12–$25 for everything—including do tors' fees—but not medicines) or a somewha cheaper "Klas I" room. If you stay in a cheape hospital room of a ward, your doctor will b some young, inexperienced kid, fresh out c medical school. Government hospitals, aprovincial capital and district level, hav improved considerably since the late 1980s.

MONEY

Best to carry travelers' checks of two leadin companies as sometimes, for mysterious resons, a bank won't cash the checks of a con pany as well known as, say, American Express U.S. dollars—checks and cash—are accepte in all banks which deal in foreign exchange, a are Australian dollars and (usually) Japanes yen, Deutsche marks, French and Swiss franc Carrying cash is not a good idea. Aside fron the possible loss, banks won't take the bil unless they are in perfect condition. Rates Jayapura are about 5–7 percent better than Wamena.

Prices quoted in this book are in U.S. do lars and were noted in September, 1989. Th Indonesian rupiah is being allowed to slow devalue, and prices stated in U.S. dollars ar more likely to remain accurate.

Bargaining

Other than airfares, package tours, prices f prepared foods and most hotels/*losmen*, price in Indonesia is a flexible thing. At the ma ket, "How much?" is not a question needing short answer, but the beginning of a convers tion. Bargaining is a highly refined art, b there are a few simple rules.

1) Never lose your temper or your sense humor. A smile is an essential weapon.

2) Always agree on a price before accepting a service.

3) Feign indifference to the charms of an item if you really want to get a good price.

4) Don't be shy about denigrating the item you want to buy: "Is this a scratch?" "But look, it's faded here."

5) It's not worth bad feelings just to knock a few cents or dollars off. You've come a long way to see Irian, why spoil it?

WEATHER

Due to Irian's mountainous body, the climate is subject to a great deal of variation. Basically, however, temperatures drop one degree centigrade with every 100 meter rise in elevation. In general, lowland temperatures fluctuate around a mean of 27°C, with an annual range seldom exceeding 8°C.

As a general rule, expect hot and muggy climates on the coasts and pleasant days and cool (even cold) nights in the highlands. Variations from this are more a matter of luck than careful planning, especially on the north coast, which is rainy, but has no real season.

The seas are more predictable. July and August are the best times to navigate off the north coast. January to March and June to October are the dangerous months for sailing off the south coast.

MOUNTAIN CLIMBING

Access to Irian's highest peaks, around Puncak Jaya, lies through Tembagapura. If you have permission to stay there, it is only a question of a one-day trek from the mine site to Puncak Jaya and other peaks in the area. You can also enter from the east, but this requires a long hike in. In either case, you will need permits from the police and military, which at the time of this writing, are not routinely granted.

Climbing Trikora is easier, and to get to the base camp, figure just a day longer than the trip to Habbema described in this book. Operators in Wamena run treks to Trikora, and you should contact them if you want to climb. (See "Highland's Practicalities," page 154.)

Those interested in climbing in Irian should contact the Indonesian Mountaineering Association. Rafia Bontoh will be most helpful and he has scads of experience with bureaucratic red tape, logistics and actual climbing. His club, MAPALA, is connected with the national university.

MAPALA. University of Indonesia, Jl. Pegangsaan Timur 17 Zaal, Jakarta Pusat, Indonesia. ℗(21) 333223.

SCUBA DIVING

Although the waters around Irian contain some of the richest reefs in Indonesia, the only organized diving is off a live-aboard, the *Tropical Princess,* stationed in Biak. If you bring your own equipment you can snorkel in most of the coastal areas, and you might even be able to scrounge up air tanks (from pearl or trepang divers) in Sorong. See "Biak Practicalities" page 78 for more information on the *Tropical Princess.*

Agent for the *Princess*: **P.T. Prima Marindo Paradise.** Jl. Pintu Masuk Pelabuan, Biak, IRJA, Indonesia. ℗(961)21008; Fax: 21804.

VISITING NATURE RESERVES

Irian Jaya has more than 50 wildlife and nature reserves, with almost a dozen more proposed. But it is a newly created system, and there has been very little development of tourist services. There are, however, a few possibilities that are not too difficult to visit.

Supiori Nature Reserve. From Biak town, one can visit the reserve areas on Supiori by chartering a boat. (There is a road, but the bridge regularly washes out.) There are lots of interesting birds here, but they are hard to spot.

Inggresau Wildlife Reserve. This reserve covers most of the interior of Yapen island, which is said to be a good place to see bird's of paradise and other interesting species. See "Yapen Island" page 76.

West Waigeo Nature Reserve. Waigeo Island is famous for bird's of paradise and other colorful species. It is not cheap, or easy to arrange, but you can visit through P.T. Makmur Thomas agency in Sorong. (See "Bird's Head Practicalities," page 109.) There are also reserves on Salawati, Batanta, Kofiau and Misool.

Wasur Wildlife Reserve. This is an unusual dry savannah, the only terrain of its kind in Irian. It is relatively easy to visit by vehicle from Merauke.

Gunung Meja Park. This small reserve is a birder's paradise, and is just north of Manokwari. The beaches here are nesting grounds for leatherback sea turtles. It is easy to reach by road or boat.

Pulau Dolok Reserve. This covers a large area of marshlands on Dolok Island (or Yos Sudarso Island). The wet season—November through April—is the best time to visit; during the dry season the area is a morass of mud, which the locals have adopted to but to which you might not. Besides, the wet season is the best time to see many waterbirds and migratory species here. To reach the reserve, hire a boat from Merauke, or fly from Merauke to Kimaam, then on to the reserve.

Mamberamo Reserve. This is a huge area including the Mamberamo, Taritatu and Tariku river drainages. Ecological zones represented here include high mountains in the Foja group and nipa swamps, and everything in between. Five species of birds of paradise and many other colorful birds inhabit this region. To see this reserve, hire a boat from Sarmi and work your way upriver, or try to fly into Lake Holmes or one of the other small mission towns.

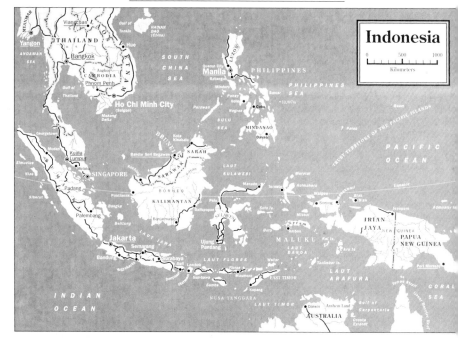

In Brief: Indonesia

The Republic of Indonesia is the world's fourth-largest country, with 190 million people. The vast majority (88 percent) are Muslims, making it the largest Islamic country. More than 350 languages are spoken, but Bahasa Indonesia, a variant of Malay, is the official language.

The nation is a republic, headed by a strong President, with a 500-member legislature and a 1,500-member People's Consultative Assembly. There are 27 provinces and special territories. The capital is Jakarta, with 9 million people.

Indonesia's U.S. $80 billion gross national product comes from oil, textiles, lumber and mining, and the country's major trading partner is Japan. Per capita income is U.S. $430. Much of the economy consists of agriculture, chiefly rice. The economic unit is the Rupiah, of which there are approximately 2,050 to U.S. $1.

The archipelago covers just over 2 million square kilometers of land. Of 18,508 islands, perhaps 6,000 are named, and 1,000 inhabited.

The Buddhist Sriwijaya maritime empire, based in southeast Sumatra, controlled parts of western Indonesia from the 7th to the 13th centuries. The Hindu Majapahit, based in eastern Java, controlled even more from the 13th to the 15th centuries. Beginning in the mid-13th century, local rulers began converting to Islam.

The Portuguese conquered Malacca in 1511, but by the early 17th century the Dutch East India Company (VOC) exclusively controlled the Indies spice trade. The VOC bankrupted in 1799, and the Dutch government ruled directly.

Anti-colonial uprisings began in the 19th century, and increased in the early 20th century, when the nationalism movement was organized around various Muslim groups, the Indonesian Communist Party (PKI) and the Indonesian Nationalist Party (PNI). The founder of the latter, Sukarno, was jailed by the Dutch.

Early in 1942, the Dutch Indies were quickly overrun by the Japanese army. Treatment by the occupiers was harsh. When Japan saw her fortunes waning toward the end of the war, Indonesian nationalists were encouraged to organize. On August 17, 1945, Sukarno proclaimed Indonesia's independence.

The Dutch sought a return to colonial rule after the war. Several years of fighting ensued between nationalists and the Dutch, and transfer, with U.S. pressure, took place in 1949.

President Sukarno's government moved steadily to the left, alienating western governments and capital. In 1963, Indonesia gained control of Irian Jaya, and began a period of confrontation with Malaysia in Borneo. On September 30, 1965 the army put down an attempted coup attributed to the communist PKI. Several hundred thousand people were killed as suspected communists in the following year.

Sukarno drifted from power, and General Suharto became president in 1968. His administration has been friendly to western and Japanese investment.

I N D O N E S I A
Travel Primer

In many ways, Indonesia is a very easy place to get around. Indonesians are as a rule hospitable and good-humored, and will always help a lost or confused traveler. The weather is warm, the pace of life is relaxed, and the air is rich with the smells of clove cigarettes, the blessed durian fruit and countless other wonders.

On the other hand, the nation's transportation infrastructure does not move with the kind of speed and efficiency that western travelers expect, which often leads to frustration and irritation.

In most cases, however, the best thing to do is adjust your way of thinking. There is nothing more pathetic than a tourist who has come all the way around the world just to shout at some poor clerk at the airport counter.

The golden rule is: things will sort themselves out. Eventually. Be persistent, of course, but relax and keep your sense of humor. Before you explode, have a *kretek* cigaret, a cup of sweet Java coffee, or a cool glass of *kelapa muda* (young coconut water). Things might look different.

GETTING TO INDONESIA

You can fly to Indonesia from just about anywhere in the world. The main international entry points are the Soekarno-Hatta airport in Jakarta, the Ngurah Rai airport in Bali, and the Polonia airport in Medan, north Sumatra. It once was the case that only Garuda, Indonesia's national airline, flew into the country, but it is now possible to arrive on a number of foreign carriers.

There are other entry points, but the paperwork can be a problem at some. For example, Kupang, West Timor is a short flight from Darwin, Australia. But Kupang cannot issue a visa-free tourist pass, and it is difficult to get a visa ahead of time in Darwin.

It is usually best to come in through the above gateways. However, if coming from the United States on the Garuda flight, you can get off at Biak, where tourist pass issue is automatic, and you can explore Irian Jaya and the eastern islands of Maluku.

Visa Formalities

Nationals of the following 30 countries are granted visa-free entry for 60 days. For other nationals, tourist visas are required. These must be obtained from an Indonesian embassy or consulate.

Argentina	Australia
Austria	Belgium
Brazil	Brunei
Canada	Denmark
Finland	France
Germany	Greece
Iceland	Ireland
Italy	Japan
Liechtenstein	Luxemburg
Malaysia	Malta
Mexico	Morocco
Netherlands	New Zealand
Norway	Philippines
Singapore	South Korea
Spain	Sweden
Switzerland	Taiwan
Thailand	United Kingdom
United States	Venezuela

To avoid any unpleasantness on arrival, check your passport before leaving for Indonesia. You need at least one empty page for your passport to be stamped. Passports must be valid for at least six months upon arrival and you should have valid proof of onward journey, either a return or through ticket. Employment is strictly forbidden on tourist visas or visa-free entry.

Visa-free entry to Indonesia means not exceeding a stay of two months (60 days). This is not extendable and is only valid when entering via the following airports: Ambon, Bali, Batam, Biak, Jakarta, Manado, Medan, Surabaya. Or the following seaports: Bali, Balikpapan, Batam, Jakarta, Kupang, Pontianak, Semarang, Tanjung Pinang.

Other visas. The two-month, single-entry, non-extendable tourist pass is not the only one offered by Indonesian immigration. It is, however, the only entry permit that comes without a great deal of paperwork and headache.

There is also a visitor's visa, which is usually given for 4–5 weeks, but can be extended for up to six months. Unfortunately, it is a real hassle to get one. You must have a reason for needing to spend time in Indonesia—academic research, relatives, religious study—and you must have a sponsor. Even with an influential sponsor, and the best of reasons, however, you still might be denied. Also, extensions are at the discretion of immigration, and the process can take days or weeks.

There is also a business visa, issued for 30 days and extendable to three months. This requires a letter from an employer that states you are performing a needed service for him or her in Indonesia.

Customs

Narcotics, firearms and ammunition are strictly prohibited. Advance approval is necessary to bring in transceivers. On entry 2 liters of alcoholic beverages, 200 cigarettes, 50 cigars or 100 grams of tobacco are allowed. There is no restriction on import and export of foreign currencies in cash or travelers checks, but there is an export limit of 50,000 Indonesian

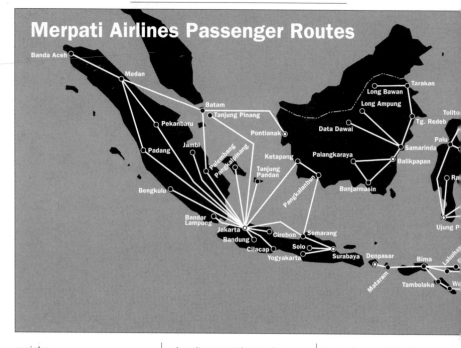

Merpati Airlines Passenger Routes

rupiahs.

All narcotics are illegal in Indonesia. The use, sale or purchase of narcotics results in long prison terms and/or huge fines—this applies to all foreigners as well as to Indonesians. Once caught, you are immediately placed in detention until trail and the sentences are very stiff.

Keep your cool

At a government offices like immigration, talking loudly and forcefully just does not make things easier. Things in Indonesia may take a little longer to accomplish than you are used to. Patience is a virtue in Indonesia that opens many doors. Good manners and dress are also to your advantage.

TRAVEL IN INDONESIA

Getting around in Indonesia is not—to Americans and Europeans used to efficient, on-time airplanes, trains and buses—particularly easy. A visitor usually has to put considerable effort into getting a booking on any form of transport, and even more to make sure that the seat is still there when it comes time to leave.

What seems at first like nerve-wracking inefficiency is really so only if one is in a hurry. Indonesia is not a fast-paced place. This, in fact, is a big part of its charm. You can not just turn off the archipelago's famous *jam karet*—"rubber time"—when it comes time to take an airplane and turn it on again when you want to relax. Take the good with the inconvenient.

Despite the maddeningly disorganized counters at the airports, the inscrutable ebb and flow of touts, passengers and employees at train and other offices, if you plan things out and are patient, you will always get where you want to go.

Air Travel

The cardinal rule for air travel in Indonesia is book early, confirm and reconfirm often. If you are told a flight is booked up, go to the airport anyway. Garuda has a modern computerized booking system, but the other airlines use a combination of written passenger lists, telexes and so forth. These "passengers" evaporate at the

last minute all the time.

The worst time for air (and any kind of) travel is during the height of the tourist season—July and August—but there may be no avoiding this. If you want to go from two well known tourist points, for example from Yogyakarta to Bali and there is simply no space on the flights, be creative take a bus to Semarang (big but not a tourist town) and then fly to Bali via Surabaya.

Garuda. Garuda is Indonesia's flagship airline, and has been in business for some 40 years. Garuda serves a couple of dozen of the largest airports in Indonesia—Jakarta Denpasar, Ujung Pandang etc.—and at least 28 cities internationally. Their planes are new and well-kept, and service is very good.

This is not a bargain air line; prices on international flights are generally 15–20 percent higher than the best deals available, and internally they are about the same percentage more expensive than Merpati. But the service and quality of equipment compares favorably to the best air lines in the world.

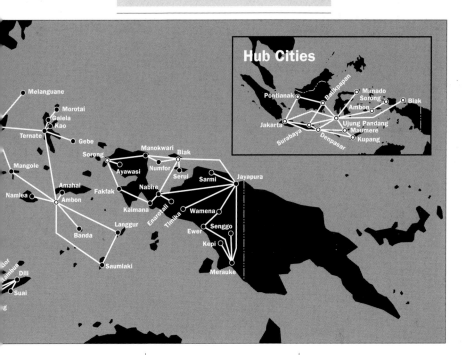

Main office: Jl. Merdeka Selatan 13, Jakarta. ✆ (21) 3801901, 3806276, 3806558.

Merpati. Merpati is by far the most useful airline for travel inside Indonesia. It and Garuda have been combined into one state airline, with Garuda flying its large jets between high-traffic hub cities, and Merpati spreading out from there with its turbo-prop and smaller aircraft. Merpati (literally "pigeon") reaches more than 160 airports and airstrips throughout Indonesia.

On the more popular routes they fly DC-9's and Fokker F-27's and F-28's, and on the more out-of-the-way places, sturdy DeHavilland of Canada Twin-Otters and Casa Nusantara 212's and 235's. The Casa's are locally made.)

Everyone who travels in Indonesia has horror stories about Merpati, flights that were cancelled at the last minute, overbooked to begin with, or cancelled three and four times in a row for strange or unfathomable reasons. But the airline does at least try to connect Indonesia's many far-flung towns and villages, and

one wonders if a U.S.-based airline would even bother in the first place to schedule a flight to a grass airstrip in a highland village of 100 people (as Merpati does in Irian Jaya).

Merpati's standard baggage allowance is 20 kilos for economy class, and on some of the smaller aircraft can be as little as 10 kilos (after which the excess baggage charges of $.50–$1.00/kilo begin to accrue). Although not always rigorously enforced, this weight limit makes another good argument for traveling light in Indonesia.

Merpati offers a fixed discount for children and students. Students (10–26 years old) receive a discount of 25% (Note: bring an international student I.D. card). Children between the ages of 2 and 10 pay 50% of the regular fare. Infants not occupying a seat pay 10% of the regular fare.

Main office: Jl. Angkasa 2 Kemayoran, Jakarta Pusat. ✆ (62) 413608, 417404. Fax: (62) 418936.

At the Soekarno–Hatta airport: ✆ (62) 5507156, 5501446, 5501446. Telex: 49020 MERPATI IA.

Other airlines. Because of the state monopoly granted Garuda/Merpati, the several smaller airlines operating in Indonesia use older equipment, and tend to concentrate on out-of-the-way areas. Their prices are usually a little cheaper than Merpati, but more important, in some areas (like Kalimantan) they offer a greater number or variety of flight options.

Bouraq. Main office: Jl. Angkasa 1–3, Jakarta. ✆ (21) 6295170, 6595179, 6595194. Bouraq is a private company, flying mainly small planes. They link many airports in Java, as well as Bali and Nusa Tenggara, Sulawesi, and Ternate. Bouraq offers a number of flights between small towns in Kalimantan.

Mandala. Main office: Jl. Veteran 1/34, Jakarta. ✆ (62) 368107. Mandala operates a few propeller-driven planes to the more out-of-the-way airstrips in Kalimantan, Sumatra and Sulawesi.

Sempati. Main office: Jl. Merdeka Timur 7, Jakarta. ✆ (21) 348760, 367743. This is a freight and passenger outfit that connects Jakarta with

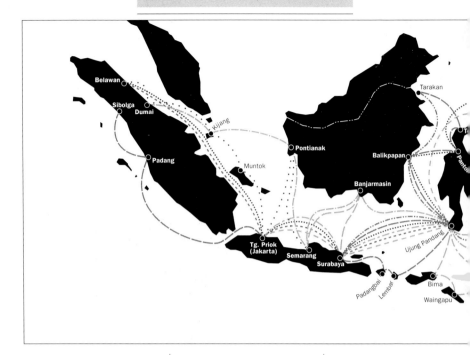

other cities in Asia, such as Singapore, Malaysia, the Philippines and Japan.

Sea Travel

There is four times as much water area in Indonesia as land, and for many centuries communications among the islands has been by boat. There are tiny ports scattered all over the archipelago, and for some of the more remote areas—for example, the Aru Islands or the southwestern Moluccas—sea travel is the only way to get there.

When traveling by boat, you have to give yourself time. Plenty of time. Most of the boats plying the islands are quite small, and are at the mercy of the seas and the seasons. Think of it as a romantic escape, and don't be in a hurry.

Pelni, the national passenger line, makes the rounds of the archipelago in 9 large ships, most holding 1,000–1,500 passengers. These boats move on schedule, and in the first or second-class cabins, can even be quite comfortable.

There are a myriad of other options. Rusty old coasters ply routes through the eastern islands, stopping at tiny ports to pick up dried coconut meat, seaweed and other small loads of cash crops. They drop off basics like tinware, fuel and the occasional outboard motor. You could find deck passage on one of these ships at just about any harbor, and for very little money.

Stock up on food—you will quickly get sick of white rice and salted fish—and bring protection from the rain, and plastic to thoroughly waterproof your gear. You could negotiate with a crewmember to rent his bunk, which could make sleeping much more comfortable.

Overnight ferries, with throbbing motors and crowded beyond belief, offer passage to many smaller islands. On these—and on deck passage on any vessel in Indonesia—it is important to use your luggage to stake out a territory early, and to set down some straw mats to have a clean place to lie down. It is almost always best to stay on deck, where the fresh sea air will keep your spirits up. Below deck tends to be loud, ver minous and smelly.

In many areas, day trips on smaller boats—*prahu*—are the best way to explore. These can be hired by the hour, with a boatman, to take you snor keling or sightseeing along the coast, or birdwatching upriver Outboard motors are ver expensive in Indonesia, and tend to be no more powerfu than is absolutely necessary These are not speedboats Inspect the boat before negoti ating a price, and if it doesn' have one, see if the boatmar can rig up a canopy to offe shelter from the blazing sun.

Pelni. Pelayaran Nasiona Indonesia is the national ship ping lines, and their 70 ships get just about everywhere i the islands. Many of the olde vessels look like floating tras cans, but the fleet of new German-built passenger ships is one of the most modern i the world. See map above fo the routes of the nine Pelr passenger ships.

The fares are fixed, an there are as many as fiv classes, depending on hov many people will be sharing room. For example:

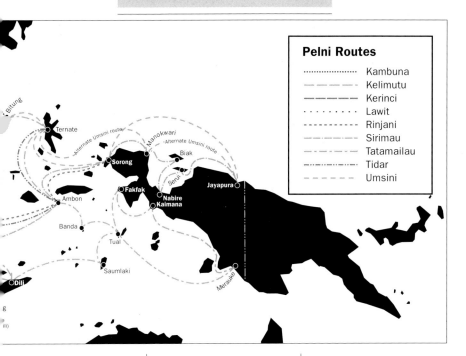

Pelni Routes

····················	Kambuna
— — — — —	Kelimutu
————————	Kerinci
· · · · · · · ·	Lawit
- - - - - - -	Rinjani
—·—·—·—·—	Sirimau
—··—··—··—	Tatamailau
■—■—■—■—■	Tidar
– – – – –	Umsini

Umsini

Class I 20 rms for 2 people
Class II 22 rms for 4 people
Class III 28 rms for 6 people
Class IV 82 rms for 8 people
Class EK Deck passage
Total: 1,729 people

The fares for the above, from Tanjung Priok harbor in Jakarta, all the way to Jayapura, Irian Jaya:

Class I $303
Class II $223
Class III $163
Class IV $127
Class EK $81

Children (1–11 years old) get a 25% discount; babies (to 1 year) get a 90% discount.

Head ticket office: Jl. Gajah Mada 14, Jakarta 10130. © (21) 343307, 344342, 344345, 344349. Fax: (21) 3810341, 345605. Telex: 44580, 45040, 45791, 45625, 45377 PELNI IA.

Travel overland

The average road in Indonesia is a paved, but rough and pot-holed thoroughfare, across which are conducted a verita-ble zoo of vehicles: fully loaded trucks, with marginal brakes and drivers going for broke anyway; full-size buses, one and three-quarters lanes wide; small public minivans, stopping anywhere and with no warning for passengers; the occasional private car; scores of motorcycles, most of them small two-stroke affairs, usually piled with goods or, at the hands of a young hotshot, screaming along at full throttle; horse-drawn passenger carts; *becak*s, bicycle rigs that carry a passenger in front; bicycles, with perhaps some children fore and aft, and almost always piled with produce, or perhaps two fighting cocks in their cages; and, of course, pedestrians of all ages.

Buses. The basic form of long, overland transportation in Indonesia is the bus. Night buses—*bis malam*—are the most comfortable for covering really long distances. They tend to leave in the late after-noon, and arrive the following morning. You can get night buses that will link up with fer-ries and take you all the way across western Indonesia. From Jakarta to Bali takes about three days. Night buses are generally in the best condi-tion, and are the fastest means of overland transport. The newest ones have air-plane style seats, on-board toi-lets and, alas, blaring video.

Intercity day buses—*bis kota*—to various destinations are ubiquitous across Indo-nesia. Some seat four across; others five. Try to get on early and pick a comfortable seat up front or in the middle. Sometimes these buses won't leave until they are full, so balance the fact of having a good seat with the time wast-ed sitting in the station. These tend to be crowded and uncomfortable, so if you are covering a really long distance, try to get a night bus. As a general rule, figure a bus can average 40 kph on Indonesia's often ratty roads.

Local buses ply all the larg-er cities, starting out from a main bus station but in many cases stopping anywhere along the route for passen-gers. Bus maps do not exist (outside of Jakarta) so you will often need to ask someone which bus you need to take.

Minibuses. The mass of local transportation in Indonesia is handled by a variety of minibuses. These can be locally assembled Mitsubishi minivans (called "colt") which can hold up to 20 people; *Oplet* or *microlet*, smaller microvans, made by Suzuki or other manufacturers, that can hold 6–10 people and which one enters and leaves through the rear; and *bemo*s, on Bali, a kind of small open-backed pickup truck with seats.

Whether in the form of a "taxi" from the airport, a vehicle of local public transportation, a tour operator's "bus," or a chartered "car," the vast majority of your local travels will be in one of these ubiquitous minivans.

Public minibuses ply regular routes, and stop anywhere along the way to pick up and drop off passengers. Even more than nature a vacuum, their drivers abhor empty seats. They are always packed. Sometimes—rarely—you can ride shotgun up front, the best seat in the house.

Prices tend to be a bit more than for buses, but you get there quicker, and there are more minibuses on the road. Tour operators use these vehicles on their guided tours, and you can often hire a minibus and driver for the hour or the day. Any hotel or losmen will have a relationship with at least one *sopir* (driver) and will arrange his services for you. Or you could just go to the station, and ask around.

Rail. Indonesia has just less than 8,000 kilometers of track, all of it on Java, Madura Island and Sumatra. Only on Java is there a complete rail system, running the entire length and breadth of the island. Indonesia's state railway system (built by the Dutch in the late 19th century) has fallen somewhat into decline.

Java used to be a destination for antique rail afficionados, but the island's several hundred steam locomotives have been gradually retired, although there are still some doing freight service.

For covering distance in Java, trains tend to be slower, but cheaper and much more relaxing than buses. On long runs, the night trains are the best, and they make fewer stops as well. Day trains stop frequently, but make an excellent way to see the country— and Java, of course, is famous for its beauty.

Like most transportation in Indonesia, trains don't hold too closely to their posted schedule. It's a good idea to keep some bottled water and a few snacks, in case you're stuck waiting somewhere.

Trains are heavily booked, and it is not usually possible to book ahead of time. This means waiting in long, confusing lines. To avoid this, you can often purchase tickets through travel agents, for a small added fee.

ACCOMMODATIONS

"Hotels" in Indonesia go by a variety of names. Theoretically, the organization is the following: "hotel," an upmarket establishment catering to westerners and tourists; "losmen," a medium-priced place, basically a cheaper hotel; "wisma," a small guesthouse; and "penginapan," very basic lodging, no frills and very cheap. In practice, however, there is often little to distinguish the many medium-range places called "losmen" and "wisma," and increasingly, even "hotel."

Whatever the name, in the $15–$40 price range, one can expect to fine comfortable rooms, good service, and a restaurant serving quality meals. Accommodations in this category have attached bathrooms, and often air-conditioning. Many of the cheaper digs ($8–$15) have only squat toilets (no toilet paper) and ladle-type baths (*mandi*), and in the cheapest *losmen* and *penginapan,* a few toilets are shared among many guests.

We suggest you bring your own towel and soap (although many places provide these for their guests) and a packet of mosquito coils. Mosquito nets are the best protection, but they're a hassle to put up in most hotel rooms. Everywhere, upon request, your room will be sprayed for insects. Be sure that this is done long before you are ready to sleep if you want to avoid the smell.

Where there are no commercial lodgings, you have to rely on local hospitality. In the *kecamatan* centers, either the police or the *camat* could help you find a place to sleep. In the villages, you should find the *kepala desa* (village chief), who will help. Although you will certainly not be treated like one, keep in mind that you are a bother. Villagers in rural Indonesia do not, routinely, maintain guest rooms.

COMMUNICATIONS

Mail. Indonesia has a large network of post offices (*kantor pos*) but it is not famous for its efficiency. If things are busy (and they usually are) it is a tedious process to go to the window for weighing, the window for stamps, etc. One should always use *kilat* or express service when posting in Indonesia. It costs a bit more, but makes a big difference. International *kilat* service gets postcards and letters to the United States in 5–7 days.

Telephone. International telecommunications to and from Indonesia are handled by satellite, and there are Kantor Telepon & Telegraph offices in most cities. While it can still be difficult to get through to Jakarta due to overloaded exchanges, most of the nightmare of telephone calls in Indonesia is past.

Many of the larger cities offer International Direct Dialing to 127 countries around the world. In fact, one can now call directly from Wamena, in the heart of the Baliem Valley of Irian Jaya, to New York City.

Faxes have become common, and you can send one from most phone offices for a reasonable rate.

Be careful of calling from hotels, as most attach a debit

itating surcharge to IDD calls made by guests. Go to the phone office instead.

Time zones. Indonesia has three time zones. Sumatra, Java and Bali are in West Indonesia Standard Time (Greenwich Mean Time plus 7 hours). Lombok to East Timor, and Kalimantan and Sulawesi are in Central Indonesia Standard Time (GMT plus 8 hours). Maluku and Irian are in East Indonesia Standard Time (GMT plus 9 hours).

INFORMATION

A very good source of information on travel in Indonesia is the Directorate General of Tourism in Jakarta. From this office one can find brochures, maps and other materials on all the provinces.

Directorate General of Tourism
Jl. Kramat Raya 81
P.O. Box 409
Tel: (21) 3103117
Fax: (21) 3101146
Telex: 61525 INTOUR IA
Cable: INTO JAKARTA

Overseas, you can contact the Indonesian embassy or one of the following Indonesia Tourist Promotion Offices:

North America)
3457 Wilshire Boulevard
Los Angeles, CA 90010
U.S.A.
Tel: (213) 387-2078
Fax: (213) 380-4876
Telex: 182192 INDOTOUR LAX

Southeast Asia)
10 Collyer Quay #15–07
Ocean Building
Singapore 0104
SINGAPORE
Tel: (65) 534-2837, 534-1795
Fax: (65) 533-4287
Telex: RS 35731 INTOUR

Australia)
Garuda Indonesia Office
4 Bligh Street
P.O. Box 3836
Sydney, NSW 2000
AUSTRALIA
Tel: 232-6044
Fax: 233-2828
Telex: 22576

Telephone Codes

From outside Indonesia, the following cities are reached by dialing 62 (the country code for Indonesia) then the city code, then the number. Within Indonesia, the city code must be preceded by a 0 (zero).

City	Code
Ambon	911
Balikpapan	542
Banda Aceh	651
Bandung	22
Banjarbaru	5119
Banjarmasin	511
Banyuwangi	333
Bekasi	99
Belawan	619
Bengkulu	736
Biak	961
Binjai	619
Blitar	342
Bogor	251
Bojonegoro	353
Bondowoso	332
Bukittinggi	752
Cianjur	263
Cibinong	99
Cilacap	282
Cimahi	229
Cipanas	255
Cirebon	231
Denpasar	361
Gadog/Cisarua	251
Garut	262
Gresik	319
Jakarta	21
Jambi	741
Jember	311
Jombang	321
Kabanjahe	628
Karawang	267
Kebumen	287
Kediri	354
Kendal	294
Kendari	401
Kisaran	623
Klaten	272
Kota Pinang	624
Kotabaru	622
Kotacane	629
Kuala Simpang	641
Kudus	291
Kupang	391
Lahat	731
Lhok Seumawe	645
Lhok Sukon	645
Lumajang	334
Madiun	351
Magelang	293
Malang	341
Manado	431
Manokwari	962
Mataram	364
Medan	61
Merauke	971
Metro	725
Mojokerto	321
Nusa Dua	361
Padang	751
Palangkaraya	514
Palembang	711
Palu	451
Pare-Pare	421
Pasuruan	343
Pati	295
Pekalongan	285
Pekanbaru	761
Pematang Siantar	622
Ponorogo	352
Pontianak	561
Prapat	625
Prigen	343
Probolinggo	335
Purwakarta	264
Purwokerto	281
Sabang	652
Salatiga	298
Samarinda	541
Sekupang	778
Semarang	24
Serang	254
Sibolga	631
Sidoarjo	319
Sigli	653
Situbondo	338
Solo	271
Sorong	951
Sukabumi	266
Sumbawa Besar	371
Sumedang	261
Surabaya	31
Tangerang	99
Tanjung Karang	271
Tapak Tuan	656
Tarakan	551
Tasikmalaya	265
Tebing Tinggi	621
Tegal	283
Ternate	921
Tulung Agung	355
Ujung Pandang	411
Ungaran	249
Wates	274
Wonosobo	286
Yogyakarta	274

Indonesian Language Primer

Pronunciation rules

Vowels
a   As in father
e   Three forms:
    1) Schwa, like the **e**
    2) Like **é** in touché
    3) Short **e**; as in b**e**t
i   Usually like long **e** (as in Bali); when bounded by consonants, like short i (h**i**t).
o   Long **o**, like go
u   Long **u**, like y**o**u
ai Long **i**, like cr**i**me
au Like **ow** in **ow**l

Consonants
c   Always like **ch** in **ch**urch
g   Always hard, like **g**uard
h   Usually soft, almost unpronounced. It is hard between like vowels, e.g. **mahal** (expensive).
k   Like **k** in **k**ind; at end of word, unvoiced stop.
kh   Like **k**ind, but harder
r   Rolled, like Spanish **r**
ng   Soft, like fli**ng**
ngg Hard, like ti**ng**le
ny   Like **ny** in So**ny**a

Spellings
In 1972, Indonesian spelling was standardized, but the old spellings are often retained in proper names.

New	Old
c	tj
y	j
j	dj
kh	ch

One also often sees romanization according to Dutch pronunciation rules, such as Soekarno (for Sukarno).

Grammer
Grammatically, Indonesian is in many ways far simpler than English. There are no articles (a, an, the). The verb form "to be" is usually not used. There is no ending for plural; sometimes the word is doubled, but often number comes from context. And Indonesian verbs are not conjugated. Tense is communicated by context or with words for time.

Personal pronouns
I	*saya*
we	*kita* (inclusive)
	kami (exclusive)
you	*anda, saudara*
	kamu (for friends and children only)
he/she	*dia*
they	*mereka*

Forms of address
Father	*Bapak* ("*Pak*")
Mother	*Ibu* ("*Bu*")
Elder brother	*Abang* ("*Bang*" or "*Bung*")
	Mas (in Java)
Younger brother/sister	*Adik* ("*Dik*")
Miss	*Nona*
Mrs.	*Nyonya*

Note: These terms are used not just within the family, but generally in polite speech.

Basic questions
How?	*Bagaimana?*
How much?	*Berapa?*
(Also: How many?)	
What?	*Apa?*
What's this?	*Apa ini?*
Who?	*Siapa?*
Who's that?	*Siapa itu?*
What is your name? (Literally: Who is your name?)	
	Siapa nama saudara?
When?	*Kapan?*
Where?	*Mana?*

Useful words
yes	*ya*
no, not	*tidak*
not	*bukan*

Note: *Tidak* is used with verbs or adverbs; *bukan* with nouns.

and	*dan*
with	*dengan*
for	*untuk*
good	*bagus*
fine	*baik*
more	*lebih*
less	*kurang*
better	*lebih baik*
worse	*kurang baik*
this (or these)	*ini*
that (or those)	*itu*
same	*sama*
different	*lain*

Civilities
Welcome	*Selamat datang*
Good morning (7–11am)	*Selamat pagi*
Good midday (11am–3pm)	*Selamat siang*
Good afternoon (3–7pm)	*Selamat sore*
Goodnight (after dark)	*Selamat malam*
Goodbye (to one leaving)	*Selamat jalan*
Goodbye (to one staying)	*Selamat tinggal*

Note: Selamat is a word from Arabic meaning "May your time (or action) be blessed."

How are you?	*Apa Khabar?*
I am fine.	*Khabar baik.*
Thank you.	*Terima kasih.*
You're welcome.	*Kembali.*
Same to you.	*Sama sama.*

Note: The above "Thank you" series is generally run all the way through in order.

Pardon me	*Ma'af*
Excuse me (when leaving a conversation, etc.)	*Permisi*

Numbers
1	*satu*	6	*enam*
2	*dua*	7	*tujuh*
3	*tiga*	8	*delapan*
4	*empat*	9	*sembilan*
5	*lima*	10	*sepuluh*

"teens"	*belas*
11	*seblas*
12	*dua belas*
13	*tiga belas*
units of ten	*puluh*
20	*dua puluh*
50	*lima puluh*
73	*tujuh puluh tiga*
hundreds	*ratus*
100	*seratus*
600	*enam ratus*
thousands	*ribu*
1,000	*seribu*
3,000	*tiga ribu*
10,000	*sepuluh ribu*
million	*juta*
2,000,000	*dua juta*
one-half	*setengah*
first	*pertama*
second	*kedua*
third	*kertiga*
fourth	*kerempat*

Time

minute	*menit*
hour	*jam* (also means clock or watch)
day	*hari*
week	*minggu*
month	*bulan*
year	*tahun*
today	*hari ini*
tomorrow	*besok*
later	*nanti*
Sunday	*Hari Minggu*
Monday	*Hari Senin*
Tuesday	*Hari Selasa*
Wednesday	*Hari Rabu*
Thursday	*Hari Kamis*
Friday	*Hari Jum'at*
Saturday	*Hari Sabtu*

What time is it?
Jam berapa?
(It is) eight thirty.
Jam setengah sembilan
(Literally "half nine")
How many hours?
Berapa jam?
When did you arrive?
Kapan saudara datang?
Four days ago.
Empat hari lang lalu.
When are you leaving?
Kapan saudara berangkat?
In a short while.
Sebentar lagi.

Basic vocabulary

to be, have	*ada*
can, to be able	*bisa*
to buy	*beli*
to know	*tahu*
to get	*dapat*
to need	*perlu*
to want	*mau*
to go	*pergi*
to wait	*tunggu*
at	*di*
to	*ke*
if	*kalau, jika*
then	*lalu, kemudian*
only	*hanya, saja*
correct	*betul*
wrong	*salah*
big	*besar*
small	*kecil*
beautiful	*cantik*
slow	*pelan*
fast	*cepat*
stop	*berhenti*
old	*tua, lama*
new	*baru*
near	*dekat*
far	*jauh*
empty	*kosong*
crowded	*ramai*

Small talk

Where are you from?
Anda berasal dari mana?
I'm from the U.S.
Saya berasal dari U.S.
How old are you?
Umur berapa tuan?
I'm 31 years old.
Saya berumur tiga puluh satu tahun.
Are you married?
Apa anda sudah kawin?
Yes, I am.
Yah, sudah.
Not yet.
Belum.
Do you have children?
Sudah punya anak?
What is your religion?
Agama apa anda?
Have you been to Bali?
Sudah pernah ke Bali?
Where are you going?
Pergi ke mana?
I'm just taking a walk.
Jalan-jalan.
Please come in.
Silahkan masuk.
This food is delicious.
Makanan ini nikmat sekali.
You are very hospitable.
Anda sangat ramah tamah.

Hotels

Where's a losmen?
Dimana ada losmen?
cheap losmen
losmen murah
average losmen
losmen lumayan
very good hotel
hotel cukup baik
Please take me to…
Tolong antar saya ke…
Are there any empty rooms?
Ada kamar kosong?
Sorry there aren't any.
Ma'af, tidak ada.
How much for one night?
Berapa harga satu malam?
One room for two of us.
Dua orang, satu kamar.
I'd like the room for 3 days.
Saya mau pakai kamar tiga hari.
hot and cold water
air panas dan dingin
Here's the key to your room.
Ini kunci kamar Tuan.
Please call a taxi.
Tolong panggilkan taksi.
Please wash these clothes.
Tolong cucikan pakaian ini.

Restaurants

Where's a good restaurant?
Rumah makan mana yang baik?
Let's have lunch.
Mari kita makan siang.
I want Indonesian food.
Saya mau makenan Indonesia.
Bring me coffee instead of tea.
Berilah saya kopi untuk gantinya teh.
May I see the menu?
Boleh saya lihat daftar makenan?
I want to wash my hands.
Saya mau cuci tangan.
Where is the toilet?
Dimana kamar kecil?
fish, squid, goat, pork
ikan, cumi, kambing, babi
salty, sour, sweet, spicy
asin, asam, manis, pedas

Shopping

I don't understand
Saya tidak mengerti.
I can't speak Indonesian.
Saya tidak bisa bicara Bahasa Indonesia.
Please, speak slowly.
Tolong, saya akan tanya.
I want to buy…
Saya mau beli…
Where can I buy…
Dimana saya bisa beli…
How much does this cost?
Berapa harga ini?
2500 Rupiah.
Dua ribu, lima ratus rupiah.
Don't give me a crazy price!
Jangan beri harga gila!
Last price.
Harga akhir.

Directions

north	*utara*
south	*selatan*
east	*timur*
west	*barat*
right	*kanan*
left	*kiri*
near	*dekat*
far	*jauh*
inside	*di dalam*
outside	*di luar*

I am looking for this address.
Saya cari alamat inin.
How far is it?
Berapa jauh dari sini?
Go straight, then turn left off the main street.
Jalan terus, lalu belok kiri di jalan raya.

Further Readings

Allen, Benedict. *Into the Crocodile Nest: A Journey Inside New Guinea.* London: Grafton Books, Paladin, 1989. This modern day adventurer flies into the Irian highlands, treks through Yali and Kim Yal country, and heads to the land of the unacculturated Obini. He gets cold feet and bugs out, and with not enough information left to finish his book, flies to the Sepik River in Papua New Guinea. A fairly thin account, with a kind of pulp journalist feel.

Archbold, Richard. "Results of the Archbold Expedition," *Bulletin of the American Museum of Natural History.* Vol. 88, Article 3. Description of Archbold's expedition to the highlands around Lake Habbema.

Asmat Sketch Books. Book 1–2, Book 3–4, Book 5A, Book 5B, Book 6, Book 7, and Book 8. Hastings, Nebraska: The Asmat Museum of Culture and Progress, copyrights 1977–1984. These paperback volumes, assembled by the Crosier mission in Agats, contain descriptions of Asmat cultural life, vocabularies, outlines of historical events in the region, Asmat mythologies, descriptions of everyday events like sago gathering, and much more. The articles are written by the missionaries, visiting ethnographers and others doing research in the Asmat lands. These are extremely valuable primary sources for anyone interested in the region. Do not think that because these are missionary products they are full of self-interested religious propaganda. They are straightforward, honest and unflinching. Available by mail from: Crosier Province, Inc., 3204 East 43d Street, Minneapolis, MN 55406. Tel: (612) 722-2223. Each volume costs $15; 40% discount on orders of five or more.

Baal, J. van. *West Irian: a Bibliography.* Dordrecht, Netherlands, 1984.

Bellwood, Peter. *Pre-History of the Indo-Malaysian Archipelago.* New York, 1985.

Bromley, Myron. "Ethnic Groups in Irian Jaya." *Bulletin for Irian Jaya Development.* 2–3:1–37, 1973.

Brongersma, L. D. *The Animal World of Netherlands New Guinea.* Gronengen: J.B. Wolters, 1958. 70 pp.

Budiardjo, Carmel and Liem Soei Liong. *West Papua: The Obliteration of a People.* Surrey, U.K.: TAPOL, 1988. A very critical look at the transfer of Irian to Indonesia and the reaction it spawned.

D'Albertis, Luigi M. *New Guinea: What I Did and What I Saw.* 2 volumes. London: Sampson Low, 1880. Worth trying to find in a good library, as naturalist D'Albertis was an always colorful figure, a keen observer, and usually behaved dispicably.

Flannery, Timothy. *The Mammals of New Guinea.* Queensland, Australia: Robert Brown and Associates, 1990. An excellent, contemporary account of New Guinea's unique mammalian fauna. Color photographs illustrate each species, and information on range, habits, etc. is complete.

Gardner, Robert and Karl G. Heider. *Gardens of War: Life and Death in the New Guinea Stone Age.* Introduction by Margaret Mead. New York: Random House, 1968. An excellent book of photographs taken during the Harvard-Peabody expedition of 1961 to the Kurelu Dani, in the eastern part of the Baliem Valley. (Out of print.)

Garnaut, Ross and Chris Manning. *Irian Jaya: The Transformation of a Melanesian Economy.* Canberra: Australian National University Press, 1974.

Gerbrands, Adrian A. *The Asmat of New Guinea. The Journal of Michael Clark Rockefeller.* The Museum of Primitive Art: New York, 1967. Based on the late Michael Rockefeller's notebooks and photographs. Particularly valuable because it shows some of the excellent art pieces Rockefeller collected in their original sites. (Out of print.)

Heider, Karl. *The Dugum Dani.* New York, 1970. The most complete ethnography of the Dani by the anthropologist who accompanied the Harvard-Peabody expedition.

———. *Grand Valley Dani, Peaceful Warriors.* New York, 1979.

Henderson, William. *West New Guinea: the Dispute and its Settlement.* Seton Hal University Press, 1987.

Hvalkof, Soren and Aaby, Peter (eds). *Is God an American?* Survival International (36 Craven St, London WC 2N/5NG), London. n.d.

Kamma, F. C. *Koreri.* The Hague, 1972. On the Koreri movement, a "cargo cult" in Biak.

Koch, K. F. *War and Peace in Jalemo.* Cambridge, 1974. A Yali ethnography.

Lawrence, Peter. *Road Belong Cargo.* Melbourne: University of Melbourne Press 1964. "Cargo cults" in Melanesia.

Matthiessen, Peter. *Under the Mountain Wall: A Chronicle of Two Seasons in Stone Age New Guinea.* New York: Penguin Books, 1987 (First published 1962). Matthiessen is among the very finest writers—both fiction and non-fiction—working today in the English language. This book is the story of the Kurelu Dani told by a novelist. It is richly descriptive, but has none of the invasive and crushing language of the ethnographer This is in fact *not* a book about the Dani; it is a book about Kurelu, U-mue, Ekapuwe, Wereklowe, and many others, including, most importantly, Tukum the swineherd.

Mitton, Robert. *The Lost World of Irian Jaya.* Melbourne: Oxford University Press, 1983. Mitton was an exploration geologist and cartographer who worked in Irian, particularly the highlands, for six years in the early and mid-'70s. He had a great knowledge of Irian, and an even greater love for the Irianese and their land. This is a book of photos and observations assembled post-humously from his notebooks; unfortunately, he died at age 30 of leukemia and was never able to properly finish the project himself. This is an excellent book, and required reading for anyone who is going to spend time in the highlands. (Out of print, but Oxford has for years been promising a re-issue.)

Mordaunt, Elinor. *The Further Venture Book.* London: John Lane the Bodley Head Limited, 1926. On a trip that criss-crossed the Dutch Indies, Ms. Mordaunt stopped at Waigeo, Sorong, Manokwari, Biak, Sarmi, Humbolt Bay (now Jayapura) and the tiny Mapia Islands. It is a standard traveler's tale of the time—that is, it says more about its British author than the people of New Guinea—and is competently written. Mordaunt doesn't always complain about the filth, and only rarely calls a Papuan woman a "hussy."

Petocz, Ronald G. *Conservation and Development in Irian Jaya.* Leiden: E.J. Brill,1989. This is a very valuable resource book developed for people in the field of conservation. It includes brief descriptions of the ecological zones and animal life of Irian, and an elaborate description of the World Wildlife Fund–prompted program of nature reserves in Irian. Some of the appendices alone are worth the price: a complete list, with runway length and coordinates, of all airstrips in the province; checklists of birds and other protected and rare species.

Pospisil, Leopold. *The Kapauku Papuans.* New York, 1978. Although some consider his "primitive capitalists" assessement overdrawn, this is the standard ethnography on the Ekagi (then called "Kapauku").

Richardson, Don. *Lords of the Earth.* Ventura, California, 1977. Protestant missionaries among the Yali. Epic, Good vs. Evil language and heavily religious in tone. Perhaps most interesting for this reason.

———. *Peace Child.* Glendale, California, 1974. Similar in style to *Lords of the Earth,* this time set among the Asmat.

Schneebaum, Tobias. *Asmat Images, From the Collection of the Asmat Museum of Culture and Progress.* Asmat Museum of Culture and Progress, 1985. This black-and-white book, illustrated with line drawings by the author, is both a catalog of the Asmat Museum's collection and a very good, compact introduction to Asmat art and culture. Schneebaum has spend considerable time in the region, and is perhaps the most knowlegeable contemporary writer on the Asmat, particularly Asmat art. In English and Indonesian. Available from the Asmat museum (in Agats) or: Crosier Province, Inc., 3204 East 43d Street, Minneapolis, MN 55406. Tel: (612) 722-2223.

———. *Where the Spirits Dwell, An Odyssey in the New Guinea Jungle.* New York: Grove Press, 1988. A well-written and rather personal account of the author's experiences in the Asmat region. Schneebaum's homosexuality makes him inherently more empathetic to many aspects of Melanesian culture, and also gives him access to a side of Asmat life that for obvious reasons is shielded from missionaries and western researchers. In addition to cultural and historical information about the Asmat, this book describes the author's personal quest for self-knowlege.

The Sky Above, the Mud Below. A film directed by Tony Saulnier. An early 1960s documentary account of an expedition across Irian, from near Pirimapun in the south to Hollandia. Mud, flies, washed out bridges and all. Some good footage of Asmat and Kim Yal. Now fairly widely available in the U.S. on video.

Souter, Gavin. *New Guinea, the Last Unknown.* New York: Taplinger, 1966. An excellent history of exploration and European involvement in New Guinea. Thoroughly researched and elegantly written. Out of print.

Velde, Van de Peter, ed. *Prehistoric Indonesia.* Dordrecht, Netherlands, 1984.

Wallace, Alfred Russel. *The Malay Archipelago.* Singapore: Graham Brash (Pte) Ltd, 1989. This is the famous account by the father of biogeography, proto-evolutionist, animal collector, and adventurer Wallace. This book covers the several years he spent in the East Indies in the mid-19th century. He spent only a few months in New Guinea, but this book is a must for anyone interested in the natural history of the region.

Wilson, Forbes. *The Conquest of Copper Mountain.* New York, 1981. About the Freeport copper mine.

Worsley, Peter. *The Trumpet Shall Sound: A Study of "Cargo" Cults in Melanesia.* 2d edition. New York: Schocken Books, 1968. One of the basic texts on "cargo cults," movements that sprang up in Melanesia as a reaction to the sudden presence of westerners and their goods and technologies.

Zegwaard, Father Gerardus Anthonius. "Headhunting Practices of the Asmat of the Netherlands New Guinea." *American Anthropologist,* Vol. 61, No. 6, Dec. 1959, pp. 1020–1041. The original description of Asmat head-hunting practices, by the pioneer missionary in the region. Zegwaard's observations still remain the standard text.

Index